KU-526-194

THE COMPLETE BOOK OF
BAKING

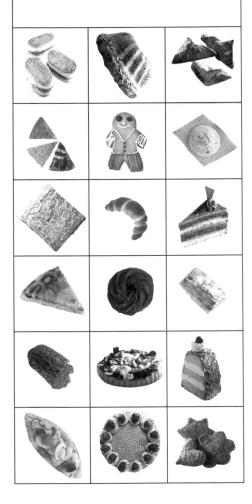

THE COMPLETE BOOK OF
BAKING

Colour
Library

Author: Monika Schumacher

English Translation: Carole Fahy, by arrangement with Bookdeals Translations,
P.O. Box 263 Taunton, TA3 6RH, England

Photography: Cover and recipes: Renate Krake, TLC-Foto-Studio GmbH, Germany
Introduction: Peter Barry, London, England

3285

This edition published 1997 by Colour Library Direct, Godalming, Surrey, England

Originally published in German as *Das Große Bassermann Backbuch*

©1991 Falken-Verlag GmbH Niedernhausen/Ts., Germany
All rights reserved
Printed in Singapore

ISBN 1 85833 085 8

CONTENTS

INTRODUCTION

Today, home baking represents the ultimate in sweet and savoury temptation. Once regarded as sheer hard work, it has now become fun, and, although cakes, gâteaux, pastries, rolls, bread and all kinds of sweet, savoury and spicy delicacies can now be bought in bakeries in almost unlimited variety, home baking is still very much alive. This is not really surprising, for home cooking these days is regarded as a very creative activity that gives plenty of scope for developing the cook's own ideas. Baking is fun twice over; firstly, there is that creative enjoyment and then the pleasure of seeing family and friends enjoy home-made cakes, delicious-smelling breads and spicy savouries. And if home-

made treats are also lovingly and imaginatively decorated, they will be doubly appreciated.

Success and praise are guaranteed by carefully following the instructions in this book. There are delicious recipes for all occasions: Christmas, Easter, family celebrations, afternoon teas and children's birthday parties.

The recipes are explained step by step, and the ingredients are listed in order of use. Just leafing through this book, with its mouthwatering illustrations, will lure the cook into the kitchen, and, with a little imagination, personal touches can be added to any recipe. We wish you lots of success in your baking, and of course in eating the delicious results!

MODERN BAKING TECHNOLOGY

Technological progress has helped to iron out the idiosyncrasies of individual cookers. Today, there is little difference between gas and electric cookers, for both work on the same principles, and are available using conventional radiated or fan-assisted heat. On the whole, all cookers these days give consistent heats, although slight variations may still occur in certain models, both gas and electric.

In order to achieve the best results, it is important to get to know the individual oven well by experimenting with small quantities before attempting to bake larger batches.

THE ELECTRIC OVEN

There are two different kinds of electric oven: conventional and fan assisted.

In a conventional oven, the heat is radiated and will vary between the top and bottom of the oven. The oven's handbook will give the appropriate shelf heights for baking individual items.

Circofan or fan-assisted ovens work with hot air. The air is heated by elements in the back of the oven, blown in through a ventilator and circulated round the oven. This circulating heat gives even cooking throughout the oven, and it can save time as well as energy, if used properly.

THE GAS OVEN

Technology has now largely eliminated the dangers of gas, and all up-to-date gas cookers/ovens are fitted with modern safety equipment. Temperature in a gas oven can be regulated with a thermostat, as in an electric oven.

BAKING TEMPERATURES

Gas oven marks and electric oven temperatures in centigrade and Fahrenheit are given in each recipe. For fan-assisted ovens and for shelf heights for individual items, always check your own oven handbook, as different models can vary. All temperatures given in the recipes are for ovens with top and bottom heat and assume the oven is preheated. For electric ovens, preheating to 200°C will take approximately 10-15 minutes. Gas ovens will reach an equivalent temperature in 5-10 minutes. Fan-assisted ovens do not need to be preheated.

OVENWARE

It is particularly difficult for the beginner to choose the right baking utensils from the vast choice on offer. Even experienced bakers and pastry cooks can get confused by the huge variety of sizes, shapes and materials available.

When choosing ovenware, bear in mind the particular oven for which it is intended. There are tins and dishes on the market specially designed for use either with gas or with electric ovens, and some which are suitable for both: read the manufacturer's instructions carefully, to avoid any unpleasant surprises!

The following is a list of the most common kinds of ovenware.

NON-STICK OVENWARE

Invented over thirty years ago, non-stick utensils are still as useful as ever today. The special plastic coating, known as PVC, that is used on pots and pans and dishes is sold under various brand names, such as Teflon. Being non-stick, the utensils are easy to clean, as well as facilitating the turning out of cakes. Non-stick tins can be used in gas, electric or fan-assisted ovens, although, if the tin is coated with black PVC, it is advisable to reduce the stated

temperature slightly if using a gas oven.

HEAVY TIN OVENWARE

Heavy tin ovenware is less suitable for gas ovens than the light variety, as the tin is inclined to get too hot. However, it is very good for use in an electric oven. As with the light tin ovenware, the heavy variety should be 'baked in' with salt before using for the first time.

LIGHT TIN OVENWARE

Light tin ovenware has been around a long time, and

is mainly recommended for gas cookers. Its only disadvantage is that the top of the cake browns before the rest, as light tin tends to resist heat. These tins should be sprinkled with salt before using for the first time and 'baked in' at very high temperatures for 15-20 minutes.

ALUMINIUM WARE

There is a wide variety of aluminium ware available; utensils with a matt finish are always preferable, as they conduct the heat better. There are aluminium utensils specially recommended for gas, electric and fan-assisted ovens. Variations also exist: some utensils are gold coloured on the outside, or have coatings on the inside; these can be used in any kind of oven.

GLASS AND STONEWARE

Heat-resistant glass, such as Pyrex, or earthenware dishes are mainly used for those recipes which need to be baked at medium or lower temperatures, as they conduct heat very slowly, but achieve a constant, even heat successfully. Cooking temperatures for glass and stoneware should not be too high for too long a period, since both materials can overheat.

RECIPES AND INGREDIENTS

YEAST DOUGH

Yeast dough is the basis of many popular recipes. For tasty breakfast rolls and breads, snacks to grace a cold buffet or as the basis of sweet pastries, yeast dough is always a favourite. And for those who like a savoury snack, yeast dough is particularly good with sausage and vegetable fillings. Recipes using yeast taste best when freshly baked. Storage is limited to a few days, for the cooked dough, unless frozen, dries out and goes stale very quickly.

Don't be put off by the fear that using yeast is very difficult — this is simply not true. Following our instructions and tips means that making yeast dough is as easy as any other form of cookery. As the name implies, the main ingredient of the dough is yeast. Yeast is a living substance that acts as a raising agent by aerating the dough and causing it to swell. However, yeast is only activated efficiently if given the right conditions, which means a temperature of around 37°C and recipe ingredients at the same temperature. When buying yeast, respect the 'best before' date because sensitive yeast cultures have a relatively short effective lifespan. Yeast is sold in both dried, powdered form and fresh. Particularly good results can be achieved with fresh yeast.

When making yeast dough, it is important not only that all the ingredients are of even temperature but also that the yeast is given sufficient rising time at each stage. The recipes in this book differentiate between light, medium and heavy yeast dough. The higher the proportion of fat and other ingredients and the stronger the type of flour used, the more yeast will have to be added. Follow these guide-lines: for a light dough, use 20-25g/¾-1oz yeast; for a medium dough, 25g/1oz yeast; and for a heavy dough, up to 50g/2oz yeast.

1. Yeast dough should be kneaded on a lightly floured board, using a regular, rhythmic action. Fold the dough towards you and then use the heel of the hand to push the dough down and away. Give the dough a quarter turn with the other hand and then repeat the folding and pushing. A firm dough is easier to work with for a beginner.

2. Continue kneading the dough for about ten minutes until it is smooth and no longer sticky. Thorough kneading is essential to distribute the yeast throughout the dough and to strengthen the gluten in the flour, both of which mean that the dough will rise more easily and be much lighter in texture, once baked.

3. Soft doughs are much stickier to work with. The temptation may be to use more flour during the kneading process, but this should be avoided or the quality of the dough will be changed. To begin with, a scraper will help to gather up the dough on the work surface. It also helps if this is kept as cool as possible.

4. The kneading action is the same as for a firm dough and the aim is also to knead until the dough is smooth and has lost its stickiness, whilst remaining soft. A food processor or mixer with a dough hook attachment will take the hard work out of kneading and produce successful doughs, provided the manufacturers instructions are followed.

BASIC SPONGE MIXTURE

A sponge mixture is easy to make, and has a wide variety of applications, including fruit flans and sponge layers for other desserts. Typically, baking powder is used as the raising agent, and successful mixtures are the result of prolonged, smooth beating. All the ingredients have to be thoroughly mixed in until a homogeneous, glutinous consistency is achieved, and the mixture drops stiffly from the spoon. The amount of fluid used should be adjusted as necessary to achieve this consistency. The main ingredients of a sponge mixture are margarine, sugar, eggs, flour and, of course, baking powder. It is most important to add the ingredients in the order given. Soft margarine and caster sugar should be thoroughly beaten, either by hand or in a mixer, until the sugar is completely dissolved and the mixture light and fluffy. Eggs are added gradually, then the flour, which has been previously sieved together with the baking powder and a pinch of salt. This is added to the mixture alternately with the liquid. Finally, any remaining ingredients are added. If the mixture curdles, possibly because ingredients are at different temperatures, the bowl should be placed over hot water and the mixture beaten again. If the recipe uses whisked egg whites, these will be added last, and should be folded very carefully into the mixture. Sponge cakes will keep fresh for a few days, and are especially suitable for freezing.

STRUDEL PASTRY

Hot apple strudel is a popular dessert, particularly in Austria and southern Germany, where it appears on every menu and is still made at home as a treat on Sundays in most households. The art of making strudel pastry is to roll it out until almost transparent, without allowing it to tear. Clever and practised hands can do this in a flash, and even beginners can achieve paper-thin results using the following little trick. Put a cloth on a kitchen table; sprinkle the cloth with flour and spread the partially rolled-out strudel

1. Using a hand-held electric beater makes light work of sponge mixtures, which require prolonged, smooth beating for the best results. After creaming together the margarine and sugar until light and fluffy, the eggs are added gradually, beating either continuously or after each addition, until they are fully incorporated.

dough on it. Now the dough can be pulled evenly in all directions, or rolled out further with a rolling pin. The sweet or savoury filling is then spread on top and the dough rolled up. Strudel dough tastes equally good hot or cold, and it is not difficult to make. Flour, oil or margarine, eggs, lukewarm water and a pinch of salt are mixed together at room temperature, and the dough beaten and kneaded until it is smooth and shiny. The more the dough is worked, the easier it is to pull. After pulling, it must rest for at least an hour in the refrigerator, during which time the filling can be prepared.

2. Baking tins should always be prepared in advance, so that the finished sponge mixture can be poured in gently and transferred to the oven as quickly as possible, to retain all the mixture's lightness. Sprinkling the greased tin with breadcrumbs or a little flour or lining with grease-proof paper are further protections against sticking.

3. Occasionally a sponge mixture may curdle. Using eggs at room temperature and beating them in thoroughly after each addition will minimise the risk of this happening. If, however, a mixture does curdle, it can be restored by placing the bowl over a pan of hot water and beating the mixture again until it regains the correct consistency.

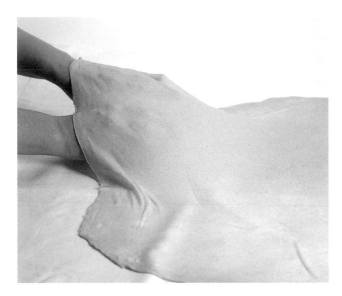

1. Strudel dough must be properly kneaded to achieve the necessary elasticity and should be allowed to rest for at least an hour before rolling out. Once the dough has been partially rolled out, place it on a cloth and use the hands to stretch it to almost transparent thinness, working gently and evenly from the centre outwards.

2. The cloth can be used to help roll up the strudel, once the filling has been spread over the pastry. The cloth acts as a support to roll the dough around the filling, swiss roll style, thus minimising the danger of tearing the pastry at this stage. Although a spiced apple filling is traditional, other fruits can be used for deliciously different variations.

SHORTCRUST PASTRY AND CRUMBLE TOPPINGS

Shortcrust pastry is the basis for numerous flans, tarts and pies. It is quickly and easily made, and has both savoury and sweet applications. Crumble topping is a variation on shortcrust pastry; it is not kneaded and has a higher proportion of fat to flour. The higher the proportion of fat, the crumblier the topping will be and the richer the taste. Shortcrust dough should stand, covered, for some time after kneading, either in a cool kitchen or in the refrigerator. For crumble toppings as used in fruit crumbles, ingredients are mixed in equal parts. Crumbles must be mixed very quickly so they stay cool, otherwise the mixture becomes sticky and unappetizing. The flour is sieved, together with the baking powder where required, and a well made in the middle. Into this are put the sugar and lightly beaten eggs, while the margarine is spread in pieces around the edge of the flour. Working, with the hands, from the outside to the middle, the ingredients are thoroughly combined. The dough is covered after mixing. If it is to be used to line a flan dish or baking tin, only a little flour should be sprinkled on the bottom of this, or the usual consistency of shortcrust pastry will be lost. Before baking, the dough should be pricked several times to stop air bubbles forming.

1. Use the fingertips only to rub the fat into the flour for the lightest and crispiest shortcrust pastry. It is often easier to work directly on a pastry board or work surface.

4. Use the rolling pin to transfer the rolled pastry to the tin. This method minimises the risk of the pastry tearing as it is lifted from the board into the tin.

1. For crumble mixtures, use the fingertips to rub the fat quickly but lightly into the flour. The mixture will resemble fine breadcrumbs, when the fat has been well rubbed in.

2. Once the sugar has been stirred in, the crumble topping is spooned over the prepared fruit. A wide variety of fruits can be used to make delicious puddings.

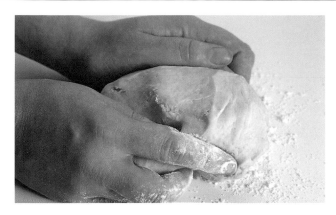

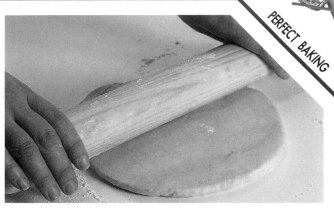

2. Light kneading will give a firm, smooth dough and a better result. Always work on a cool, lightly floured surface and flour your hands to avoid stickiness.

3. Rolling out is easier on a floured surface, using a floured rolling pin. A cool surface is also important to prevent sticking — marble is ideal.

5. Once the pastry circle has been positioned centrally over the tin, ease it gently in without stretching, and leave a slight overhang.

6. Remove the excess pastry and give a neat, even edge to the pastry case by rolling the pin over the top of the tin and gathering up the trimmings.

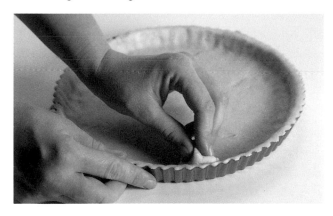

7. Press the pastry gently into the ridges of the tin. Using a wedge of the excess pastry makes this easier to do without stretching the dough or making it sticky.

8. When baking blind, prick the base all over with a fork first. Then line the pastry case with greaseproof paper and weigh this down with a layer of ceramic 'beans'.

FAT-FREE SPONGE

This mixture starts as a creamy mass of eggs, sugar and flour. Since no fat is added, these sponge cakes are light and easily digested. As with other mixtures, there are many methods of preparation and numerous combinations of ingredients according to personal preference and eventual use. However, one thing is absolutely fundamental: the more the eggs are beaten, the more voluminous the cake will be. For this reason, the use of an electric beater is recommended, as the right consistency will be achieved in a very short time and with very little effort. The remaining ingredients then have only to be folded carefully into the mixture. The flour must be sieved very finely before it is folded in. This mixture should go into the oven as quickly as possible, since it will collapse, if left standing for long. Use a loose-bottomed cake tin, the base of which must either be greased well or lined with greaseproof paper. After baking, brush the paper with cold water to remove easily. Wrapping the cooled cake in foil or cling film and leaving it for a day will bring out its full flavour. For flan cases or gâteaux layers, cut a round cake into several horizontal layers. This is easily done by inserting a long, sharp knife into the cake, holding the knife steady and turning the cake through 360 degrees with the other hand. A strong piece of cotton can also be used to slice as many layers as required quickly and easily; the different layers can be lifted apart with the aid of a palette knife.

PUFF PASTRY

Puff pastry is delicious and versatile, tasting as delicious with sweet fillings as with meat, cheese or vegetables. Ready-made puff pastry is very convenient, as making it from scratch is a difficult and time-consuming process. When rolling out the dough, remember to roll it in two different directions alternately. Use only a little flour when rolling out, or the pastry will become tough and dry instead of light and flaky. When cutting into shape, use a sharp knife or the individual layers may stick together and

1. A fat-free sponge relies on lengthy whisking to achieve the best results. To cut down on the time involved, an electric beater is recommended. The eggs and sugar must be whisked until they are thick, creamy and doubled in volume. The ideal consistency has been reached when the whisk leaves a thin trail in the mixture, if lifted.

fail to puff up during baking. The high fat content of puff pastry means that the baking tin is not greased but simply rinsed with cold water. Since puff pastry does not contain any sugar, it browns slowly and can stand high baking temperatures. For a golden finish, lightly beat an egg yolk with a little water and brush the pastry with this before baking, to glaze.

WAFFLE MIXTURE

In grandmother's day, waffles were cooked in heavy, cast-iron pans which were placed either on top of the stove or in the oven. Today electric waffle irons are easy to use and spread the heat evenly. Many recipes and secret tricks for making delicious waffles have been handed down from mother to daughter, and experienced cooks still swear by their own little idiosyncrasies, such as only using fresh farm eggs or

2. If the egg whites are to be added separately, they should be whisked until stiff but not dry. A metal spoon should be used to fold them in gently but thoroughly into the rest of the ingredients, so that the whites are fully incorporated without losing any of their lightness or volume. It is important to work quite quickly.

3. The flour must be sieved very finely before being folded in, to retain as much lightness as possible in the mixture. Fold the flour in carefully, using a metal spoon. Then transfer the mixture to pre-prepared tins. This sponge mixture should go into the oven as quickly as possible, to prevent it collapsing.

spring water. The waffle iron should be greased with oil or margarine. Waffles taste best fresh, eaten either with cream or a mixture of cinnamon and sugar. They also freeze well. When freezing, keep the waffles separate between sheets of greaseproof paper. It is important that the basic waffle mixture is beaten until light and airy; this is achieved more easily using an electric beater. The flour is then added, spoonful by spoonful, until the mixture is glutinous.

CURD CHEESE/QUARK DOUGH

This dough is easily and quickly made. It is suitable for many different recipes, and can be shaped and filled as desired. The addition of curd cheese makes deliciously light pastries which should be eaten on the day of baking.

CHOUX PASTRY

Doughnuts, cream buns and the famous éclair make quick and easy surprises for afternoon tea. Take care not to let a draught near the choux pastries whilst they are still hot, however, or these delicate treats will collapse. This is really the only point to watch when making and using choux pastry. In Switzerland it is known as 'boiled pastry', because flour is simply stirred into margarine and water that has been heated to boiling point. When the mixture has formed a ball, it is 'burned off', i.e: stirred until a white layer has formed at the bottom of the pan, indicating that all superfluous liquid has evaporated. The mixture is then taken off the heat and one egg is beaten in immediately; stirring continuously, the remaining eggs are beaten in gradually. The right consistency has been reached when the mixture hangs from the spoon. The mixture must be cooled before adding baking powder, otherwise this will lose its raising power. Choux pastry cannot be rolled or shaped by hand. It is piped from a forcing bag in rosettes, strips, letters etc. onto a baking tray which has been lightly greased and floured. Leave cooked items to cool down very slowly to keep them light. With cream buns and éclairs a 'hat' must be cut off the top immediately, using scissors, to let the steam escape. Choux pastry must be eaten the day it is made or it becomes tough and rubbery.

1. The flour is beaten into the boiled water and fat until it comes smoothly away from the sides and base of the pan in a ball. Once this stage has been reached, stop beating, or the mixture will become fatty.

PIZZA DOUGH

The popularity of pizza has spread from its native Italy throughout the world. There is a huge range of ingredients that are suitable for toppings, so why not design your own combinations? The pizza base is a flat circle of one of several possible doughs, the most common of which is a yeast dough. Different flours can be used, and all pizza doughs can be prepared quickly and easily.

1. Pizza dough should be rolled out to a circle slightly larger than required and placed on a greased and floured baking tray. The excess dough is then folded in and pressed down gently to give a slightly raised edge.

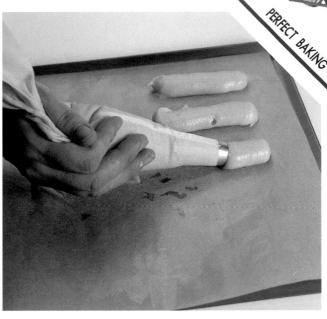

2. Beat in the eggs gradually. They may either be lightly beaten in advance and added a little at a time, or added whole, one by one. In both cases, the mixture must be well beaten after each addition, to incorporate the egg fully.

3. Choux pastry is too soft to be rolled out and is either piped or spooned onto the prepared baking tray. For éclairs, it is piped out in strips about 7cm/3-inches long. Choux pastry can also be deep-fried.

2. The raised edge helps to contain the topping and makes it easier to spread this over the base. Although a tomato mixture is the basis of most toppings, the variations, using extra ingredients, are almost limitless.

BAKING TIPS

Get all ingredients and utensils ready before starting. Weigh out all the required ingredients in advance and, if necessary, bring them to room temperature. If baking tins have rust marks, sprinkle these with salt, rub down with salad oil and wipe off with paper. Spring-release or loose-bottomed tins don't always fit together exactly, so line the base with a circle of greaseproof paper cut slightly larger than necessary and folded up the edge of the tin, so the cake mixture can't leak out. One-piece cake tins can also be lined with greaseproof paper, in which case the tin should be greased well first, as should the lining paper, to prevent it sticking either to the tin or to the cake. Remove the paper as soon as the cooked cake has been turned out to cool. When making sponge-cake layers, only grease the base of the cake tin. As a general rule, all tins, except the non-stick variety, should be lightly greased with margarine before use. Never use strong-smelling fats such as lard or bacon fat.

• Cakes will turn out of the tin more easily if the tin is placed in the refrigerator for about 15 minutes after greasing, or if it is sprinkled with golden bread-crumbs or flour before the cake mixture is put in.

• Margarine straight from the refrigerator is normally too hard to work with, except when making short-crust pastry and puff pastry. To make smooth beating easier, rinse the mixing bowl with hot water first.

• Caster sugar is usually better for baking than granulated. It is easier to work into the mixture and combines better with the other ingredients.

• Always break eggs into a cup first to check they are fresh.

• Traces of yolk in egg white impair the whisking/stiffening process.

• Egg whites are sometimes difficult to beat to a stiff consistency. A few drops of water added at the start can help, but it is important to watch continuously in case the water separates from the egg foam. The addition of a few drops of lemon juice or a pinch of salt may save the day.

• Always sieve flour, baking powder and icing sugar before use, as any small lumps may not dissolve later.

• Always slide the mixture slowly into the baking tin, and fill to a few centimetres below the rim of the tin to give the cake room to rise.

• Always wipe off any drops of mixture from the rim or the outside of the tin, as otherwise they will burn during baking and damage the tin.

• It is easier to roll out kneaded dough and puff pastry between two sheets of greaseproof paper.

• Cutting out shapes is easier if the pastry cutter is first dipped in flour.

• If you want to open the oven door to check on progress, kitchen windows and doors must be closed to avoid draughts, otherwise the cake may collapse. If, after testing, a cake needs more baking time, but is already becoming too dark, cover the top with greaseproof paper. Never reduce the temperature significantly since this may cause the cake to collapse.

• At the end of baking time, turn the oven off and leave the cake in, with the door closed, for 5 minutes before removing.

• Generally, turn the cake out of the tin whilst still warm, although there are a few exceptions that prove this rule. Place a wire rack on top of the cake and, holding the tin with a kitchen towel, turn it and the wire rack over.

• Leave cakes to cool before working further on them. If possible, leave, covered with a tea towel, overnight.

1. Kneaded doughs and puff pastry are easier to roll out between two sheets of greaseproof paper. This method is also useful for some of the softer biscuit or cookie doughs. Keeping the doughs cool also makes the process easier.

2. Cutting out shapes is much easier if the cutters are dipped in flour first. This also gives a cleaner, more distinct edge to the shapes. Cutters are now available in many different shapes and sizes.

• Always soak sheet gelatine in cold water.

• If gelatine is lumpy after dissolving, heat slightly and then strain before use.

• Sliced fruit, particularly apples, pears and bananas, turns dark very quickly. To avoid this keep the slices in water with a slice of lemon added.

• If the top of a cake is too dark, rub it over with a cheese grater and then cover thickly with icing or icing sugar.

• Trim uneven surfaces of gâteau layers with a sharp knife and turn over.

• When making fruit flans and gâteaux, make sure the fruit for the filling is quite dry, as any juice will soak in and cause sogginess. To avoid this, bake flan cases blind.

BASIC SHORTCRUST PASTRY

Suitable for:
Sweet or savoury flans
Sweet or savoury tarts
(Exclude sugar for savoury items)

Ingredients:
250g/8oz flour
65g/2½ oz sugar
Pinch of salt
125g/4oz margarine, chilled
1 egg

Method:
1. Sieve the flour and baking powder onto a pastry board and add the sugar and salt. Dot the margarine over the top in small pieces and dredge more flour over.
2. Using a palette knife, cut the fat into the flour until the mixture resembles fine breadcrumbs.
3. Make a well in the middle, drop in the egg with a little flour and mix in well.
4. Work the mixture to a smooth dough by hand. Leave to stand in a cool place before using.

Quick Method:
On low speed, mix all the ingredients together using an electric mixer or the pastry hook attachment of a handmixer. Increase the speed to knead thoroughly. Leave to stand as above before using.

1.

2.

3.

4.

Tips for Shortcrust Pastry:
• Using icing sugar instead of caster sugar gives a smoother finish to your pastry.
• Wrap the rolled-out pastry round a rolling pin to lift it off the board and over the prepared baking tin.

BASIC VICTORIA SPONGE

Suitable for:
Large and small cakes
Sponge flan cases

Ingredients:
125g/4oz margarine
125g/4oz sugar
Pinch of salt
2 eggs
250g/8oz flour
½ sachet baking powder
Scant 125ml/4floz milk

Method:
1. Beat the margarine in electric mixer until smooth and creamy, then gradually add sugar and eggs, and continue to beat until the sugar is dissolved and mixture is light and fluffy.
2. Sieve together the flour and baking powder, and fold this into the mixture alternately with the milk. The baking powder should not be lumpy or it will create large air pockets in the mixture.
3. The mixture is ready when it drops slowly and stickily from the spoon.
4. Grease the cake tin and sprinkle breadcrumbs on the base. Turn the mixture into the tin and bake as instructed.

Variation:
If the recipe requires the egg yolk and white to be added separately, beat the egg with the margarine and sugar until the mixture is light and fluffy, and fold in the stiffly beaten egg white at the end.

Quick Method:
Beat all the ingredients together using an electric whisk, beginning on a low setting and then beating for 1½ minutes on the highest setting.

1.

2.

3.

4.

Variation

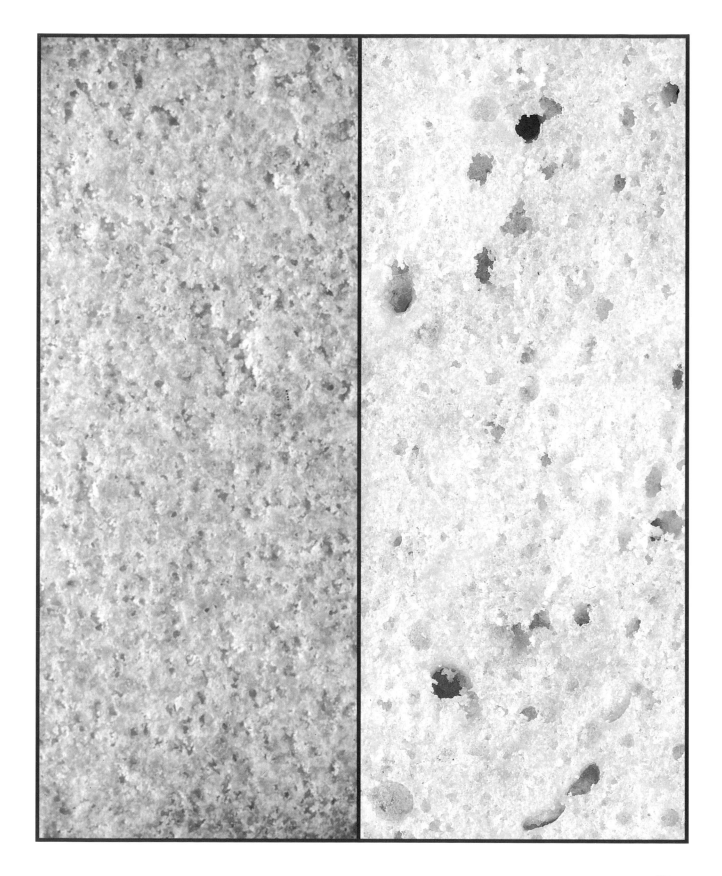

BASIC YEAST DOUGH

Suitable for:
Sugar cakes
Sponge with crumble topping
Almond slices
Yeast cakes
Fruit cakes
Fruit loaf
Yeast Rings
Savoury biscuits (use only a pinch of sugar to help the yeast work)
Bread
Rolls
Pizza dough

Ingredients:
25g/1oz yeast
300ml/½ pint lukewarm milk
1 pinch of salt
65g/2½oz margarine
500g/1 lb plain flour
40g/1½oz sugar
1 pinch salt (savoury biscuits: 1 tsp)
1-2 eggs

Method:
1. Crumble the yeast into the lukewarm milk, add pinch of sugar, cover and leave to work for 5-10 minutes in a warm place.
2. Melt margarine and leave to cool.
3. Put flour, sugar, salt and margarine into a bowl. Break in eggs, add dissolved yeast and mix well together.
4. Knock down and knead dough until you have a homogeneous mixture which is smooth and supple.
5. Cover with aluminium foil or a cloth and leave to rise until doubled in volume (20-30 minutes).
6. Knead thoroughly once more.

1.

2.

3.

4.

5.

6.

Quick Method:
Put all the ingredients except milk into an electric mixer bowl. Mix and then knead using kneading hook, first on low speed and then on high until dough is smooth and soft. Add milk only after mixer is running. Leave to rise to double original volume — approximately 1 hour as yeast has been crumbled straight into dough mixture.

Tips for Yeast Dough:
Ensure yeast dough does not become more than luke-warm. Yeast develops best at 37°C and at 60°C it dies.
• When dough is prepared and shaped to your requirements it should be left again to rise. This applies to both dried and fresh yeast.
• Yeast dough can be kept frozen for up to 3 months. For dough which is to be frozen use only half the quantity of yeast and add a little more sugar. Allow to rise for a short time only before freezing. After defrosting proceed with preparation as before.

BASIC CURD DOUGH

Suitable for:
Pizza dough
Vegetable tarts
Yeast cakes

Ingredients:
200g/7oz cottage cheese
1 pinch of salt
6 tbsps milk
8 tbsps oil
1-2 eggs
1 pinch baking powder
400g/13oz plain flour

Method:
1. Mix cottage cheese, salt, milk, oil and eggs well together.
2. Mix flour and baking powder. Put half into food mixer bowl and, using the kneading hook attachment, mix into the cheese mixture.
3. Turn dough out onto a floured board and knead in the remaining flour by hand.

1.

2.

3.

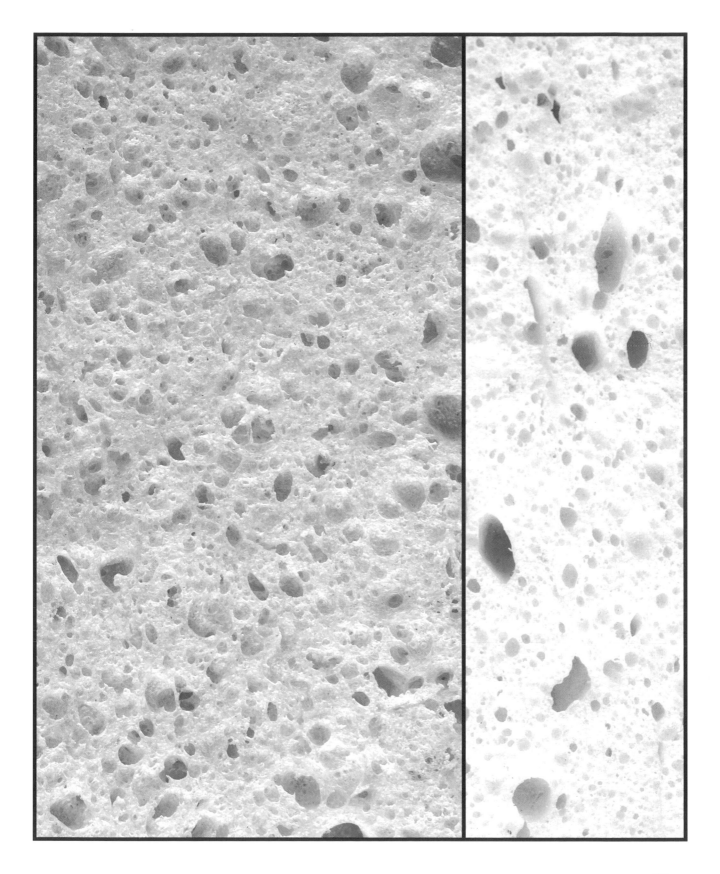

BASIC WHISKED SPONGE

Suitable For:
Gâteaux
Swiss rolls
Cream cakes

Ingredients:

4 eggs, separated
4 tbsps water
125g/4oz sugar
Pinch of salt
Margarine, where specified
75g/3oz flour
Pinch of baking powder

Method:
1. Using either a balloon whisk or an electric mixer with whisk attachment, beat the egg yolks, water, sugar and salt together in a bowl until the mixture is thick and creamy.
2. If the recipe specifies margarine, melt this, allow it to cool, then beat it into the mixture in a thin trickle.
3. Beat the egg whites until stiff, and fold into the egg yolk mixture. Mix the flour, cornflour and baking powder together and sieve onto the egg mixture.
4. Fold the flour carefully into the egg mixture; do not stir or the air beaten into the mixture will be lost and the cake will be heavy.
5. For a sponge gâteau, grease the base of a spring-release tin and line it with greaseproof paper. Turn the cake mixture into this, and bake according to recipe. Once cooked, leave the cake to stand in the tin for about 20 minutes. Turn out and remove the greaseproof paper.
6. When completely cold, slice the cake into layers as required using strong cotton thread.

1.

2.

3.

4.

5.

6.

BASIC CHOUX PASTRY

Suitable For:
Cream Puffs
Crullers

Ingredients:

250ml/8 fl oz water
50g/2oz margarine
1 tsp sugar (if required)
Pinch of salt
150g/5oz flour
4-5 eggs
1 tsp baking powder

Method:
1. In a saucepan, bring the water, margarine, sugar and salt to the boil. Remove from the heat and add all the flour at once, beating the mixture until smooth.
2. Replace on a medium heat and stir the mixture until it comes away from the sides of the pan to form a ball in the centre. Remove from the heat.
3. Beat in one egg immediately and turn the mixture into a bowl. Gradually beat in the remaining eggs one by one, incorporating them well into the mixture.
4. Finally, add the baking powder as per the recipe's instructions.

1.

2.

3.

4.

Choux Pastry Tips
• Choux pastry is not suitable for freezing.
• For baking, the tin must either be greased or lined with greaseproof paper.
• As soon as choux pastry is removed from the oven after baking, it should be pierced so the steam can escape. This prevents the finished pastries becoming rubbery.

THE
MAGIC OF
CAKES

This delicious collection of recipes begins with unusual Continental ring cakes and other popular favourites. These are followed by mouthwatering tarts and pies that no one can resist.

LEMON CAKE

Makes approximately 8 portions

125g/4oz margarine
Grated zest of ¼ lemon
100g/3½oz caster sugar
2 eggs
4 tbsps milk
200g/7oz flour
50g/2oz cornflour
½ tsp baking powder
Margarine, for greasing

To Moisten

4 tbsps lemon juice
50g/2oz sugar
2 tbsps water
1 tbsp brandy

Icing

100g/3½oz icing sugar
1 tbsp lemon juice
Zest of 1 lemon

1 Beat the margarine with grated lemon zest, sugar, eggs and milk until fluffy. Mix together the flour, cornflour and baking powder and gradually fold this into the margarine mixture.

2 Grease a 20-cm/8-inch decorative baking tin, e.g. cloverleaf shape. Turn the mixture into this and bake in a preheated oven, Gas Mark 4/180°C/350°F for 45-50 minutes. Leave to cool.

3 Boil the lemon juice with the sugar and water, add the brandy and sprinkle liberally over the cake to moisten.

4 Mix the icing sugar with the lemon juice and spread over top and sides of cake. Decorate with finely cut strips of lemon zest.

GRANDMOTHER'S CHOCOLATE CAKE

Makes approximately 20 portions

250g/8oz margarine
250g/8oz caster sugar
3 tsps vanilla sugar
4 eggs
Pinch of salt
75g/3oz cocoa powder
1 tsp instant coffee
500g/1lb flour
3 tsps baking powder
125 ml/4 fl oz milk
125g/4oz cocktail cherries
50g/2oz chopped walnuts
Margarine for greasing

Icing

200g/7oz icing sugar
2-3 tbsps water
75g/3oz walnut kernels

1 Beat the margarine until creamy, then gradually add the sugar, vanilla sugar and, finally, the eggs one by one. Continue beating until the sugar has dissolved. Add the salt, cocoa powder and coffee powder. Sieve together the flour and baking powder and fold into the mixture, alternating with the milk.

2 Halve the cocktail cherries, roll them in flour and fold them into the mixture together with the walnuts.

3 Grease a 22-cm/8½-inch ring tin, pour in the mixture and bake in a preheated oven, Gas Mark 5/190°C/375°F for about 1 hour 15 minutes.

4 Mix the water and icing sugar together and spread onto the cake while this is still warm. Decorate with the walnuts.

CURD CHEESE CAKE

Makes 20 portions

250g/8oz margarine
250g/8oz caster sugar
4 eggs
Juice and grated zest of 1 lemon
375g/12oz low fat curd cheese
500g/1lb flour
3 tsps baking powder
125g/4oz raisins
75g/3oz chopped almonds
3 tbsps rum
Margarine for greasing
Breadcrumbs

1 Beat the margarine until pale and fluffy. One by one, beat in the sugar, eggs, lemon juice and grated zest.

2 Wrap the low fat curd cheese in a cloth, and squeeze to remove any moisture. Incorporate the cheese into the mixture. Sieve together the flour and baking powder and gradually fold into the mixture. Finally stir in the raisins, chopped almonds and rum.

3 Grease a 22-cm/8½-inch ring tin and sprinkle with breadcrumbs. Pour in the mixture and bake in preheated oven, Gas Mark 5/200°C/400°F for 60-70 minutes.

Note: This cake only works with very dry curd cheese.

MANDARIN CAKE

Makes approximately 20 portions

190g/6oz tin mandarin oranges
1 packet lemon cake mix
20g/3/4oz ground hazelnuts
Margarine for greasing

Icing
250g/8oz icing sugar
5 tbsps orange juice
2 tbsps coconut oil
Grated zest of 1 orange

1 Strain the mandarins. Make up the cake mixture according to the instructions on the packet. Halve the mandarin seg-ments and fold them into the mixture, together with the hazelnuts.
2 Turn the mixture into a greased 22-cm/8½-inch ring tin. Bake for 50 minutes in a preheated oven, Gas Mark 4/180°C/340°F.
3 Mix the icing sugar to a smooth consistency with the orange juice and coconut oil. Set one third aside. Mix the remainder with the orange zest and spread over the cooled cake. Leave to harden. Spread the remaining icing over the cake, to form a second layer.

PINEAPPLE CAKE

Makes approximately 20 portions

200g/7oz margarine
300g/10oz caster sugar
6 tsps vanilla sugar
Pinch of salt
6 eggs
Grated zest of 1 lemon
3 tbsps lemon juice
450g/15oz flour
3 tbsps baking powder
250g/8oz fresh or tinned pineapple slices, cut into chunks
Margarine for greasing
Breadcrumbs

1 Make a basic sponge mixture using the margarine, sugar, vanilla sugar, salt, eggs, flour, baking powder, lemon juice and zest.
2 Dust the well-drained pineapple chunks lightly with a little flour and fold them into the mixture.
3 Grease a 22-cm/8½-inch ring tin. Sprinkle with breadcrumbs and turn the mixture into this. Bake for 65-70 minutes in a preheated oven, Gas Mark 2-3/150-170°C/300-325°F.

WALNUT CAKE

Makes approximately 20 portions

375g/12oz margarine
300g/10oz caster sugar
Pinch of salt
6 tsps vanilla sugar
6 eggs
250 g/8oz walnuts, ground
3 tsps baking powder
375g/12oz flour
4 tbsps brandy
Fine breadcrumbs
Margarine for greasing
Icing sugar

1 Beat the margarine, sugar, salt, vanilla sugar and eggs until light and fluffy. Mix together the nuts, baking powder and flour and incorporate them gradually into the mixture, together with the brandy.
2 Grease a 22-cm/8½-inch ring tin and sprinkle with breadcrumbs. Turn the mixture into this. Bake for 50 minutes in a preheated oven, Gas Mark 4/180°C/340°F.
3 When cool, dust the walnut cake with icing sugar.

GRANNY'S RED JAM CAKE

Makes approximately 20 portions

250g/8oz margarine
200g/7oz caster sugar
3 tsps vanilla sugar
Pinch of salt
4 eggs
3 tbsps rum
3 tsps baking powder
500g/1lb flour
300g/10oz thick red-fruit jam
Margarine for greasing
Breadcrumbs

1 Beat together the margarine, sugar, vanilla sugar, salt and eggs until light and fluffy, then add the rum. Sieve together the flour and baking powder and incorporate them gradually to make a fairly solid sponge mixture.
2 Turn half the sponge mixture into a 22-cm/8½-inch ring tin, which has been greased and sprinkled with breadcrumbs, and use the back of a spoon to create a hollow in the middle of the mixture.
3 Pile the jam into the hollow, and cover with the remaining sponge mixture. Swirl a fork through the mixture, to create a marble effect.
4 Bake for about 60 minutes in a preheated oven, Gas Mark 4/175°C/340°F.

the instant coffee and vanilla sugar, and mix together well.

2 Sieve together the flour and baking powder, and gradually fold into the cake mixture. Stir in the milk; the dough should be of a sticky consistency.

3 Beat the egg whites stiffly and fold them gently into the mixture.

4 Line a 30-cm/12-inch square cake tin with buttered grease-proof paper and turn the mixture into this. Bake for about 50 minutes in a preheated oven, Gas Mark 4/180°C/350°F.

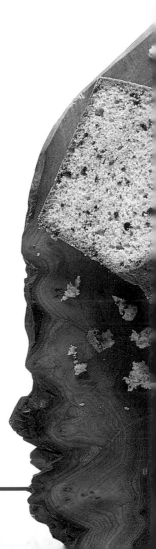

FRUIT RING

Makes approximately 20 portions

250g/8oz margarine
250g/8 oz caster sugar
4 eggs
Grated zest of 1 lemon
4 tbsps lemon juice
500g/1lb flour
3 tsps baking powder
125 ml/4 fl oz milk
125g/4oz raisins
125g/4oz currants
75g/3oz almonds
Margarine for greasing

1 Beat the margarine and sugar until light and fluffy. Beat in the eggs one at a time, then add the lemon zest and juice.

2 Sieve together the flour and baking powder, and fold into the mixture, alternating with the milk.

3 Sprinkle the raisins and currants with a little flour and stir these into the mixture together with the almonds.

4 Grease a 22-cm/8½-inch ring tin with margarine, turn the mixture into this and bake for about 60 minutes in a preheated oven, Gas Mark 4/180°C/350°F.

MOCHA CAKE

Makes approximately 20 portions

150g/5oz margarine
200g/7oz caster sugar
Pinch of salt
4 eggs, separated
2 tbsps instant coffee
3 tsps vanilla sugar
250g/8oz flour
2 tsps baking powder
6 tbsps milk
Margarine for greasing

1 Beat the margarine until creamy; one by one, beat in the sugar, salt and egg yolks. Stir in

KING'S CAKE

Makes approximately 16 portions

200g/7oz margarine
150g/5oz caster sugar
Pinch of salt
3 eggs
Grated zest of 1 lemon
4 tbsps lemon juice
2 tbsps rum
100g/3½oz marzipan, chopped

375g/12oz flour
3 tsps baking powder
125 ml/4 fl oz milk
125g/4oz raisins
125g/4oz currants
50g/2oz glacé cherries
100g/3½oz mixed orange and lemon peel
Margarine for greasing

Icing
200g/7oz icing sugar
5 tbsps rum
2 tbsps coconut oil, warmed
100g/3½oz flaked almonds, toasted

1 Beat the margarine with the sugar and salt until light and fluffy. Gradually beat in the eggs, lemon peel and juice, rum and marzipan.

2 Sieve together three-quarters of the flour and the baking powder and fold into the mixture, alternating with the milk.

3 Add the raisins, currants, halved cherries and peel to the remaining flour, mix well and stir into the cake mixture.

4 Turn the mixture into a greased loaf tin and bake for approximately 70 minutes in a preheated oven, Gas Mark 4/180°C/350°F. Turn out and leave to cool.

5 Mix together the icing sugar, rum and coconut oil. Spread over the cooled cake and sprinkle with the flaked almonds.

ORANGE LOAF CAKE

Makes approximately 16 portions

250g/8oz margarine
250g/8oz caster sugar
Pinch of salt
3 eggs
4 egg yolks
100 g/3½oz flour
2 tbsps orange liqueur
Grated zest of 1 orange and 1 lemon
100g/3½oz cornflour
2 tbsps orange juice
1 tbsp lemon juice
100g/3½oz ground almonds
80g/3oz candied orange peel, chopped
Margarine for greasing
Breadcrumbs

Icing

100g/3½oz clear marmalade
200g/7oz icing sugar
3 tbsps orange juice
25g/1oz candied orange peel, chopped

1 Beat the margarine, sugar and salt until light and fluffy, then gradually blend in the eggs and egg yolks adding a little flour as you work. Stir in the orange liqueur and grated orange and lemon zest. Add the remaining flour, cornflour, orange and lemon juice, almonds and candied orange peel.
2 Grease a loaf tin and sprinkle with breadcrumbs. Turn the mixture into this and bake for 75-90 minutes in a preheated oven, Gas Mark 4/80°C/350°F.
3 Heat the marmalade and spread over the cold cake. Mix the icing sugar and orange juice to a smooth paste and spread over the top and sides of cake. Decorate with the chopped candied orange peel.

MARBLE CAKE

Makes approximately 20 portions

250g/8oz margarine
275g/9oz caster sugar
3 tsps vanilla sugar
4 eggs
2 tbsps rum
Pinch of salt
500g/1lb flour
3 tsps baking powder
125 ml/4 fl oz milk + 2 tbsps milk
25g/1oz cocoa
25 g/1oz chopped almonds
Margarine for greasing

1 Cream together the margarine, 250g/8oz of the caster sugar and the vanilla sugar. Beat in the eggs one at a time, then add the rum and salt. Sieve together the flour and baking powder, and add gradually to the mixture, alternating with the 125 ml/4 fl oz milk. Divide into portions of one-third and two-thirds.
2 Mix the one-third portion with the cocoa, almonds, remaining caster sugar and 2 tbsps milk. Set aside.
3 Grease a 30-cm/12-inch ring or loaf tin and spoon the two mixtures alternately into this. Swirl a fork through the layers, to create the marbled effect.
4 Bake the cake for 60-70 minutes in a preheated oven, Gas Mark 4/180°C/350°F.

SPICY CAKE

Makes approximately 20 portions

4 eggs
200g/7oz caster sugar
125g/4oz margarine, softened
Grated zest of ½ lemon
2 heaped tsps cinnamon
1 heaped tsp ground cloves
1 level tsp cardamom
½ tsp aniseed
½ tsp ginger
Pinch of nutmeg
250g/8oz flour
2 tsps baking powder
25g/1oz chopped almonds
50g/2oz grated chocolate
50g/2oz finely sliced candied peel
50g/2oz maraschino cherries, chopped
Margarine for greasing
Icing sugar for dusting.

1 Beat the eggs until foamy, then gradully beat in the sugar. Stir in the softened margarine, then, one by one, the grated lemon peel, spices, the flour sieved together with the baking powder, the almonds, chocolate, lemon zest and cherries.
2 Grease a 25-cm/10-inch loaf tin, and line with grease-proof paper. Turn the cake mixture into this and bake for about 50 minutes in a preheated oven, Gas Mark 5-6/190°-200°C/375°-400°F.

YEAST RING

Makes approximately 20 portions

25g/1oz fresh yeast
125 ml/4 fl oz lukewarm milk
250g/8oz margarine
500g/1lb flour
Pinch of salt
250g/8oz caster sugar
150g/5oz chopped almonds
Grated zest of 1 lemon
4 tbsps lemon juice
4 eggs
50g/2oz candied peel
200g/7oz raisins
Margarine for greasing
Icing sugar for dusting

1 Crumble the yeast into the lukewarm milk, and leave in a warm place until frothy. Soften the margarine.
2 Mix together the flour, salt, sugar and 125g/4oz of the almonds in a bowl. Add the yeast mixture, the softened margarine, the lemon zest and juice and the eggs. In a mixer, work to a smooth dough. Add the candied peel and raisins.
3 Grease a loaf tin or a 22-cm/8½-inch ring tin. Sprinkle with the remaining almonds and turn the cake mixture into this. Leave to rise in a warm place.
4 Bake for approximately 75 minutes in a preheated oven, Gas Mark 4/180°C /350°F.
5 Turn out and leave to cool before dusting with icing sugar.

CHOCOLATE SPONGE CAKE

Makes Approximately 20 portions

200g/7oz flour
1½ tsps baking powder
25g/1oz cocoa powder
25g/1oz chopped almonds
150g/5oz caster sugar
Pinch of salt
3 tsps vanilla sugar
150g/5oz margarine, softened
3 eggs
4 tbsps milk
Margarine for greasing

Icing

2 tbsps apricot jam
100g/3½oz chocolate icing
25g/1oz white icing
25g/1oz pink icing
Sugar pearls, etc. to decorate

1 Sieve together the flour, baking powder, and cocoa. Add the almonds, sugar, salt, vanilla sugar, margarine, eggs and milk, and mix together well either by hand or in an electric mixer.

2 Grease a 22-cm/8½-inch star-shaped tin and turn the mixture into this. Bake for about 50 minutes in a preheated oven, Gas Mark 4/180°C/350°F.

3 Spread the cooled cake thinly with the jam, and cover with the chocolate icing. Decorate with sugar pearls, etc.

Note: This chocolate cake makes an attractive gift presented in a decorative box.

RUM SANDCAKE

Makes approximately 20 portions

250g/8oz margarine
250g/8oz caster sugar
Grated zest of ½ lemon
2 tbsps rum
Pinch of salt
4 eggs
125g/4oz self-raising flour
125g/4oz cornflour
Margarine for greasing

NOUGAT CAKE

Makes approximately 16 portions

150g/5oz margarine
150g/5oz caster sugar
3 tsps vanilla sugar
Pinch of salt
3 eggs
250g/8oz flour
3 tsps baking powder
3 tbsps rum
3 tbsps milk
50g/2oz chopped almonds
100g/3½oz nougat
Margarine for greasing

1 Beat the margarine with the caster sugar, vanilla sugar and salt until light and fluffy. Beat in the eggs one at a time. Sieve together the flour and baking powder and fold into the mixture, alternating with the rum, milk and almonds.

2 Turn two-thirds of the mixture into a greased 20-cm/8-inch ring tin. Melt the nougat in a double boiler over a pan of hot water, leave to cool, then stir into the remaining mixture. Spread this over the mixture in the ring tin, and swirl a fork through both layers to give a partly marbled effect.

3 Bake for about 60 minutes in a preheated oven, Gas Mark 4/180°C/350°F.

1 Cream the margarine until light. One by one, beat in the sugar, vanilla sugar, grated lemon zest, rum, salt and eggs. Continue to stir until the sugar has dissolved.

2 Sieve together the flour and cornflour and fold gradually into the mixture.

3 Grease a 25-cm/10-inch loaf tin and line with greaseproof paper. Turn the mixture into this and bake for about 60 minutes in a preheated oven, Gas Mark 4/180°C/350°F.

MARZIPAN SPONGE SLICES

Makes approximately 40 slices

Shortcrust Pastry
200g/7oz flour
100g/3½oz margarine
50g/2oz caster sugar
1 egg
Pinch of salt
Margarine for greasing

Sponge Mixture
250g/8oz margarine
250g/8oz caster sugar
Pinch of salt
4 eggs
Grated zest of 2 lemons
100g/3½oz marzipan
500g/1lb self-raising flour
Scant 250 ml/8 fl oz milk

Decoration
125g/4oz red jam
125g/4oz icing sugar
3 tbsps water
100g/3½oz almond slivers

1 Use the flour, sugar, margarine and salt to make a basic shortcrust pastry. Knead and chill for 30 minutes. Roll out to fit a greased baking tray, and bake for 15 minutes in a preheated oven, Gas Mark 6/200°C/400°F. Remove and leave to cool.

2 Meanwhile, beat the margarine with the sugar and.salt, until light and fluffy. Beat in the eggs, one at a time, then add the lemon zest and the marzipan, worked to a paste. Sieve together the flour and baking powder and fold gradually into mixture, alternating with the milk.

3 Spread the cooled pastry with the jam, spoon over the sponge mixture and return to the oven for a further 30 minutes.

4 Mix the icing sugar and water to a smooth paste and spread over the warm cake. Sprinkle almond slivers on top, and cut the cake into small squares immediately.

SPICY CHOCOLATE CAKE

Makes approximately 20 portions

250g/8oz margarine
300g/10oz brown sugar
3 tsps vanilla sugar
3 eggs
4 tbsps crème fraîche
80g/3oz golden syrup
Pinch of ground cloves
2 tbsps cinnamon
Pinch of nutmeg
100g/3½oz plain chocolate, grated
3 tbsps cocoa
2 tsps baking powder
200g/7oz flour
200g/7oz ground almonds
150g/5oz ground walnuts
2 tbsps rum
Margarine for greasing

Filling

250g/8oz plain chocolate
150g/5oz margarine
150g/5oz icing sugar
1 tbsp almond liqueur
1 tbsp instant coffee

To Decorate

Chocolate icing
Cocoa beans

1 Beat the margarine until creamy, gradually adding the sugar, vanilla sugar, crème fraîche, golden syrup, spices, grated chocolate, the flour and baking powder sieved together, and the cocoa, almonds, nuts and rum, in that order.

2 Spread the mixture into a greased square or rectangular baking tin and bake for 25 minutes in a preheated oven, Gas Mark 6/200°C/400°F. Turn out and leave to cool.

3 Melt the chocolate in a bowl over a pan of hot water. Beat the margarine and icing sugar until light and fluffy, then stir in, one by one, the liqueur, coffee and melted chocolate.

4 Slice the cooled cake in half horizontally. Spread the bottom layer with the chocolate filling and replace the top layer.

5 Decorate with the chocolate icing and cocoa beans.

GRANDMOTHER'S CRUMBLE CAKE

Makes approximately 30 portions

40g/1½oz fresh yeast
Scant 250 ml/8 fl oz lukewarm milk
350g/12oz caster sugar
400g/13oz margarine
1kg/2lb flour
Salt
2 eggs
2 vanilla pods
Margarine for greasing

1 Crumble the yeast into the lukewarm milk, add a pinch of sugar and leave, covered, in a warm place until frothy. Melt 125g/4oz of the margarine and leave to cool.
2 Mix together 500g/1lb of the flour, a pinch of salt, 100g/3½oz of the caster sugar, the eggs, the softened margarine and the yeast mixture. Using an electric mixer, mix and knead to a smooth dough. Cover and set aside in a warm place to rise.
3 Meanwhile, mix the remaining flour with a pinch of salt, the vanilla pith, and the remaining caster sugar. Rub in the remaining margarine to make a coarse crumble mixture.
4 Knead the risen yeast dough briefly. Place on a greased baking tray and use a spatula to flatten the dough out. Sprinkle the crumble mixture on top and leave to stand for a short while.
5 Bake for about 20 minutes in a preheated oven, Gas Mark 5-6/190°-200°C/375°-400°F.

CHOCOLATE CAKE

Makes approximately 24 portions

375g/12½oz margarine
375g/12½oz caster sugar
7 eggs
300g/10oz chocolate, grated
400g/13oz self-raising flour
150g/5oz ground almonds
Margarine for greasing

Topping
200g/7oz marzipan paste
4 tbsps water
250g/8oz icing sugar

1 Beat the margarine until creamy. Gradually beat in the sugar. Beat in the eggs one by one. Add the grated chocolate, flour and ground almonds.
2 Turn the mixture into a greased baking tin and bake for 40 minutes in a preheated oven, Gas Mark 4/180°C/350°F. Turn out and leave to cool.
3 Mix the marzipan paste with the icing sugar and water, roll it out between two sheets of greaseproof paper, then spread over the cooled cake. Cut into squares.

MARZIPAN CAKE

Makes approximately 24 portions

250g/8oz margarine
250g/8oz caster sugar
Pinch of salt
4 eggs
250g/8oz self-raising flour
Margarine for greasing

Topping
7 tbsps redcurrant jelly
450g/14oz marzipan
Egg white

1 Beat the margarine, caster sugar and salt until light and fluffy. Beat in the eggs, one by one. Fold in the flour thoroughly.
2 Turn the mixture into a greased baking tin and bake for 30 minutes in a preheated oven, Gas Mark 4/180°C/350°F. Turn out and leave to cool.
3 Spread the redcurrant jelly over the cooled cake. Mix the marzipan paste with the icing sugar and water and roll the mixture out between two sheets of greaseproof paper. Cover the top of cake with the marzipan and brush with a little beaten egg white.

HONEY SLICES

Makes approximately 24 slices

500g/1lb plain flour
150g/5oz hazelnuts, chopped
1 tsp cinnamon
Pinch ground cloves
Grated zest of ½ lemon
50g/2oz ground almonds
325g/11oz clear honey
150g/5oz caster sugar
½ tsp bicarbonate of soda

½ tsp potash
1 tbsp rose water
1 egg
Margarine for the tin

Icing

250g/8oz icing sugar
2-3 tbs water
100g/4oz almonds, flaked

1 Mix flour, nuts, cinnamon, cloves, grated lemon zest and almonds in a bowl. Heat the honey and sugar together, stirring until sugar is dissolved. Leave to cool and stir into mixture. Dissolve bicarbonate of soda and potash in the rosewater. Beat in the egg and add to the cake mixture.

2 Knead the cake mixture into a smooth dough and roll out to a thickness of 1 cm/½ inch. Turn into a greased baking tin and bake for 40 minutes in a preheated oven, Gas Mark 4/180°C/350°F.

3 Cut the cake into squares while still warm. Mix the icing sugar with the water and use to ice the squares. Sprinkle with flaked almonds.

DUTCH ALMOND CAKE

Makes approximately 24 portions

Pastry Base

600g/1lb 4oz plain flour
250g/8oz margarine
150g/5oz caster sugar
Pinch of salt
2 eggs
3-4 tbsps milk
Margarine for greasing

Cake Topping

150g/5oz margarine
200g/7oz caster sugar
6 tsps vanilla sugar
6 eggs
Grated zest of 1 lemon
300g/10oz ground almonds
60g/2½oz plain flour
1 tsp baking powder
3 tbsps whipping cream
100g/3½oz apricot jam

1 Make the pastry base by mixing the flour, margarine, sugar, salt, eggs and milk to a smooth dough. Chill for 30 minutes.

2 Roll out the dough, and use to line a greased baking tray 30 cm x 40 cm/12 inches x 16 inches. Prick the pastry all over with a fork and bake blind for 15 minutes in a preheated oven, Gas Mark 7/220°C/425°F. Remove the pastry base and reduce the heat to Gas Mark 4/180°C/350°F.

3 Meanwhile, beat together the margarine, sugar, vanilla sugar, eggs, grated lemon zest and almonds until light and fluffy. Sieve together the flour and baking powder and fold into the cake mixture. Stir in the cream.

4 Spread the apricot jam over the cooked pastry base, pour over the cake mixture and bake for about 40 minutes at the reduced heat.

ORANGE CAKE

Makes approximately 32 portions

Coconut Mixture
250g/8oz flour
75g/3oz caster sugar
Pinch of salt
150g/5oz margarine
50g/2oz desiccated coconut
Margarine for greasing

Sponge Mixture
250g/8oz margarine
200g/7oz caster sugar
4 eggs
Grated zest of 1 orange
200g/7oz flour
2 tsps baking powder
3 tbsps orange juice

Glaze
125g/4oz clear marmalade
2 tbsps orange juice

BEE STINGS

Makes approximately 24

40g/1½oz fresh yeast
250 ml/8 fl oz lukewarm milk
100g/3½oz caster sugar
500g/1lb plain flour
Pinch of salt
1 egg
Grated zest of 1 lemon
100g/3½oz margarine, melted
Margarine for greasing

Topping
150g/5oz margarine
150g/5oz brown sugar
150g/5oz flaked almonds
1 tbsp flour
2 tbsps whipping cream
1 tbsp clear honey

Filling
1 packet confectioner's custard,
vanilla flavour

1 Crumble the yeast into the lukewarm milk and leave in a warm place until frothy. Mix the sugar, flour, salt, margarine, lemon zest and frothy yeast mixture into a dough. Leave in a warm place to rise. Spread out onto a baking tray.

2 Put all the ingredients for the topping into a saucepan, bring to the boil, stirring, then remove from the heat and leave to cool. Spread the cooled topping over the dough base. Leave in a warm place to rise again. Bake for about 20 minutes in a pre-heated oven, Gas Mark 6/ 200°C/400°F.

3 Make up the confectioner's custard according to the instructions on the packet and set aside.

4 Once cooled, cut the cake into squares. Cut each slice in half and sandwich together with confectioner's custard.

To Moisten

100 ml/3½ fl oz orange juice
2 tbsps lemon juice
2 tbsps orange liqueur
25g/1oz icing sugar

To Decorate

Peel of 2 thinly pared oranges
Sugar water
100g/3½oz icing sugar
3 tbsps orange juice

1 To make the coconut mixture, mix the flour, sugar and salt on a pastry board. Using a palette knife, cut in the chilled margarine in small pieces. Mix well together. Add the desiccated coconut, quickly mix in and knead to a smooth dough. Chill.

2 Roll out the dough and use to line a greased baking tray 30 cm x 40 cm/12 inches x 16 inches. Prick the dough all over with a fork and bake for about 10 minutes in a preheated oven, Gas Mark 6/200°C/400°F.

3 Beat together the margarine and sugar until light and fluffy. Gradually beat in the eggs and orange zest. Sieve together the flour and baking powder and fold into the sponge mixture, together with the orange juice.

4 Combine the orange juice and marmalade and brush over the warm coconut dough. Pour over the sponge mixture, and bake for a further 15-20 minutes.

5 Mix together the orange juice, lemon juice, orange liqueur and icing sugar and use to moisten the warm cake. Set aside to cool.

6 Cut the orange zest into thin strips, bring to the boil in the sugar water and then drain. Mix the icing sugar with the orange juice, and use to ice the cake. Sprinkle orange zest on top.

PLUM FLAN

Makes approximately 24 portions

40g/1½oz fresh yeast
250 ml/8 fl oz lukewarm milk
125g/4oz caster sugar
500g/1lb flour
Pinch of salt
125g/4oz margarine
1 egg
Margarine for greasing

Topping

1 ½kg/3lb plums, stoned
2 eggs
100g/3½oz caster sugar
Cinnamon to taste
250 ml/8 fl oz soured cream

1 Crumble the yeast into the lukewarm milk, add a pinch of sugar and leave in a warm place until frothy. Mix together the flour, sugar, salt and melted margarine, then add the yeast mixture and the egg. Knead together well. Cover with foil and leave to rise in warm place.

2 Use the dough to line a greased baking tin. Arrange the plums on top and bake for about 20 minutes in a pre-heated oven, Gas Mark 6-7/200-220°C/400-425°F.

3 Meanwhile, stir together the eggs, sugar, cinnamon and soured cream. Spread over the flan and return to the oven for a further 30 minutes.

APRICOT MERINGUE CAKE

Makes approximately 12 portions

Topping

750g/1½lb apricots
75g/3oz caster sugar

Sponge Flan

125g/4oz margarine
125g/4oz caster sugar
3 tsps vanilla sugar
Pinch of salt
Grated zest of 1 lemon
3 eggs
2 tsps baking powder
200g/7oz plain flour
2 tbsps whipping cream
2 tbsps rum
Margarine for greasing

Meringue

2 egg whites
100g/3½oz caster sugar
40g/1½oz desiccated coconut/ground almonds

1 Pour boiling water over the apricots, then skin, halve and stone them. Cover the fruit with the sugar and set aside.

2 Beat the margarine until fluffy. Gradually beat in the sugar, vanilla sugar, salt, grated lemon zest and the eggs, one by one. Sieve together the flour and baking powder and fold into the mixture, alternating with the cream and rum.

3 Grease and line a 26-cm/10-inch loose-bottomed tin and turn the mixture into it. Arrange the apricots on top and bake for about 50 minutes in a preheated oven, Gas Mark 4/180°C/350°F.

4 Meanwhile, make the meringue. Whisk the egg whites until stiff, and gradually fold in the sugar and desiccated coconut/almonds. Using a piping bag, decorate the hot cake with the meringue mixture, and return to the oven for a further 10 minutes.

CURD CHEESE AND PLUM FLAN

Makes approximately 24 portions

200g/7oz low fat curd cheese
6 tbsps milk
1 egg
3 tbsps vegetable oil
100g/3½oz caster sugar
3 tsps vanilla sugar
Salt
400g/13oz plain flour
3 tsps baking powder
Margarine for greasing

Topping

1½kg/3lb plums, stoned
2 eggs
100g/3½oz caster sugar
Cinnamon to taste
250 ml/8 fl oz thick soured cream

1 Mix together the curd cheese, milk, egg, vegetable oil, caster sugar, vanilla sugar and salt. Sieve together the flour and baking powder and stir one half into the mixture. Knead in the second half. Roll out the dough and use to line a greased baking tin.

2 Arrange the plums on top of the dough. Bake for 20 minutes in a preheated oven, Gas Mark 6/200°C/400°F.

3 Meanwhile, beat together the eggs, sugar, cinnamon and soured cream. Pour over the flan and return to the oven for a further 30 minutes.

BLUEBERRY FLAN WITH CRUMBLE

Makes approximately 24 portions

25g/1oz fresh yeast
250 ml/8 fl oz lukewarm milk
Pinch of sugar
500g/1lb flour
125g/4oz caster sugar
Pinch of salt
150g/5oz margarine
2 eggs
Margarine for greasing

Crumble

500g/1lb flour
250g/8oz caster sugar
1 vanilla pod
300g/10oz margarine
2 tsps cinnamon

Topping

1kg/2lb blueberries

1 Crumble the yeast into the lukewarm milk with a pinch of sugar, stir, cover and leave for 20 minutes in a warm place until frothy.

2 Mix together the flour, sugar, salt and melted margarine. Stir in the yeast mixture. Knead the dough well. Cover and leave in a warm place until it has doubled in size.

3 Use the crumble ingredients to make a basic crumble mixture. Set aside. Wash and pick over the blueberries.

4 Roll out the dough and use to line a greased baking tray. Spread half the crumble mixture evenly on top, followed by the drained blueberries and then the remaining crumble mixture.

5 Bake for 20-25 minutes in a preheated oven, Gas Mark 6/ 200°C./400°F.

Note: Packet yeast dough and crumble mixture may be substituted in this recipe.

SHORTCRUST APPLE DUMPLINGS

Makes 8 dumplings

Pastry

250g/8oz flour
125g/4oz margarine
65g/2½oz caster sugar
Pinch of salt
Grated zest of 1 lemon
1 egg
Margarine for greasing

Filling

8 small apples
25g/1oz raisins
25g/1oz chopped walnuts
2 tbsps rum
1 tbsp caster sugar

Glaze

1 egg yolk, beaten
Icing sugar to dust

1 Use the pastry ingredients to make a basic shortcrust, knead and chill.
2 Peel and core the apples. Fill the centres with the raisins, walnuts, rum and sugar.
3 Roll out the pastry and cut out 8 circles large enough to cover the apples. Place an apple in the middle of each pastry circle. Pull the pastry up around each apple, pinch the edges together firmly to

seal and decorate with pastry shapes made from the trimmings.
4 Brush the beaten egg yolk over the pastry to glaze. Place the apple dumplings on a greased baking tray and bake for 45 minutes at Gas Mark 7/220°C/425°F.
5 Before serving, dust the apple dumplings with icing sugar.

GOOSEBERRY FLAN WITH CRUMBLE TOPPING

Makes approximately 24 portions

Pastry

375g/12oz flour
1 tsp baking powder
175g/6oz margarine
100g/3½oz caster sugar
2 eggs
1 tbsp milk
Margarine for greasing
Breadcrumbs

Filling

500 ml/18 fl oz milk
2 packets blancmange powder
125 ml/4 fl oz water
1 egg yolk
750g/1½lb low fat curd cheese
300g/10oz caster sugar
6 tsps vanilla sugar
1 egg white, beaten
750g/1½lb gooseberries

Crumble

175g/6oz flour
125g/4oz margarine
125g/4oz caster sugar

1 Mix the pastry ingredients to a firm dough, knead and chill.
2 Mix the milk, blancmange powder, water and egg yolk and cook until thick, following the instructions on packet. Stir in the low fat curd cheese, caster sugar, vanilla sugar and beaten egg white.
3 Grease a baking tin and sprinkle with breadcrumbs. Roll out the pastry and use to line the tin. Spread the blancmange mixture evenly over and top with the gooseberries.
4 Make a crumble topping with the flour, margarine and sugar and sprinkle this over the gooseberries. Bake for approximately 45 minutes in a preheated oven, Gas Mark 7/220°C/425°F.

CHERRY PIE

Makes approximately 24 portions

40g/1½oz fresh yeast
250 ml/8 fl oz lukewarm milk
Pinch of salt
750g/1½lb flour
150g/5oz caster sugar
Pinch of salt
Grated zest of ½ lemon
125g/4oz margarine
Margarine for greasing

Filling

2 eggs
2kg/4lb sweet cherries, stoned
200g/7oz ground almonds
125g/4oz granulated sugar
1-2 tsps cinnamon
Icing sugar

1 Crumble the yeast into the lukewarm milk, add a pinch of sugar and a little flour and leave in a warm place until frothy.
2 Mix together the flour, sugar salt and grated lemon zest. Alternately add the frothy yeast, melted margarine and eggs, mixing well after each addition. Knead the dough well and leave to rise in a warm place.
3 Roll out half the dough, and use to line a greased baking tray, pulling the dough up the sides of the tray. Sprinkle over the gound almonds and spread cherries on top.
4 Mix together the sugar and cinnamon and sprinkle over the cherries. Roll out the remaining dough and use to cover the pie. Wet the edges and press together firmly to seal.
5 Cover the pie with foil and leave to rise in a warm place. Bake for approximately 30 minutes in a preheated oven, Gas Mark 6/200°C/400°F. When cold, dredge with icing sugar.

UPSIDE DOWN APPLE CAKE

Makes approximately 12 portions

Filling

20g/3/4oz margarine
40g/1½oz chopped walnuts
25g/1oz caster sugar

500g/1lb cooking apples
100g/3½oz margarine
175g/6oz caster sugar
Grated zest of 1 lemon
Pinch of salt
2 egg
4 tbsps lemon juice
200g/7oz flour
2 tsps baking powder

1 Line a shallow 26-cm/10-inch spring-release tin with grease-proof paper. Melt the margarine and spread over the paper.
2 Mix together the chopped walnuts and sugar. Peel and core the apples, cut them into thick slices and arrange these over the bottom of the tin. Sprinkle over the nut mixture.

COCONUT SPONGE WITH PLUMS

Makes approximately 12 portions

100g/3½oz margarine
100g/3½oz caster sugar
3 tsps vanilla sugar
Pinch of salt
2 eggs
2 tbsps rum
150g/5oz flour
1 tsp baking powder

100g/3½oz desiccated coconut
1 kg/2 lb plums, stoned
Icing sugar
Margarine for greasing
Breadcrumbs

1 Beat together the margarine, sugar, vanilla sugar, salt, eggs and rum until light and fluffy. Sieve together the flour and baking powder and fold into the mixture, together with the desiccated coconut.
2 Grease a shallow 26-cm/ 10-inch cake tin with a remov-able base. Sprinkle with breadcrumbs. Turn the mixture into the tin, mounding it up slightly at the edges.
3 Arrange the plums close together on top of the cake mixture.
4 Bake the cake for approximately 60 minutes in a preheated oven, Gas Mark 4/ 180°C/350°F. Before serving, dust with icing sugar.

3 Beat the margarine, sugar, grated lemon zest and salt until light and fluffy. Gradually beat in the eggs and lemon juice. Sieve together the flour and baking powder and incorporate gradually into mixture. Spread the cake mixture over the apples.

4 Bake for approximately 45 minutes in a preheated oven, Gas Mark 6/200°C/400°F.

5 Remove from the oven and leave to cool for approximately 10 minutes after baking. Release the tin. Place a serving plate over the cake, turn it up-side down and remove the tin's base and the greaseproof paper.

WINTER STRAWBERRY GATEAU

Makes 12 portions

200g/7oz flour
1 tsp baking powder
100g/3½oz margarine
50g/2oz caster sugar
2 egg yolks
Margarine for greasing

Filling

2 egg whites
25g/1oz ground almonds
25g/1oz candied orange peel
25g/1oz candied lemon peel
50g/2oz icing sugar
1-2 tbsps fine breadcrumbs
750g/1½lb frozen strawberries, thawed

1 Sieve together the flour and baking powder. Cut in the margarine, then work in the sugar and egg yolks quickly and thoroughly to make a smooth dough. Grease a 26-cm/10-inch flan tin with a removable base. Roll out the dough and use to line the base and sides of the tin. Prick the pastry case several times with a fork. Bake for approximately 15-20 minutes in a preheated oven, Gas Mark 6/200°C/400°F. Remove from the oven and raise the heat to Gas Mark 8/230°C/450°F.

2 Whisk the egg whites until stiff, then fold in the almonds, finely chopped orange and lemon peel and icing sugar.

3 Sprinkle the cooled pastry case with breadcrumbs, fill with the strawberries and pile the meringue mixture on top.

4 Return to the oven for about 10 minutes, until the meringue is a pale gold colour. Leave to cool slightly, then serve immediately.

APRICOT BEIGNETS

Makes approximately 18

100g/3½oz margarine
50g/2oz caster sugar
3 tsps vanilla sugar
2 eggs
4 tbsps soured cream
350g/12oz flour
2 tsps baking powder

Filling

240g/8oz tinned apricots
25g/1oz desiccated coconut
1 egg yolk
Vegetable oil for deep-frying
Icing sugar to dredge

1 Beat together the margarine, sugar, vanilla sugar, salt and eggs until light and fluffy. Add the cream. Sieve together the flour and baking powder, stir a little into the mixture, then mix in the remainder by hand. Knead, then leave to stand. Roll out the dough to a thickness of 5 mm/ ¼ inch.
2 Drain the apricots, roll them in desiccated coconut and arrange on one half of the dough, well spaced out.
3 Beat the egg yolk and brush it round the apricots. Fold the second half of the pastry over the apricots. Press the two layers together well around each apricot half.
4 Cut out the apricot beignets with a pastry cutter. Make sure the edges are firmly sealed.
5 Heat the vegetable oil in a large saucepan or deep frying pan to approximately 180°C/ 350°F. Fry the apricot beignets a few at a time for about 4 minutes. Drain on kitchen paper and dust with icing sugar.

GOOSEBERRY AND YOGHURT TARTLETS

Makes 8

175g/6oz flour
Pinch of salt
3 tsps vanilla sugar
1 tbsp anisette
175g/6oz margarine
175g/6oz low fat curd cheese
Margarine for greasing

Filling

750g/1½lb tinned gooseberries
40g/1½oz granulated sugar
2 eggs
150g/5oz full fat natural yoghurt
1 tbsp anisette
Sugar for sprinkling

1 Working quickly, mix the flour, salt, vanilla sugar, anisette, margarine and curd cheese to a dough and set aside in the refrigerator to chill.
2 Drain the gooseberries. Add sugar to taste if desired. Toast the desiccated coconut with 2 tbsps sugar until golden brown.
3 Roll out dough and use to line 8 greased 11-cm/4-inch tartlet tins. Sprinkle each tin with the toasted coconut and fill with the gooseberries. Beat together the eggs, yoghurt, anisette and remaining sugar and pour this over the gooseberries.
4 Bake the tartlets for about 25 minutes in a preheated oven, Gas Mark 6/200°C/400°F. Turn the tartlets out immediately, and sprinkle with sugar before serving.

PLUM FLAN

Makes approximately 24 portions

40g/1½oz fresh yeast
250 ml/8 fl oz lukewarm milk
125g/4oz caster sugar
500g/1lb flour
Pinch of salt
125g/4oz margarine, melted
1 egg
Margarine for greasing

Topping

1½ kg/3lb plums, stoned
75g/3oz soft brown sugar
Cinnamon
50 g/2oz almonds, chopped

1 Crumble the yeast into the milk, stir in a pinch of both sugar and flour. Cover, and leave for 5-10 minutes in a warm place until frothy.
2 Put the flour, sugar, salt, the cooled margarine and the beaten egg into a bowl. Add the frothy yeast, mix well and thoroughly knead the dough, using an electric mixer if possible. Cover with foil and leave in a warm place until doubled in size. Knead again and use to line a greased baking tin.
3 Arrange the plums on top of the dough. Leave in warm place to rise again, then bake for 25-30 minutes in a preheated oven, Gas Mark 7/220°C/425°F.
4 Mix the soft brown sugar with the cinnamon and sprinkle over the warm cake. Dust with the almonds.

RHUBARB FLAN BOURBON

Makes approximately 12 portions

Filling

750g/1½lb rhubarb

Flan base

100g/3½oz margarine
200g/7oz caster sugar
3 tsps vanilla sugar
Pinch of salt
2 eggs
175g/6oz flour
2 tsps baking powder
2-3 tbsps whipping cream

Margarine for greasing

Topping

25g/1oz caster sugar
1 packet blancmange powder, vanilla flavour
600 ml/1 pt milk
1 egg

1 Wash and trim the rhubarb and cut into 8-cm/3-inch pieces.
2 Beat the margarine with the sugar, vanilla sugar and salt until light and fluffy, then beat in the eggs, one by one. Sieve together the flour and baking powder and fold into the mixture, alternating with the whipping cream.
3 Grease a 24-cm/9-inch flan tin with a removable base. Spread the flan mixture into it and top with the rhubarb. Bake for about 40 minutes in a preheated oven, Gas Mark 4/180°C/350°F.
4 Mix the sugar and the blancmange powder with a little milk, then add the egg. Bring the remaining milk to the boil and stir in the blancmange mixture. Stirring continuously, bring back to the boil. Remove from the heat, leave to cool, then spread over the rhubarb.

STRAWBERRY SUMMER DREAM

Makes 12 portions

1 x 24-cm/9-inch sponge flan base

Topping
250g/8oz curd cheese
125g/4oz caster sugar
3 tsps vanilla sugar
Grated zest of 1 lemon
3 tbsps lemon juice
3 sheets gelatine
125 ml/4 fl oz whipping cream
1kg/2lb strawberries

Glaze
125 ml/4 fl oz apple juice
125 ml/4 fl oz red wine
2 tbsps lemon juice
25g/1oz caster sugar
1 packet quick-setting gelatine, strawberry flavour

1 Place the sponge flan base on a serving dish.

2 Mix the curd cheese with the sugar, vanilla sugar, lemon juice and grated lemon zest. Stir in the dissolved sheet gelatine; set aside in the refrigerator. Whip the cream until stiff, and mix into the half-set curd cheese and gelatine.

3 Pile the mixture onto the flan base and arrange the drained and halved strawberries on top.

4 Mix the apple juice, red wine, lemon juice and sugar with the quick-setting gelatine, following the instructions on the packet, and drizzle carefully over the strawberries. Allow to set.

TYROLEAN APPLE STRUDEL

Makes 4-6 portions

250g/8oz flour, ½ tsp salt
125 ml/4 fl oz lukewarm water
40g/1½oz margarine, melted
1 tbsp fine breadcrumbs

Filling

1kg/2lb apples
125g/4oz caster sugar
½ tsp cinnamon
3 tsps vanilla sugar
75g/3oz raisins and currants, mixed
50g/2oz chopped almonds
Margarine for greasing
50g/2oz icing sugar to dredge

1 Mix the flour, salt, water and margarine to a firm dough and knead until smooth and elastic. Brush with warm water and leave to stand in a warmed pan for 30 minutes.

2 Roll out the pastry on a floured cloth and carefully pull until very thin, using the backs of the hands, and working from the centre to the outside: you should be able to see the cloth through the pastry. Trim to form a rectangle and sprinkle with the breadcrumbs.

3 Slice the peeled apples very thinly, and mix with the sugar, cinnamon, raisins, vanilla sugar and almonds. Arrange this mixture over the pastry, leaving 5 cm/2 inches clear all round the edge. Fold these edges inwards over the apple mixture. Use the cloth to roll the strudel up fairly loosely, patting it into shape occasionally. Brush with melted margarine and bake for 50-60 minutes in a pre-heated oven, Gas Mark 6-7/200°-220°C/400°-425°F. Once or twice during cooking, brush the strudel with more melted margarine.

4 Dust the strudel with icing sugar, slice and serve warm as a dessert or cold for afternoon tea.

GOOSEBERRY FLAN

Makes approximately 16 portions

1 packet Victoria sponge mix

Filling

1kg/2lb gooseberries

125g/4oz caster sugar

40g/1½oz cornflour

Topping

100g/3½oz marzipan paste

50g/2oz caster sugar

1 egg white

1 Wash and pick over the gooseberries, then cook them in a little water for a few minutes without allowing them to soften. Make a paste with the cornflour and a little cold water and stir this into the gooseberries to thicken. Leave to cool.

2 Make up the Victoria sponge mixture according to the packet instructions. Turn the mixture into a greased 28-cm/11-inch pie dish, heaping the mixture upwards slightly around the outside edgs.

3 Pile the gooseberries onto the sponge and bake for 20-25 minutes in a preheated oven, Gas Mark 6/200°C/400°F.

4 Cream the marzipan paste with the sugar and egg white. Fill a piping bag with the marzipan mixture and use to decorate the cooked flan. Pop under a preheated grill for a few minutes, until the marzipan turns golden brown.

RHUBARB RING

Makes approximately 20 portions

250g/8oz margarine

250g/8oz caster sugar

6 tsps vanilla sugar

Pinch of salt

5 eggs, separated

100g/3½oz ground almonds

375 g/12oz rhubarb

250g/8oz flour

3 tsps baking powder

Margarine for greasing

Breadcrumbs

Icing sugar for dusting

1 Beat the margarine with the sugar, vanilla sugar, salt and egg yolks until light and fluffy. Cut the rhubarb into small pieces, and add to the mixture with the almonds. Sieve together the flour and baking powder, then fold into the mixture. Whisk the egg whites until stiff, then carefully fold into the cake mixture.

2 Grease a 25-cm/10-inch ring mould, and sprinkle with breadcrumbs. Turn the mixture into this and bake for 60 minutes in a preheated oven, Gas Mark 4/180°C/350°F.

3 When cooked, turn the rhubarb ring out of the mould, and dust with icing sugar before serving.

CHERRY MARZIPAN CAKE

Makes approximately 20 portions

125g/4oz margarine
200g/7oz caster sugar
6 tsps vanilla sugar
4 eggs
Pinch of salt
Grated zest of 1 lemon
300g/10oz flour
1 tsp baking powder
250g/8oz marzipan paste, crumbled
200g/7oz bottle or tinned morello cherries
Margarine for greasing
Breadcrumbs
150g/5oz icing, if desired

1 Beat together the margarine, sugar and vanilla sugar until light and fluffy, then beat in the eggs, salt and lemon zest. Sieve together the flour and baking powder and gradually fold into the mixture. Stir in the crumbled marzipan paste. Lastly, carefully fold in the well-drained cherries.
2 Grease a 28-cm/11-inch loaf tin, and sprinkle with breadcrumbs. Turn the mixture into this and bake for 70-80 minutes in a preheated oven, Gas Mark 2-3/150°-170°C/ 300°-325°F. Leave to cool slightly before turning out. Ice, if desired.

REDCURRANT FLAN

Makes approximately 12 portions

250g/8oz flour
125g/4oz margarine
100g/3½oz caster sugar
Pinch of salt
2 egg yolks
Grated zest of ½ lemon
Margarine for greasing

Filling

500g/1lb redcurrants
4 egg whites
150g/5oz caster sugar
1 tbsp cornflour

1 Mix the flour, margarine, sugar, salt, egg yolks and lemon zest to a dough. Chill for 30 minutes. Roll out, and use to line a 26-cm/10-inch flan ring with a removable base. Bake for 20-30 minutes in a preheated oven, Gas Mark 6/200°C/ 400°F. Remove the cooked flan base and reduce the heat to Gas Mark 2-3/150°-170°C/ 300°-325°F.
2 Wash and pick over the redcurrants, draining them well.
3 Whisk the egg whites until very stiff, fold in the sugar and cornflour and whisk for a further 5 minutes. Fold the redcurrants carefully into the egg white mixture and pile onto the flan base.
4 Return the redcurrant flan to the oven for about 40 minutes.

61

BLACKBERRY SLICES

Makes approximately 24 slices

250g/8oz flour
150g/5oz caster sugar
Pinch of salt
150g/5oz margarine, chilled
1 egg
40g/1½oz ground almonds
2 tbsps rum
Margarine for greasing

Filling

5 tbsps blackberry jam
1 tbsp maraschino
500g/1lb blackberries
20g/3/4oz desiccated coconut
2 tsps caster sugar

Topping

500g/1lb curd cheese
125g/4oz caster sugar
3 tsps vanilla sugar
Grated rind of 1 lemon
6 tbsps lemon juice
7 sheets gelatine
250 ml/8 fl oz cream, whipped

Glaze

2 tbsps blackberry jam
Scant 250 ml/8 fl oz blackberry juice
3 sheets gelatine

1 Mix together the flour, sugar and salt on a pastry board, then dot with the chilled margarine cut into small pieces. Cut in with a pastry knife. Make a well in the mixture and put in the egg, almonds and rum. Working quickly, mix to a dough with your hands. Chill for 30 minutes.

2 Roll out the dough twice. Use to line a rectangular baking tin. Prick the base several times with a fork and bake for 10-15 minutes in a preheated oven, Gas Mark 6-7/200°-220°C/ 400°-425°F.

3 Mix the blackberry jam and maraschino together. Spread onto the warm pastry base and arrange the blackberries on top. Toast the desiccated coconut and sugar under the grill until golden, then sprinkle over the blackberries.

4 Mix together the curd cheese, sugar, vanilla sugar, lemon zest and juice. Soak the gelatine and dissolve in a little water over a low heat. Stir into the curd cheese mixture. When this is half set, fold in the whipped cream and spread evenly over the blackberries.

5 Stir together the blackberry jam and a little of the blackberry juice, then make up to 250 ml/8 fl oz with the remaining blackberry juice. Soak the gelatine, dissolve it in a little water over a low heat and add to the blackberry juice and jam mixture. Leave until lightly set, then spread over the topping. Leave to chill in the refrigerator. Cut into squares before serving.

CALVADOS APPLECAKE

Makes 16 portions

Pastry

750g/1½lb flour
175g/6oz caster sugar
5 tsps vanilla sugar
375g/12oz margarine
3 eggs
Margarine for greasing

Filling

2½kg/5lb cooking apples
375 ml/12 fl oz white wine
375 ml/12 fl oz water
Grated zest of 1 lemon
125g/4oz caster sugar
90g/3oz chopped almonds
150g/5oz currants
500 ml/18 fl oz apple juice from cooking
25g/1oz cornflour

Icing

200g/7oz icing sugar
6 tbsps calvados
2 tsps coconut oil

1 Mix the pastry ingredients to a dough and chill, covered, in the refrigerator.

2 Meanwhile, peel and core the apples and cut them into thick slices. Bring the white wine, water, grated lemon peel and sugar to the boil and stew the apples in this until part-cooked but still firm. Drain in a colander.

3 Roll out half the pastry and use to line a greased baking tray. Sprinkle over the almonds. Spread the cooled apple on top and sprinkle the currants over. Thicken the apple juice with the cornflour, adding a little extra liquid, if necessary, and spread over the apples.

4 Roll out the remaining pastry, and lay it over the apples. Press the edges together to seal, and prick the top all over with a fork. Bake for about 30 minutes in a preheated oven, Gas Mark 7/ 220°C/425°F.

5 Mix together the icing sugar, calvados and coconut oil. Brush this icing over the cooled cake. Cut into slices.

GATEAUX FOR THE GOURMET

A dream come true: you don't need to be a brilliant cook to spoil yourself and your family with these tempting and exotically decorated gâteaux. Just follow the simple recipes in this chapter for certain success.

CHOCOLATE WINDMILL GATEAU

Makes approximately 12 portions

250g/8oz margarine
250g/8oz caster sugar
Pinch of salt
5 eggs
300g/10oz flour
1½ tsps baking powder
1 tbsp instant coffee
3 tbsps warm water
Margarine for greasing
1½ tbsps cocoa
1 tbsp warm water
1 tbsps crème de cacao liqueur

Filling

500 ml/18 fl oz milk
1 packet custard powder
150g/5oz caster sugar
1/2 tbsp cocoa
200g/7oz margarine

Decoration

Grated chocolate
Wafer-thin chocolate leaves

1 Make a sponge mixture with the margarine, sugar, salt, eggs, flour and baking powder. Dissolve the coffee in the 3 tbsps warm water and stir into the sponge mixture.

2 Turn half the mixture into a greased 24-cm/9-inch tin with a removable base and bake for about 35 minutes at Gas Mark 4/180°C/350°F.

3 Meanwhile, mix the cocoa with the remaining warm water and the crème de cacao and stir into the reserved sponge mixture.

4 Leave the first sponge layer to cool. Cut it in half horizontally. Bake and slice the second batch of mixture in the same way.

5 Make a thick custard with the milk, custard powder, sugar and cocoa. Leave to cool. Beat margarine until light and fluffy and incorporate into the custard.

6 Spread the cake layers with the chocolate custard cream and stack together, alternating light and dark layers of sponge. Reserve a little of the cream to pipe a windmill design on the top of the cake and fill in the shapes with grated chocolate. Decorate the outer edge of cake with wafer-thin chocolate leaves.

CINNAMON GATEAU

Makes approximately 12 portions

4 eggs, separated
3 tbsps warm water
125g/4oz caster sugar
3 tsps vanilla sugar
Pinch of salt
2 tbsps cinnamon
75g/3oz flour
50g/2oz cornflour
Margarine for greasing

Filling

500 ml/18 fl oz milk
1 packet custard powder
2 egg yolks
125g/4oz caster sugar
3 tbsps white rum
3 tbsps cinnamon
250g/8oz margarine

Icing

100g/3oz icing sugar
2-3 tbsps white rum
Grated chocolate to decorate

2 tbsps rum
200g/7oz whipping cream
1 tbsp margarine
2 tbsps caster sugar
100g/3½oz almond cracknel

1 Strain the chestnuts and set aside 6 for decoration. Purée the remainder in an electric blender. Bring the purée to the boil with the milk, sugar and vanilla pod. Season with salt and simmer for about 40 minutes, stirring continuously. Remove the vanilla pod and leave the mixture to cool. Stir in the softened margarine, the cocoa and 1 tbsp rum.
2 Crumble the macaroons into a bowl, moisten with the 2 tbsps rum and leave to soak.
3 Line an 18-cm/7-inch tin with a removable base with damp greaseproof paper. Spread a layer of chestnut cream in the bottom, sprinkle over half the soaked macaroons, add a second layer of chestnut cream, followed by the remaining soaked macaroons and a final layer of chestnut cream. Place the gâteau in the

freezer for about 8 minutes.
4 Whip the cream until stiff, then use to cover the top and sides of the chilled gâteau.
5 Melt the 1 tbsp margarine in a frying pan, toss the 6 reserved chestnuts in this and then add the 2 tbsps sugar to glaze. Sprinkle the gâteau with the cracknel, decorate with the chestnuts and serve immediately.

1 Beat the egg yolks with the water, sugar, vanilla sugar and salt until light and foamy. Stir in the cinnamon. Whisk the egg whites until stiff, and fold them into the yolk mixture. Sieve the flour, cornflour and baking powder over the mixture, then fold in very gently using a balloon whisk. Turn the mixture into a greased 24-cm/9-inch tin with a removable base and bake for about 40 minutes in a preheated oven, Gas Mark 6/ 200°C/400°F.

2 Make up the milk, custard powder and sugar, egg yolks, rum and cinnamon into a thick custard. Melt the margarine, let it cool, then stir it slowly into the warm custard.
3 Slice the gâteau base in three horizontally and sandwich the layers together with the custard cream.
4 Mix the icing sugar with the rum and use to ice the gâteau. Decorate with grated chocolate.

CHILLED CHESTNUT GATEAU

Makes 8 portions

630g/1¾lb tinned whole chestnuts
375 ml/13 fl oz milk
125g/4oz caster sugar
1 vanilla pod
Pinch of salt
125g/4oz margarine, softened
50g/2oz cocoa
1 tbsp rum
150g-200g/5oz-7oz macaroons

COFFEE AND MERINGUE GATEAU

Makes 12 portions

3 eggs, separated
3 tbsps lukewarm water
Pinch of salt
150g/5oz caster sugar
50g/2oz margarine, melted and cooled
75g/3oz cornflour
1 tsp baking powder
Margarine for greasing

Meringue
1 egg white
50g/2oz caster sugar

Filling
125 ml/4 fl oz egg flip
1 tsp instant coffee
1 tsp cocoa

50g/2oz icing sugar
5 sheets gelatine
500 ml/18 fl oz whipping cream

1 Beat the egg yolks, water, salt and sugar until light and foamy, and add the melted and cooled margarine. Whisk the egg whites until stiff, and spoon onto the mixture. Sieve the flour, cornflour and baking powder over the egg whites. Gently fold everything together.

2 Grease the bottom of a 24-cm/9-inch cake tin with a removable base, turn the mixture into this and bake for 25-30 minutes in a preheated oven, Gas Mark 4/180°C/350°F. Remove the cake and reduce the heat to Gas Mark ¼/110°C/225°F.

3 Cut out a sheet of greaseproof paper the size of the tin. Mark out 12 wedges on this to act as a guide. Grease the paper and place on a baking tray. Whisk the egg white until stiff, gradually whisking in the sugar. Spoon the meringue into a piping bag and pipe decorations onto the greaseproof guide. Dry the meringue out for 40 minutes in the oven, leaving the door slightly open.

4 Slice the cake in two horizontally. Mix together the egg flip, coffee, cocoa and icing sugar. Soak the gelatine, dissolve it in a little water over a low heat and mix into the coffee mixture. Whip the cream until stiff and fold into coffee mixture as it begins to set.

5 Place one cake layer in ring of cake tin. Spread half the filling over this layer. Place the second cake layer on top and spread with the remaining filling. Arrange the meringue decorations on top and chill the finished gâteau.

Note: This gâteau may also be served semi chilled.

PEACH GATEAU WITH ALMOND CREAM

Makes approximately 12 portions

100g/3oz margarine
100g/3oz caster sugar
Pinch of salt
3 eggs
40g/1½oz ground almonds
150g/5oz plain flour
1 tsp baking powder
Margarine for greasing

Cream

1 packet custard powder
250 ml/8 fl oz milk
50g/2oz caster sugar
2 eggs
250ml/8 fl oz whipping cream

Topping

3 kiwi fruit
1 large tin peach halves
4 tbsps apricot jam
Toasted flaked almonds

1 Beat the margarine, sugar, salt and eggs until light and fluffy. Add the almonds and the flour sieved together with the baking powder. Turn the mixture into a greased 24-cm/9-inch cake tin with a removable base and bake for about 25 minutes in a preheated oven, Gas Mark 4-5/180-190°C/350-375°F. Leave to cool, before turning out.

2 Mix the custard powder with a little milk, the sugar and eggs. Bring the whipping cream and the remaining milk to the boil, stir in the mixed custard powder and boil for 1 minute. Leave to cool, stirring occasionally.

3 Replace the cooled sponge in the cake tin ring, without the base, and pour the almost set cream on top. Leave to set in the refrigerator.

4 Peel and slice the kiwi fruit. Drain the peaches and arrange both fruits on top of the cream.

5 Heat the apricot jam, rub through a sieve and brush over the fruit. Sprinkle the toasted almonds on top and decorate with whipped cream, if desired.

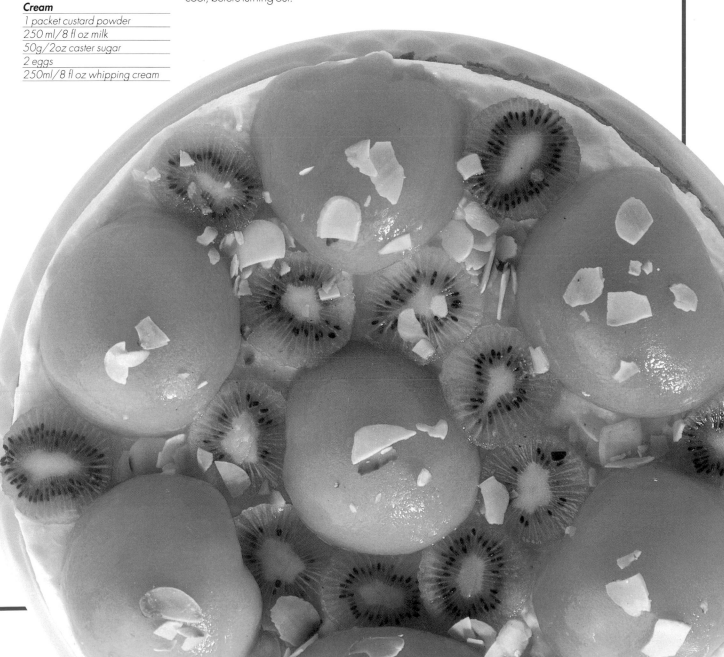

PINEAPPLE MARZIPAN GATEAU

Makes approximately 12 portions

150g/5oz marzipan paste
175g/6oz margarine
175g/6oz sugar
3 tsps vanilla sugar
3 eggs
300g/10oz plain flour
2 tbsps baking powder
50g/2oz ground almonds
4 slices fresh pineapple or 200g/7oz pineapple chunks, tinned

Decoration

100g/3oz marzipan paste
50g/2oz icing sugar
Red and green colouring
1 packet chocolate icing

1 Cream the marzipan paste and margarine to a soft consistency by hand. Gradually beat in the sugar, vanilla sugar and eggs. Sieve together the flour and baking powder, and fold into the mixture, a spoonful at a time. Add the almonds. Drain the pineapple well, cut into small pieces, and add to mixture.

2 Line a 26-cm/10-inch cake tin with a removable base with greaseproof paper. Turn the mixture into this and bake for 60-70 minutes in the centre of a preheated oven, Gas Mark 4/ 180°C/350°F.

3 For the decoration, mix the marzipan paste to a smooth paste with the icing sugar. Colour half red and a quarter green, and leave the rest white.

4 Make up the chocolate icing and spread over the top and sides of the gâteau.

5 Roll out the white marzipan paste thinly and cut out 2 hearts. Roll out the green paste and cut out a few leaf shapes. Draw veins on the leaves with the back of a knife blade.

6 To make the roses, firstly shape some of the red paste into cones, about 2 cm/¾ inch high. Roll out the remaining red paste and cut out a number of small circles 3½ cm/1¼ inches in diameter. Cut the circles in half.

7 Press the semicircles around the cones in layers, shaping the top edges to form petals. Press the layers firmly together at the base. Arrange the roses, leaves and hearts attractively on top of the gâteau.

MARZIPAN CAKE

Makes approximately 12 portions

Mixture

4 eggs, separated
3 tbsps warm water
125g/4oz caster sugar
3 tsps vanilla sugar
Pinch of salt
75g/3oz margarine, melted
75g/3oz flour
75g/3oz cornflour
Pinch of baking powder
Margarine for greasing

Filling

100g/3oz clear marmalade
400g/13oz marzipan paste

2 tbsps rum
600 ml/1 pt whipping cream
25g/1oz caster sugar
3 tsps vanilla sugar
6oz ground hazelnuts
4 tsps chocolate powder

1 Whisk the egg yolks with the water, sugar, vanilla sugar and salt until light and foamy, then whisk in the cooled margarine. whisk the egg whites until stiff and pile on top of the mixture. Sieve the flour, cornflour and baking powder over the egg whites and gently fold everything together.

2 Turn the mixture into a greased 26-cm/10-inch cake tin with a removable base and bake for 35-40 minutes in a preheated oven, Gas Mark 7/220°C/425°F. Turn out and leave to cool.

3 When cold, cut in half horizontally and spread the marmalade over one layer.

4 Mix the marzipan paste with the rum and roll out into two circles to fit the cake layers. Place one layer of marzipan on top of the marmalade-covered cake base.

5 Whip the cream with the sugar and vanilla sugar, and stir in the hazelnuts and chocolate powder. Divide into three equal portions.

6 Spread one-third of the cream over the marzipan. Cover with the second layer of cake. Spread the second portion of cream on top of this. Use the remaining cream to cover the sides of the gâteau, reserving a little for decoration if desired. Place the second marzipan layer on top of the gâteau.

7 Knead the marzipan trimmings together. Roll out and cut into decorative shapes, then pop them under a preheated grill to brown. Decorate the gâteau with piped cream, if desired, and with the marzipan shapes.

ORANGE MONT BLANC

Makes 12 portions

100g/3oz margarine
2 eggs
125g/4oz caster sugar
3 tsps vanilla sugar
Pinch of salt
100g/3oz flour
1½ tsps baking powder
2-3 tbsps whipping cream
Margarine for greasing
Breadcrumbs

Topping

4 tbsps apricot brandy
5 sheets gelatine

3 oranges
600 ml/1 pt whipping cream
25g/1oz caster sugar
3 tsps vanilla sugar
1 tbsp grated orange zest

Icing

125 ml/4 fl oz orange juice
40g/1½oz sugar
1 packet quick-setting gelatine
Pistachios for decorating

1 Melt the margarine and leave to cool. Whisk the eggs, sugar, vanilla sugar and salt until light and foamy. Whisk in the margarine. Sieve together the flour and baking powder. Fold into the mixture, together with the whipping cream.

2 Grease a 26-cm/10-inch flan ring and sprinkle with breadcrumbs. Turn the mixture into this and bake for 20-25 minutes in a preheated oven, Gas Mark 4/180°C/350°F. Leave to cool.

3 Moisten the flan base with the apricot brandy. Soak the gelatine sheets.

4 Peel and slice the oranges. Drain, reserving the juice. Whip the cream with the sugar, vanilla sugar and grated orange zest until stiff.

5 Drain the gelatine, dissolve over a low heat and mix with the cream mixture. Put a little cream into a piping bag and use to decorate the edge of the

gâteau. Pile the remaining cream onto the flan base. Arrange the orange slices on top.
6 Using additional unsweetened orange juice if necessary, make up the reserved orange juice to 125 ml/4 fl oz. Add the sugar. Use this liquid to make up the quick-setting gelatine according to the instructions on the packet. Spoon over the oranges. Decorate the piped edge of the gâteau with chopped pistachios.

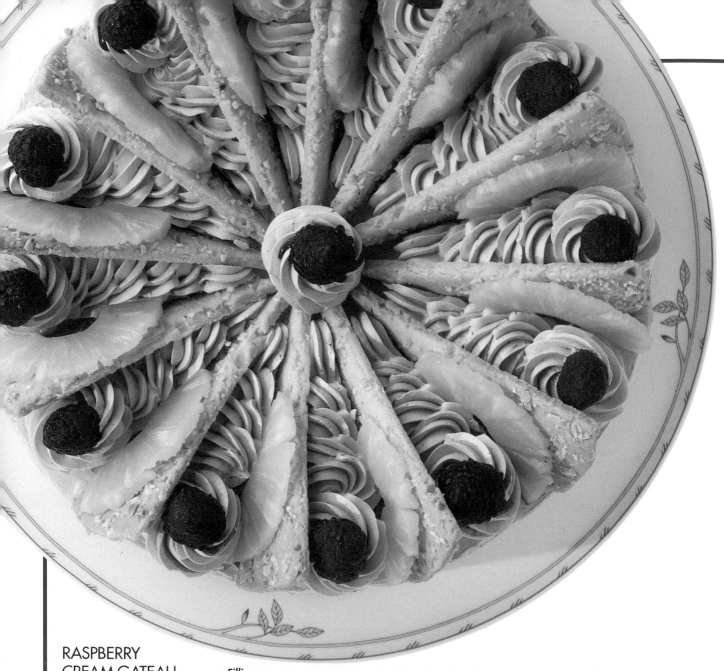

RASPBERRY CREAM GATEAU WITH PINEAPPLE

Makes approximately 12 portions

175g/6oz margarine
150g/5oz caster sugar
3 tsps vanilla sugar
5 eggs
Pinch of salt
Grated zest of 1 lemon
300g/10oz flour
2 tsps baking powder
80g/3oz finely chopped walnuts
Margarine for greasing

Filling

250g/8oz raspberries
25g/1oz caster sugar
1 l/1¾ pints whipping cream
2½ tbsps vanilla sugar
12 slices fresh pineapple

1 Make a basic sponge mixture using the margarine, 125g/4oz of the caster sugar, the vanilla sugar, eggs, salt, grated lemon zest, flour and baking powder. Mix together the walnuts and the remaining caster sugar.

2 Divide the mixture into six portions. Turn one portion into a greased 26-cm/10-inch cake or flan tin with a removable base. Sprinkle with a little of the walnut/sugar mixture and bake for 8-10 minutes in a preheated oven, Gas Mark 6/200°C/400°F, until golden brown. Immediately after baking, slide the sponge layer carefully onto greaseproof paper and leave to cool. Bake five more layers in the same way. While still warm, cut one layer into twelve wedge-shaped pieces.

3 Sprinkle the raspberries with the sugar. Reserve a few for decoration and purée the rest. Whip the cream with the vanilla sugar, and fold in the raspberry purée. Reserve some of the raspberry cream for piping.

4 Sandwich the layers together with raspberry cream. Arrange the twelve cake wedges in a fan shape on top of the gâteau (see illustration) and pipe the reserved cream between them. Decorate with the pineapple slices and the reserved raspberries.

CARIBBEAN FRUIT GATEAU

Makes approximately 12 portions

100g/3½oz flour
65g/2½oz icing sugar
Pinch of salt
65g/2½oz ground almonds
65g/2½oz margarine
Margarine for greasing

Topping

1 tin creamed coconut
6 sheets gelatine
250 ml/8 fl oz whipping cream
425g/14oz pineapple slices, tinned
2 bananas
Lemon juice
3 kiwi fruit
425g/14oz tinned mandarin oranges

Glaze

125 ml/4 fl oz pineapple juice
1 tsps sugar
1 packet quick-setting gelatine

1 Make a firm dough using the flour, icing sugar, salt, ground almonds and margarine. Roll out and use to line a greased 26-cm/10-inch cake tin with a removable base. Bake for 12-15 minutes in a preheated oven, Gas Mark 6/200°C/400°F. Leave to cool, then remove the base and place the gâteau back in the cake ring.

2 Soak the gelatine according to the instructions. Put 250 ml/8 fl oz of the creamed coconut into a bowl and stir in the prepared gelatine. Whip the cream until stiff and fold into the partly-set coconut cream. Spread evenly over the gâteau base.

3 Drain the pineapple slices and cut them into semicircles. Slice the bananas and brush them with a little lemon juice. Peel and slice the kiwi fruit, halving them if necessary, and drain the mandarins.

4 Arrange the fruit on the gâteau base, lightly pressing them into the cream. Make up the glaze using the pineapple juice, sugar and quick-setting gelatine, according to the instructions on the gelatine packet. Spoon evenly over the fruit.

Note: You can store any remaining creamed coconut for a short time in a screw-top jar in the refrigerator. It is good in fruit salads, summer drinks, etc.

PEAR GATEAU

Makes approximately 12 portions

Pastry
150g/5oz flour
½ tsp baking powder
65g/2½oz caster sugar
60-80g/2½-3oz margarine
1 small egg

Fruit Filling
485g/1lb tinned pears, or
approximately 600g/1¼lb fresh
dessert pears

Sponge Filling
3 large eggs, separated
2-3 tbsps pear brandy
150g/5oz caster sugar
75g/3oz flour
75g/3oz ground almonds
20g/3/4oz cocoa
3 level tsps baking powder

Decoration
2 pears, cut in half
Chocolate icing
1 packet lemon or chocolate icing

1 Make a firm dough from the pastry ingredients and chill for 30 minutes. Roll out, and use to line a greased deep flan tin, 26cm/10 inches in diameter. Bake blind for 10 minutes in a preheated oven, Gas Mark 6/200°C/400°F.
2 Arrange the well-drained fruit filling on the pastry case, cut edge downwards.
3 To make the sponge filling, whisk the egg yolks with the brandy until light and foamy. Whisk in the sugar and continue whisking until it has dissolved. Whisk the egg whites until stiff. Pile on top of mixture. Sieve the flour, cornflour, almonds, cocoa and baking powder over the egg whites. Using a balloon whisk, very gently fold everything together.
4 Pour the sponge filling over the pears and bake for about 50 minutes in a preheated oven, Gas Mark 4-6/175°-200°C/350°-400°F.
5 Coat the reserved pear halves with chocolate icing. Spread lemon or chocolate icing over the

gâteau, sprinkle the cracknel round the edge and arrange the chocolate pears on top.

TROPICAL TART

Makes approximately 12 portions

Pastry Base
125g/4oz margarine
75g/3oz icing sugar
3 tsps vanilla sugar
1 egg
Pinch of salt
250g/8oz flour
½ bottle rum flavouring
Margarine for greasing

Filling
200g/7oz dates
100g/3½oz margarine
100g/3½oz brown sugar
100g/3½oz coco-crisps
425g/14oz tinned pineapple slices
2 packets quick-setting gelatine
4 rum-flavoured chocolate truffles

SACHERTORTE

Makes approximately 12 portions

125g/4oz plain chocolate
60g/2½oz almonds, unskinned
125g/4oz margarine
125g/4oz caster sugar
5 eggs, separated
125g/4oz flour
1 heaped tsp baking powder
Margarine for greasing

Icing

125 ml/4 fl oz brandy
200g/7oz apricot jam
125g/4oz chocolate icing

1 Grate the chocolate and grind the almonds. Beat the margarine, sugar, egg yolks and chocolate until light and fluffy. Sieve together the flour and baking powder, and fold in first this mixture, then the ground almonds and finally the stiffly-beaten egg whites.

2 Grease the bottom of a 24-cm/9-inch cake tin with a removable base. Turn the mixture into this and bake for 40-45 minutes in a preheated oven, Gas Mark 6/200°C/400°F.

3 Slice the cake in half horizontally. Sprinkle brandy over both layers and leave to cool.

4 Sandwich the layers together with some of the jam. Spread the remaining jam all over the cake. Prepare the chocolate icing and coat the cake with it.

1 Cream the margarine until fluffy, then beat in the icing sugar and vanilla sugar. Add the egg, salt, flour and rum flavouring and mix to make a light dough. Chill.

2 Use to line a greased 26-cm/10-inch flan tin and bake for 15-20 minutes in a preheated oven, Gas Mark 6/200°C/400°F. Leave to cool.

3 Stone and dice the dates. Heat the margarine in a pan, put in the dates and cook them slowly until soft. Stir in the sugar and lastly the coco-crisps.

4 Spread the above mixture evenly into the pastry case, pressing it down well. Arrange the pineapple slices on top and coat with the quick-setting gelatine, prepared according to the packet instructions. Decorate with the rum truffles.

BLACK FOREST GATEAU

Makes approximately 12 portions

75g/3oz margarine
75g/3oz caster sugar
Pinch of salt
4 eggs, separated
2 tbsps kirsch
75g/3oz ground almonds
75g/3oz flour
1 heaped tsp baking powder
Margarine for greasing

Filling and Decoration

200g/7oz sour cherries, tinned or preserved
4 tbsps kirsch
4 sheets gelatine
500ml/18 fl oz sweetened cream, whipped
25g/1oz plain chocolate, coarsely grated

1 Beat the margarine, sugar, vanilla sugar, salt, and egg yolks until light and fluffy. Break the chocolate into small pieces, pour hot water over and leave to stand. Drain, retaining about 2 tbsps of water. Beat the chocolate until smooth, then fold it into the sponge mixture, together with the kirsch and almonds.

2 Whisk the egg whites until stiff, and pile on top of the cake mixture. Sieve the flour and baking powder over the egg whites. Carefully fold everything together.

3 Grease a 24-cm/9-inch cake tin with a removable base. Turn the mixture into this and bake for about 50 minutes in a preheated oven, Gas Mark 4/ 180°C/350°F.

4 Drain the cherries. Slice the cooled sponge in half horizontally and sprinkle liberally with kirsch. Soak the gelatine, dissolve over a low heat and incorporate well into the whipped cream.

5 Spread the cream over the first sponge layer. Arrange the cherries on top, cover with the second sponge layer and spread the remaining cream all over and round the gâteau. Decorate with coarsely-grated chocolate.

SOUTH SEAS GATEAU

Makes approximately 12 portions

Pastry

125g/4oz flour
40g/1½oz caster sugar
25g/1oz desiccated coconut
75g/3oz margarine
Margarine for greasing

Sponge Mixture

2 eggs, separated
2 tbsps water
65g/2½oz caster sugar
50g/2oz flour
25g/1oz cornflour

Filling

500g/1lb apples
125 ml/4 fl oz white wine
40g/1½oz caster sugar
Grated zest of 1 lemon
260g/8oz pawpaw cubes, tinned
approximately 4 tbsps white wine
5 kiwi fruits
2 tbsps lemon juice
3 packets quick-setting gelatine

Meringue

2 egg whites
75g/3oz caster sugar
Pinch of cinnamon
25g/1oz desiccated coconut

Glaze

25g/1oz apricot jam

1 Make a dough from the pastry ingredients. Leave to stand for 1 hour. Roll out and use to line a shallow 24-cm/9-inch cake tin with a removable base. Prick the base in several places with a fork and bake for about 10 minutes in a preheated oven, Gas Mark 7/220°C/425°F.
2 Meanwhile, whisk the egg yolks, water and sugar until light and foamy. Whisk the egg whites until stiff, spoon onto the sugar mixture. Sieve the flour and cornflour over the egg whites, and carefully fold everything together.
3 Brush the jam over the hot pastry base, diluting it with a little water if it is too thick. Spread the sponge mixture on top and bake for a further 10-15 minutes. Leave to cool, then remove from the tin.
4 Peel and core the apples, and cut each apple into eight pieces. Simmer gently for about 5 minutes in the white wine with the sugar and grated lemon zest. Drain, reserving the liquid.
5 Drain the pawpaw cubes, reserving the juice. Make up the reserved liquids to 500 ml/18 fl oz. Add lemon juice to taste and use to make up the quick-setting gelatine, according to the instructions on the packet.
6 Place the gâteau on a heatproof dish and place the ring of the cake tin over it again. Spread a little of the gelatine mixture over and arrange the fruit on it, covering the gâteau right up to the edge of the ring. Spoon over the remaining gelatine mixture. Leave until almost set.
7 Whisk the egg whites until stiff, whisk in the sugar and fold in the cinnamon and desiccated coconut. Spread this over the gâteau and put under a preheated low grill until lightly coloured. Remove cake tin ring and leave the gâteau to cool.

ALMOND CAKE

Makes 12 portions

150g/5oz ground almonds
150g/5oz caster sugar
3 tsps vanilla sugar
2 eggs
5 eggs, separated
50g/2oz flour
50g/2oz cornflour
Grated zest of 1 lemon
Margarine for greasing

To Moisten
2 tbsps brandy

Filling
200g/7oz margarine
4 egg yolks
180g/6oz icing sugar
6 tbsps strong, cold coffee
200g/7oz hazelnut cracknel

Decoration
2 egg whites
Icing sugar
Food colouring
100g/3½oz marzipan
Icing flowers, if desired

1 Whisk the almonds, sugar, vanilla sugar, eggs and egg yolks until light and thick. Sieve over the flour, cornflour and grated lemon zest and fold in carefully with a balloon whisk. Whisk the egg whites until stiff and fold in.

2 Turn the mixture in a greased 26-cm/10-inch cake tin with a removable base, and bake for about 50 minutes in a preheated oven, Gas Mark 4/180°C/350°F.

3 Slice the cooled cake horizontally into three layers, sprinkle each layer with brandy and leave to soak in.

4 Cream the margarine until light and fluffy, then beat in the egg yolks, icing sugar and coffee one after the other. Continue beating until mixture is of a thick, foamy consistency. Stir in the cracknel. Use this coffee cream to sandwich together the cake layers.

5 Whisk the remaining egg whites until light and foamy. Stir in the icing sugar to make a thick, hard icing. Use to ice the top and sides of the cake.

6 Colour the marzipan as required and shape into flowers, leaves and stems. Decorate the cake, adding ready-made icing flowers if desired.

ALASKA SPONGE

Makes approximately 7 portions

Sponge

1 egg, separated
50g/2oz caster sugar
3 tsps vanilla sugar
1 tbsp water
40g/1½oz flour
Margarine for greasing

Filling

100g/3½oz raisins
5 tbsps rum
375 ml/12 fl oz whipping cream
25g/1oz caster sugar
50g/2oz chocolate, coarsely grated
1 packet chocolate ice cream
1 packet lemon ice cream

Decoration

Chocolate, coarsely grated

1 Use the sponge ingredients to make up a basic sponge mixture. Line a loaf tin with a 12-cm/4½-inch-wide strip of foil or greaseproof paper. Grease with margarine and turn the sponge mixture into this. Lay another strip of foil or greaseproof paper on top, to cover the sponge. Bake for 12-15 minutes in a preheated oven, Gas Mark 7/220°C/425°F. Remove the top foil or greaseproof paper, turn out the sponge, pull off the second piece of foil or paper and leave the sponge to cool. Cut into two 15-cm/6-inch-long rectangles.

2 In a saucepan, heat the raisins with the rum, then remove from the heat and allow to cool. If the raisins do not absorb all the rum, sprinkle the sponge with remainder. Whip the cream until stiff, adding sugar to taste. Divide into two portions, adding the grated chocolate and rum raisins to one portion.

3 Build up the gâteau as follows: a layer of sponge, a layer of raisin cream, a layer of chocolate ice cream, another layer of raisin cream, a layer of lemon ice cream, another layer of raisin cream and a final layer of sponge.

4 Spread the plain whipped cream all round the cake, decorate with coarsely grated chocolate and put into the freezer for at least 3 hours. Slice before serving.

STRAWBERRY AND LEMON CREAM GATEAU

Makes approximately 12 portions

250g/8oz flour
50g/2oz caster sugar
Pinch of salt
Grated zest of 1 lemon
125g/4oz margarine
1 egg

Topping

750g/1½lb strawberries
50g/2oz caster sugar
2 tbsps syrup of pomegranate
2 packets quick-setting gelatine, strawberry flavour
1 packet lemon trifle topping mix
125 ml/4 fl oz white wine
175g/6oz caster sugar
200g/7oz full fat soft cheese
6 tbsps vanilla sugar
4 tbsps lemon juice
500g/1lb whipping cream
Lemon slices, to decorate

1 Mix the flour, sugar, salt, lemon zest and egg together well. Knead to a light dough. Leave to stand in a cool place.

2 Meanwhile, wash, hull and halve the strawberries and sprinkle with sugar.

3 Roll out the dough. Line the base and sides of a 26-cm/10-inch cake tin with a removable base with greaseproof paper. Line with the pastry and bake for about 20 minutes in a preheated oven, Gas Mark 6/200°C/400°F. Leave to cool in the tin.

4 Drain the strawberries, and make up the liquid to 500 ml/18 fl oz with water. Add the syrup of pomegranate. Arrange half the strawberries over the gâteau base. Make up 1 packet of quick-setting gelatine with 250 ml/8 fl oz of the strawberry juice, according to the packet instructions. Spread over the strawberries.

5 Mix the trifle topping with the white wine and leave to soak for 10 minutes. Add the sugar and dissolve over a low heat, stirring constantly. Leave to cool.

6 Mix the soft cheese with the vanilla sugar and lemon juice, then stir in the trifle topping. Whip the cream until stiff and fold it into the half-set mixture. Spread over the strawberries, smoothing the top. Leave to set. Arrange the remaining strawberries on top.

7 Make up the second packet of quick-setting gelatine with the remaining strawberry juice and spoon over the gâteau. Carefully remove the greaseproof paper from the sides and bottom of the gâteau. Decorate with the lemon slices.

BANANA TOWER

Makes approximately 12 portions

Mixture

5 eggs
225g/7½oz caster sugar
Pinch of salt
6 tbsps single cream
125g/4oz margarine, melted and cooled
250g/8oz flour
3 tsps baking powder

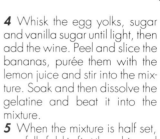

4 Whisk the egg yolks, sugar and vanilla sugar until light, then add the wine. Peel and slice the bananas, purée them with the lemon juice and stir into the mixture. Soak and then dissolve the gelatine and beat it into the mixture.

5 When the mixture is half set, carefully fold in first the whipped cream and then the stiffly beaten egg whites. Divide into two portions.

6 Replace the cake tin ring around one of the larger cake layers and cover thickly with one portion of cream.

7 Divide the second portion of cream in two. Spread one half over the second large cake layer. Place this second layer on top of first. Use the remaining cream to sandwich together the two smaller cake layers and place these on top of the larger ones.

8 Make up the chocolate couverture according to the instructions, add the coconut oil and cover the gâteau with it. Decorate with whipped cream.

Filling

5 eggs, separated
175g/6oz caster sugar
3 tsps vanilla sugar
Grated zest of 1 lemon
3 tbsps white wine
750g/1½lb ripe bananas
7 tbsps lemon juice
8 sheets gelatine
250g/8oz cream, whipped
5 tbsps maraschino

Icing

200g/7oz chocolate couverture
25g/1oz coconut oil

For Decoration

250 ml/8 fl oz whipping cream

1 Whisk the eggs, sugar and salt until light and foamy, then gradually whisk in the cream and margarine. Sieve together the flour and baking powder, and fold into the mixture.

2 Grease two cake tins with removable bases, one 16 cm/6 inches in diameter and the other 24 cm/9 inches in diameter. Divide the mixture between these and bake for 20-25 minutes in a preheated oven, Gas Mark 6-7/200-220°C/400-425°F. Leave to cool.

3 Slice each cake in half horizontally and moisten liberally with maraschino.

AN INVITATION TO AFTERNOON TEA

Do you enjoy a good, old-fashioned tea? Then why not invite a few friends round and treat them to delicious, crunchy biscuits and cookies, and three different kinds of cake, made from one basic mixture.

ALMOND TRIANGLES

*Makes approximately
45 triangles*

250g/8oz flour
125g/4oz margarine
1 egg
75g/3oz caster sugar
Margarine for greasing

Filling
100g/3½oz ground almonds
150g/5oz caster sugar
1 egg, separated

Icing
25g/1oz coconut oil
75g/3oz icing sugar
15g/1/2oz cocoa powder
1-2 tbsps rum

1 Make a dough from the flour, margarine, egg and sugar. Knead lightly and leave to stand in a cold place for 30 minutes.
2 Mix the almonds, sugar and egg white to a firm consistency.
3 Roll out the dough thinly. Cut out 6-cm/2½-inch rounds and arrange them on a greased baking tray. Place a ball of almond mixture on top of each round. Brush the pastry edges with beaten egg yolk. Fold the pastry inwards on three sides and press the edges lightly into the almond filling.
4 Bake in a preheated oven, Gas Mark 6/200°C/400°F for 10-15 minutes.
5 Meanwhile mix the coconut oil with the icing sugar, cocoa and rum. Ice the warm triangles at the point where the folded edges meet.

RUM RINGS

Makes approximately 40 rings

300g/10oz flour
50g/2oz cocoa powder
Pinch of salt
100g/3½oz caster sugar
200g/7oz margarine
2 tbsps rum

Margarine for greasing
1 egg
25g/1oz chopped almonds

1 Make a dough from the flour, cocoa, salt, sugar, margarine and rum. Knead lightly and leave to stand in a cold place for at least 60 minutes.
2 Roll small pieces of the dough into thin coils. Twist two coils together to form a ring. Make about 40 rings in this way.
3 Arrange the rings on a greased baking tray, brush with beaten egg and sprinkle with chopped almonds.
4 Bake in a preheated oven, Gas Mark 6-7/200-225°C/400-425°F. for 12-14 minutes. When cooked, they should be golden brown in colour.

DUTCH SHORTBREAD

Makes approximately 25 biscuits

200g/7oz margarine
125g/4oz caster sugar
6 tsps vanilla sugar
Pinch of salt
2 tbsps rum
100g/3½oz ground almonds
300g/10oz flour
Good pinch of baking powder
Margarine for greasing

1 Beat the margarine, sugar, vanilla sugar and salt until light and fluffy. Add the rum, almonds and the flour, sieved together with the baking powder.
2 Using a piping bag, pipe wide strips onto a greased baking tray.
3 Bake the shortbread in a preheated oven, Gas Mark 7/220°C/425°F for 10-15 minutes.

SWEET CARAWAY BISCUITS

Makes approximately 40 biscuits

250g/8oz flour
125g/4oz margarine
125g/4oz caster sugar
1 tbsp caraway seeds
Pinch of ground nutmeg
Grated zest of 1 lemon
1 small egg
1 tbsp sherry
Sugar

LEMON HEARTS

Makes approximately 40 hearts

250g/8oz flour
125g/4oz margarine
150g/5oz caster sugar
3 egg yolks
Grated zest of 1 lemon
Good pinch of baking powder

Margarine for greasing
50g/2oz icing sugar
1 tbsp lemon juice
Approximately 1 tbsp water

1 Make a dough from the flour, margarine, sugar, egg yolks, grated lemon zest and baking powder, working the ingredients together quickly but thoroughly. Leave to stand in a cold place for a short time.
2 Roll out the dough fairly thickly. Using a heart-shaped cutter, cut out biscuits and arrange on a greased baking tray. Bake in a preheated oven, Gas Mark 7/220°C/425°F for about 12 minutes, until golden brown.
3 Mix the icing sugar, lemon juice and water and use to ice the hearts.

1 Make a dough from the flour, margarine, sugar, caraway seeds, nutmeg, grated lemon zest, egg and sherry and chill.
2 Roll out the dough to 1 cm/ ³⁄₈ inch thick, and cut out various shapes using biscuit cutters.
3 Line a baking tray with greaseproof paper, arrange the biscuits on it and bake in a preheated oven, Gas Mark 6/200°C/400°F for 10-15 minutes.
4 Whilst they are still hot, sprinkle the biscuits with sugar.

HALF-'N-HALVES

Makes approximately 25 biscuits

250g/8oz flour
125g/4oz margarine
100g/3½oz caster sugar
6 tsps vanilla sugar
1 egg
25g/1oz ground hazelnuts
Margarine for greasing
200g/7oz icing sugar
2-3 tbsps redcurrant syrup

1 Make a dough from the flour, margarine, sugar, vanilla sugar, egg and hazelnuts. Leave in a cold place for 15 minutes.
2 Roll out the dough to the thickness of a knife blade, and cut out 4-cm/1½-inch rounds. Arrange the rounds on a greased baking tray and bake in a preheated oven, Gas Mark 7/220°C/425°F for about 12 minutes until golden brown.
3 Mix half the icing sugar to a thick consistency with the redcurrant syrup and 1 tsp water. Mix the remaining icing sugar with plain water.
4 Ice each biscuit half in red icing and half in white, and leave to set.

COCONUT DROPS

Makes approximately 60 biscuits

200g/7oz margarine
200g/7oz caster sugar
3 tsps vanilla sugar
Pinch of salt
4 egg whites
200g/7oz flour
½ tsp baking powder
200g/7oz desiccated coconut
Margarine for greasing

1 Beat the margarine, sugar, vanilla sugar, salt and egg whites until light and fluffy. Sieve together the flour and baking powder and fold into the mixture alternately with the coconut.
2 Using a piping bag fitted with a plain nozzle, pipe out small amounts of the mixture onto a greased baking tray.

Bake in a preheated oven, Gas Mark 6/200°C/400°F for about 10 minutes.

Note: A teaspoon may also be used to drop the mixture onto the tray.

CREAM BISCUITS

Makes approximately 40 biscuits

500g/1lb flour
½ tsp baking powder
Pinch of salt
Pith of 2 vanilla pods
375g/12oz margarine
200g/7oz soured cream
Demerara sugar

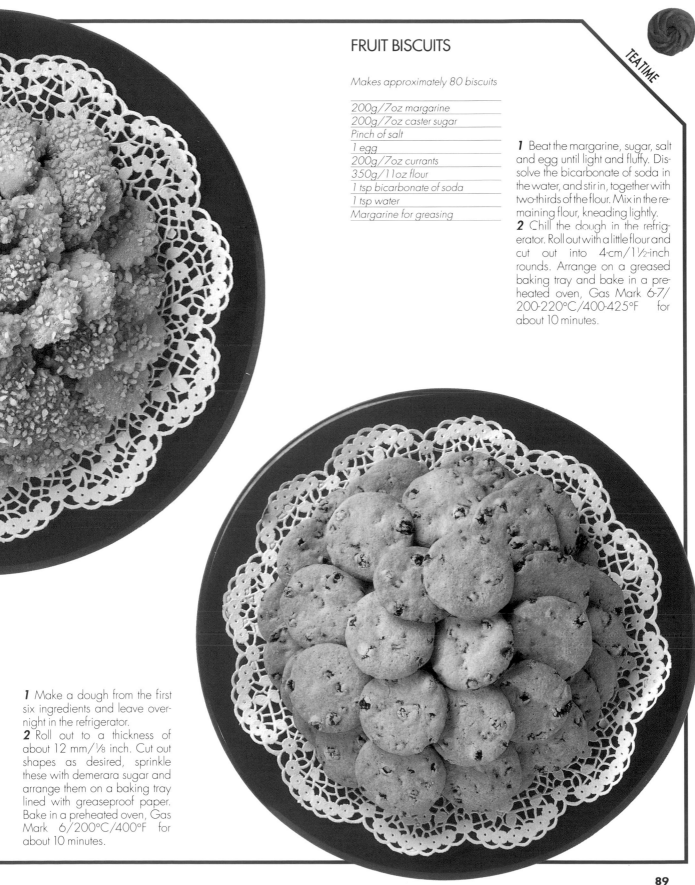

FRUIT BISCUITS

Makes approximately 80 biscuits

200g/7oz margarine
200g/7oz caster sugar
Pinch of salt
1 egg
200g/7oz currants
350g/11oz flour
1 tsp bicarbonate of soda
1 tsp water
Margarine for greasing

1 Beat the margarine, sugar, salt and egg until light and fluffy. Dissolve the bicarbonate of soda in the water, and stir in, together with two-thirds of the flour. Mix in the remaining flour, kneading lightly.

2 Chill the dough in the refrigerator. Roll out with a little flour and cut out into 4-cm/1½-inch rounds. Arrange on a greased baking tray and bake in a preheated oven, Gas Mark 6-7/200-220°C/400-425°F for about 10 minutes.

1 Make a dough from the first six ingredients and leave overnight in the refrigerator.

2 Roll out to a thickness of about 12 mm/⅛ inch. Cut out shapes as desired, sprinkle these with demerara sugar and arrange them on a baking tray lined with greaseproof paper. Bake in a preheated oven, Gas Mark 6/200°C/400°F for about 10 minutes.

ALMOND FLAKES

Makes approximately 15 biscuits

100g/3½oz flaked almonds
1 tbsp clear honey
3 tsps vanilla sugar
75g/3oz chocolate, coarsely grated
25g/1oz coconut oil
4 tbsps whipped cream

1 Toast the flaked almonds with the honey and vanilla sugar until golden brown, then leave to cool.
2 Melt the grated chocolate with the coconut oil in a bowl over a pan of hot water. Stir in the flaked almonds. Leave the mixture to cool slightly, then fold in the whipped cream. Line a baking tray with greased foil or greaseproof paper. Arrange dollops of the mixture on this.
3 Place in the refrigerator to set.

SPANISH CINNAMON BUNS

Makes approximately 12 buns

250g/8oz margarine
250g/8oz caster sugar
Pinch of salt
6 eggs
3 tsps cinnamon
250g/8oz flour
Margarine for greasing

1 Beat the margarine, sugar, salt and eggs until light and fluffy, then fold in the cinnamon and flour.
2 Divide the mixture between twelve greased bun tins and bake on the lowest shelf in a pre-heated oven, Gas Mark 6-7/200°-220°C/400°-425°F for about 15 minutes.

CHOCOLATE RINGS

Makes approximately 50 biscuits

175g/6oz margarine
150g/5oz icing sugar
1 egg yolk
3 tsps vanilla sugar
2 tbsps cocoa powder
1 tsp instant coffee
250g/8oz flour
Margarine for greasing

1 Beat the margarine, icing sugar, egg yolk, vanilla sugar, cocoa and coffee until light and fluffy. Fold in the sieved flour.
2 Using a piping bag fitted with a star nozzle, pipe out rings of the mixture onto a baking tray lined with greased foil or greaseproof paper.
3 Bake in a preheated oven, Gas Mark 6-7/200°-220°C/ 400°-425°F for about 8-10 minutes.

CHOCOLATE ALMOND TREATS

Makes approximately 45 biscuits

200g/7oz almonds
100g/3½oz plain chocolate
200g/7oz caster sugar
3 level tsps cinnamon
3 eggs
Margarine for greasing

1 Grind the almonds and grate the chocolate. Mix together with the sugar, cinnamon, flour and eggs to make a dough.
2 Using two teaspoons, drop spoonfuls of the mixture onto a greased and floured baking tray.
3 Bake the biscuits in a pre-heated oven, Gas Mark 4/ 180°C/350°F for about 20 minutes.

SWISS COOKIES

Makes approximately 50 cookies

175g/6oz flour
85g/3¼oz margarine
75g/3oz caster sugar
3 tsps vanilla sugar
1 egg
Pinch of salt
50g/2oz raisins
60g/2½oz hazelnut kernels
Margarine for greasing

1 Make a dough from the flour, margarine, sugar, vanilla sugar, egg and salt. Stir in the raisins and hazelnut kernels.
2 Shape into rolls about 4 cm/ 1½ inches thick and either put into the freezer or leave for 24 hours in a very cold place. Cut the rolls into ½-cm/¼-inch-thick slices. Arrange the cookies on a greased baking tray and bake in a preheated oven, Gas Mark 6-7/200°-220°C/

400°-425°F for 15-20 minutes, until golden brown.

GREEK WALNUT TRIANGLES

Makes approximately 40 triangles

250g/8oz margarine
100g/3½oz icing sugar
Pinch of salt
300g/10oz flour
1½ tsps baking powder
50g/2oz walnuts, chopped
Margarine for greasing
Icing sugar for dredging

1 Stir together the margarine, icing sugar and salt, without beating. Sieve together the flour and baking powder and add to the mixture, together with the walnuts.

2 Shape the dough into rolls the thickness of a finger, and cut into 15-cm/6-inch lengths.

3 Bend each length into a triangle, place on a greased baking tray and bake in a preheated oven, Gas Mark 6/200°C/400°F for 10-12 minutes.

4 When cold, dredge with icing sugar.

MINI ROCK CAKES

Makes approximately 80 cakes

450g/15oz flour
3 tsps baking powder
150g/5oz caster sugar
250g/8oz margarine
150g/5oz sultanas or currants
2 eggs
4 tbsps milk
Margarine for greasing

1 Mix the flour, baking powder and sugar on a pastry board. Dot with the cold margarine cut into small pieces. Cut the margarine into the flour with a palette knife. Add the sultanas.

2 Beat the eggs with the milk. Make a well in the flour mixture, pour in the egg mixture, and quickly work the two together to make a soft dough.

3 Using a teaspoon, drop spoonfuls of the mixture onto a greased baking tray and bake in a preheated oven, Gas Mark 6/200°C/400°F for 20-25 minutes.

CRUMBLE COOKIES

Makes approximately 40 cookies

250g/8oz flour
1 tsp baking powder
200g/7oz margarine
3 tbsps whipping cream
3 tsps vanilla sugar
Egg yolk
Demerara sugar
Margarine for greasing

1 Sieve together the flour and baking powder. Make a smooth dough from this, the margarine, cream and vanilla sugar. Chill.
2 Roll out the dough, cut out hearts or stars, brush thinly with egg yolk and sprinkle with demerara sugar.
3 Arrange the biscuits on a greased baking tray and bake in a preheated oven, Gas Mark 6-7/200-225°C/400-425°F for about 8 minutes until just golden.

ALMOND SNAPS

Makes approximately 50 biscuits

75g/3oz margarine
100g/3½oz caster sugar
100g/3½oz golden syrup
1 tsp cinnamon
40g/1½oz chopped almonds
150g/5oz flour
2 tbsps whipping cream
100g/3½oz chocolate couverture

1 Beat the margarine, sugar and syrup until light and fluffy.

Fold in the cinnamon, almonds, flour and cream.
2 Bake the mixture in batches. Place four teaspoonfuls of the mixture at a time on a greased baking tray, leaving large gaps in between. Dip a knife in hot water and flatten each spoonful of mixture.
3 Bake in a preheated oven, Gas Mark 6-7/200°-220°C/400°-425°F. for 3-5 minutes.
4 Leave to cool slightly. Whilst still warm, take each biscuit carefully off the tray and shape by bending round a rolling pin.
5 Coat half of each biscuit by dipping in the chocolate couverture.

CHOCOLATE PRALINES

Makes approximately 20 biscuits

125g/4oz caster sugar
125g/4oz chopped almonds
250g/8oz whipping cream
50g/2oz candied lemon zest
25g/1oz margarine
5 tbsps orange liqueur
Vegetable oil for greasing
Plain chocolate couverture
Strips of orange zest

1 Melt the sugar in a pan, without allowing it to colour. Stir in the almonds, cream and lemon zest, and bring to the boil, stirring constantly until the mixture starts to thicken. Add the margarine and orange liqueur and continue to boil until the mixture shrinks away from the bottom of the saucepan and the spoon leaves a mark. Pour the mixture quickly into an oiled baking tin.
2 When the mixture has hardened, cut it into small squares, using a knife dipped in water.
3 Leave to go quite cold, then coat thinly with the melted chocolate couverture and leave to harden.
4 When the chocolate is almost hard, decorate the pralines with paper-thin strips of orange zest.

CHOCOLATE CHIP BISCUITS

Makes approximately 30 biscuits

100g/3½oz margarine
75g/3oz caster sugar
75g/3oz brown sugar
1 tsp vanilla sugar
Pinch of salt
1 egg
1 tbsp water
175g/6oz flour
100g/3½oz plain chocolate
50g/2oz hazelnut kernels
Margarine for greasing

1 Beat the margarine, sugar, brown sugar and vanilla sugar until light and fluffy. Add the salt, egg and water and mix together well. Fold in the sieved flour. Cut the chocolate into small cubes, chop the hazelnut kernels roughly and stir both into the mixture.

2 Drop teaspoonfuls of the mixture onto a greased baking tray and flatten each one lightly. Bake in a preheated oven, Gas Mark 6/200°C/400°F for about 12 minutes.

GINGER BISCUITS

Makes approximately 30 biscuits

225g/7½oz flour
Pinch of salt
50g/2oz ground almonds
1 tsp ground ginger
1 tsp cinnamon
20g/¾oz fresh ginger, grated
125g/4oz caster sugar
125g/4oz margarine
1 egg, beaten
Margarine for greasing
1 egg yolk for brushing
Almonds, glacé cherries or crystallized ginger to decorate

1 Mix together the flour, salt, ground almonds, ginger, cinnamon, grated ginger and sugar on a pastry board. Dot with flakes of margarine and cut these in using a palette knife. Make a well in the mixture, drop in the beaten egg and mix together well with the palette knife. Knead quickly to a smooth dough. Cover and chill.
2 Roll out the dough and cut into shapes. Arrange on a baking tray lined with a sheet of greaseproof paper. Mix the egg yolk with a little water and brush over the biscuits to glaze. Bake in a preheated oven, Gas Mark 6/200°C/400°F for about 8 minutes.

SWISS BISCUIT SQUARES

Makes approximately 50 biscuits

250g/8oz flour
250g/8oz caster sugar
Pinch of salt
2 tsps cinnamon
125g/4oz ground almonds
125g/4oz margarine
1 egg, beaten
Margarine for greasing
1 egg yolk

1 Mix together the flour, sugar, salt, cinnamon and almonds on a pastry board. Using a palette knife, cut in the margarine. Add the beaten egg, mix and knead together well.
2 Roll out the dough on a greased baking tray to a thickness of ½ cm/¾ inch. Mix the egg yolk with a little water and brush over the dough. Use a fork to mark a criss-cross pattern on top.
3 Bake in a preheated oven, Gas Mark 4-6/180°C-200°C/350°-400°F for about 20 minutes. Cut into 4-cm/1½ -inch squares whilst still hot.

CHOCOLATE DROPS

Makes approximately 40 biscuits

200g/7oz margarine
250g/8oz flour
50g/2oz cornflour
125g/4oz caster sugar
3 tsps vanilla sugar
25g/1oz cocoa powder
2 level tsps baking powder
Flour
Almond halves

1 Melt the margarine and set aside to cool. Mix together the flour, cornflour, sugar, vanilla sugar, cocoa powder, baking powder and liquid margarine to a smooth dough.

2 Roll walnut-sized pieces of the dough into balls and arrange them on a floured baking tray.

3 Press an almond half onto each biscuit. Bake in a pre-heated oven, Gas Mark 6/200°C/400°F for about 20 minutes.

Note: These chocolate drops may also be iced if desired.

FLORENTINES

Makes approximately 30 biscuits

200g/7oz flaked almonds

100g/3½oz candied orange peel, roughly chopped

50g/2oz margarine

125g/4oz whipping cream

200g/7oz caster sugar

125g/7oz flour

Margarine for greasing

Flour

125g/4oz plain chocolate couverture

1 Put the almonds, orange peel, margarine, cream, sugar and flour into a saucepan and bring to the boil, stirring continuously.

2 Grease and flour a baking tray. Drop teaspoonfuls of the mixture onto the tray, leaving large gaps between. Using the back of a teaspoon, press each biscuit flat.

3 Bake in a preheated oven, Gas Mark 6-7/200°-220°C/400° 425°F for 7-10 minutes.

4 Melt the chocolate couverture in a bowl over a pan of hot water. Coat the undersides of the florentines with the couverture, and pattern with a fork if desired.

THREE-IN-ONE LOW FAT SPONGES

Basic Low Fat Sponge Mixture

75g/3oz margarine, softened
6 eggs, separated
6 tbsps warm water
200g/7oz caster sugar
Pinch of salt
100g/3½oz plain flour
75g/3oz cornflour
1 tsp baking powder

1 Whisk the egg yolks with the water, sugar and salt until light and foamy. Carefully incorporate the margarine.
2 Whisk the egg whites until stiff and fold into the mixture.
3 Sieve the flour, cornflour and baking powder over the mixture. Using a balloon whisk, carefully fold everything together.
5 Divide the sponge cake mixture into three equal portions.

CRANBERRY CREAM SPONGE

Makes 8 portions

1 portion low fat sponge cake mixture
250g/8oz whipping cream
1 tbsp caster sugar
100g/3½oz cranberries
Margarine for greasing
Icing sugar

1 Grease a 20-cm/8-inch cake tin and turn the sponge mixture into it. Bake for 20-25 minutes in a preheated oven, Gas Mark 6/200°C/400°F. Turn out and leave to cool.
2 Whip the cream until stiff. Lightly crush the cranberries with a fork and fold them into the cream.
3 Slice the cooled sponge cake in half horizontally. Sandwich together again with the cream and cranberry mixture. Dust the cake with icing sugar. Slice.

COFFEE SPONGE

Makes approximately 6 portions

1 portion low fat sponge cake mixture
250g/8oz whipping cream
2 tbsps caster sugar
1 tbsp coffee powder
Margarine for greasing

1 Grease a 16-cm/6-inch spring-release cake tin and turn the sponge mixture into it. Bake for 20-25 minutes in a preheated oven, Gas Mark 6/200°C/400°F. Turn out and leave to cool.
2 Whip the cream and sugar together until stiff. Mix in the coffee powder.
3 Slice the cake in half horizontally. Sandwich together again with the coffee cream, reserving enough for decoration. Using a piping bag, decorate the cake with the remaining cream.

PEACH GATEAU

Makes approximately 6 portions

1 portion low fat sponge cake mixture
400g/13oz tinned peaches
4 tbsps apricot jam
1 tbsp gin
250g/8oz whipping cream
1 tbsp caster sugar
Margarine for greasing
Peach slices to decorate

1 Grease an 18-cm/7-inch spring-release cake tin and turn the sponge mixture into it. Bake for 20-25 minutes in a preheated oven Gas Mark 6/200°C/400°F. Turn out and leave to cool.
2 Put the peaches in a colander to drain. Heat the apricot jam and stir in the gin.
3 Cut the cooled sponge cake in half horizontally. Arrange the drained peach slices on the bottom sponge layer and spread the apricot jam over them. Replace the top sponge layer.
4 Whip the cream and sugar until stiff, then spread over the top and sides of the gâteau. Decorate with the additional peach slices.

THREE-IN-ONE YEAST-DOUGH DELIGHTS

Basic Yeast Dough Mixture

1 packet yeast
250 ml/8 fl oz lukewarm milk
75g/3oz caster sugar
600g/1¼lb flour

Pinch of salt
150g/5oz margarine, melted
1 egg

1 Crumble the yeast into the milk, add a little sugar, cover and leave in a warm place until frothy.
2 Put the flour, remaining sugar and salt into a bowl. Add the frothy yeast, margarine and egg. Mix to a dough then knead well, using an electric mixer for preference. Cover and leave to rise in a warm place.
3 Knead the risen dough well and divide into three equal portions.

ROSE BUN ROUND

Makes 8 portions

1 portion yeast dough
20g/3/4oz margarine, melted
25g/1oz cinnamon sugar
25g/1oz hazelnut brittle
Margarine for greasing

Roll out the dough to a 20-cm x 25-cm/8-inch x 10-inch rectangle. Brush with the melted margarine and sprinkle over the cinnamon sugar and hazelnut brittle. Roll up along the long side, and slice into eight equal rounds. Grease a shallow 16-cm/6-in cake tin with a removable base. Arrange the slices, cut edges upwards, in a circle in the tin, with one slice in the centre. Cover and leave to rise in a warm place. See Yeast Plait for cooking instructions.

GUGELHUPF

Makes approximately 4 portions

1 portion yeast dough
20g/3/4oz caster sugar
Grated lemon zest
25g/1oz raisins
25g/1oz candied lemon peel
25g/1oz glacé cherries, quartered
3 tbsps lukewarm milk
Margarine for greasing
Icing sugar for dusting

YEAST PLAIT

Makes approximately 8 portions

1 portion yeast dough
Margarine for greasing
Milk for glazing
Demerara sugar and flaked almonds

1 Divide the dough into three, make each portion into a roll of equal length and thickness, and plait them together. Place on a small, greased baking tray, cover and leave to rise in a warm place. Before baking, brush with milk, then sprinkle with flaked almonds and demerara sugar.

2 All three recipes are baked in a preheated oven, Gas Mark 6 - 7/200° - 220°C/400° - 425°F. The Plait should be baked for about 20 minutes, whilst the Rose cake and Gugelhupf need about 30-40 minutes. Dust the Gugelhupf with icing sugar, before serving.

Note: All three recipes are suitable for freezing.

Add the sugar, lemon zest, raisins, candied lemon peel, glacé cherries and lukewarm milk to the yeast dough. Mix together well. Press the dough into a greased 16-cm/6-inch ring mould, cover and leave to rise in a warm place. See Yeast Plait for cooking instructions.

THREE-IN-ONE PLAIN SPONGES

2 Bake all three cakes in a pre-heated oven, Gas Mark 6-7/ 200° - 220°C/400° - 425°F. The Orange Cake requires 40 minutes and the Spicy Cake and Hazelnut Sponge require about 50 minutes.

3 Dust the hazelnut sponge with icing sugar before serving. Cover the cooled Spicy Cake with the melted chocolate couverture and decorate with candied fruit. For the Orange Cake, mix the icing sugar with the orange juice and coconut oil and use to ice the cooled cake.

ORANGE CAKE

Makes approximately 8 portions

1 portion sponge mixture
Grated zest of ½ orange
2 tbsps orange liqueur
Margarine for greasing
Breadcrumbs
100g/3½oz icing sugar
2 tbsps orange juice
1 tsp coconut oil
Candied fruit to decorate

1 Stir the grated orange zest and orange liqueur into the third portion of sponge mixture. Grease a 16-cm/6-inch ring mould, sprinkle with breadcrumbs and turn the mixture into it.

Note: All three cakes are suitable for freezing.

Basic Sponge Mixture

375g/12oz margarine
375g/12oz caster sugar
7 eggs
375g/12oz flour
1½ tsps baking powder
Breadcrumbs

Beat the margarine, sugar and eggs until light and fluffy. Sieve together the flour and baking powder, and fold into the mixture. Divide the mixture between three bowls.

HAZELNUT SPONGE

Makes approximately 4 portions

1 portion sponge mixture
50g/2oz toasted hazelnuts, ground
2 tbsps rum
Margarine for greasing
Breadcrumbs
Icing sugar

Stir the hazelnuts and rum into one portion of the sponge mixture. Turn into a 16-cm/6-inch ring mould, which has been greased and sprinkled with breadcrumbs. See Orange Cake for baking instructions.

SPICY SPONGE

Makes approximately 8 portions

1 portion sponge mixture
4 tbsps mixed spice
1 tbsp rum
2 tbsps chocolate buttons
Margarine for greasing
Breadcrumbs
150g/5oz chocolate couverture, melted
Candied fruit

Stir the mixed spice and rum into the second portion of sponge mixture. Fold in the chocolate buttons. Grease a 20-cm/8-inch loaf tin and sprinkle with breadcrumbs. Turn the mixture into this. See Orange Cake for baking instructions.

CREAM POT TREATS

Mixture

1 pot whipping cream
200g/7oz caster sugar
Pinch of salt
3 tsps vanilla sugar
4 eggs
200g/7oz flour
3 tsps baking powder
Grated zest of 1 lemon
Margarine for greasing

Topping 1

Makes approximately 8 portions

75g/3oz margarine
100g/3½oz caster sugar
3 tsps vanilla sugar
2 tbsps milk
100g/3½oz flaked almonds

Topping 2

Makes approximately 8 portions

500g/1lb apples, peeled
2 tbsps caster sugar
1 tsp cinnamon

1 Beat together the cream, sugar, salt, vanilla sugar and eggs. Sieve the flour with the baking powder, and fold into the mixture with the grated lemon zest.

2 Pour half the mixture into a greased baking tin and bake in a preheated oven, Gas Mark 6/200°C/400°F for about 15 minutes.

3 Meanwhile, prepare the first topping. Put the margarine, sugar and vanilla sugar, milk and almonds into a saucepan and bring to the boil. Leave to cool. Spread over the cake and bake for a further 15 minutes.

4 Cut the peeled apples into wedges ready for the second cake.

5 Put the second portion of mixture into a shallow 22-cm/8½-inch cake tin with a removable base. Arrange the apple wedges close together on top, mix the cinnamon with the sugar and sprinkle over the apples. Bake in the preheated oven, Gas Mark 6/200°C/400°F, for about 35 minutes.

MORE VARIETY SPONGES

Basic Sponge Mixture

125g/4oz margarine
5 eggs
200g/7oz caster sugar
3 tsps vanilla sugar
Pinch of salt
250g/8oz flour
3 tsps baking powder
3 tbsps whipping cream
Margarine for greasing
Breadcrumbs

Melt the margarine and leave to cool. Whisk the eggs, sugar, vanilla sugar and salt until light and foamy; gradually whisk in the melted margarine. Sieve together the flour and baking powder and fold into the mixture with the cream. Divide the mixture as follows:

For the Fruit Gâteau, put a scant one-third of the mixture into a 16-cm/6-inch flan ring with a removable base, which has been greased and sprinkled with breadcrumbs. Baking time will be about 45 minutes.

For the Nougat Sponge, grease a 20-cm/8-inch loaf tin and sprinkle with breadcrumbs. Turn one-third of the mixture into it. Baking time will be about 45 minutes.

For the Bumble Bee Cake, grease a shallow 16-cm/6-inch cake tin with a removable base and sprinkle with breadcrumbs. Turn the remaining mixture into it. Part bake for about 15 minutes.

Bake all the cakes together in a preheated oven, Gas Mark 6-7/ 200°-220°C/400°-425°F.

BUMBLE BEE CAKE

Makes approximately 4 portions

50g/2oz margarine
50g/2oz caster sugar
50g/2oz flaked almonds
1 tbsp cream, 10g/½oz flour

Put all the ingredients in a saucepan, bring to the boil, stirring, and spread over the part-baked cake. Return to the oven for a further 15 minutes.

NOUGAT SPONGE

Makes 8 portions

2 eggs
25g/1oz caster sugar
9 tbsps vanilla sugar
Pinch of salt
125g/4oz margarine

Topping

½ packet chocolate nougat with nuts
1 tbsp coconut oil
Candied fruit

1 Slice the cooled cake in three, horizontally.

2 Whisk the eggs, sugar, vanilla sugar and salt in a bowl over hot water, until thickened. Leave to cool, stirring occasionally.

3 Meanwhile, beat the margarine until light and fluffy, and beat gradually into the cooled mixture.

4 Sandwich together the three cake layers with the cream.

5 Pour hot water on the chocolate nougat, leave to stand for a little while, then drain. Stir the coconut oil into the melted nougat and use to coat the cake. Decorate with candied fruit.

FRUIT GATEAU

Makes approximately 4 portions

3 tbsps kirsch
200g/7oz white grapes
2 kiwi fruit
1 small banana
2 tbsps lemon juice
125 ml/4 fl oz white wine
40g/1½oz caster sugar
Grated zest of ½ lemon
1 packet quick-setting gelatine

1 Sprinkle the kirsch over the cooled cake. Scald the grapes, peel and deseed. Peel and thickly slice the kiwi fruit. Slice the banana, and briefly turn in the lemon juice. Arrange the fruit on top of the gâteau.

2 Make up a glaze with the white wine, sugar, grated lemon zest and quick-setting gelatine according to the packet instructions. Pour the glaze over

the fruit and leave to set. Serve cold, with whipped cream if desired.

THREE-IN-ONE SHORTCRUST FLANS

Shortcrust Mixture

375g/12oz flour
100g/3½oz caster sugar
Pinch of salt
3 tsps vanilla sugar
175g/6oz margarine
2 small eggs, beaten

CHERRY FLAN

Makes approximately 6 portions

1 small jar sour cherries, stoned
1 portion shortcrust pastry
Margarine for greasing
40g/1½oz desiccated coconut
1 egg
1 tbsp caster sugar
1½ tsps vanilla sugar
100g/3½oz quark

Mix the flour, sugar, salt and vanilla sugar together on a pastry board. Dot with small flakes of cold margarine and cut these in with a palette knife. Add the beaten eggs, mix together thoroughly and knead to a smooth dough. Divide into three equal portions and chill.

1 Drain the cherries.
2 Roll out pastry and use to line a greased 18-cm/7-inch flan tin with a removable base. Sprinkle with the coconut and arrange the cherries on top. Beat the egg, sugar, vanilla sugar and quark until light and fluffy and spread over the cherries.
3 Bake in a preheated oven, Gas Mark 6/200°C/400°F for about 30 minutes.

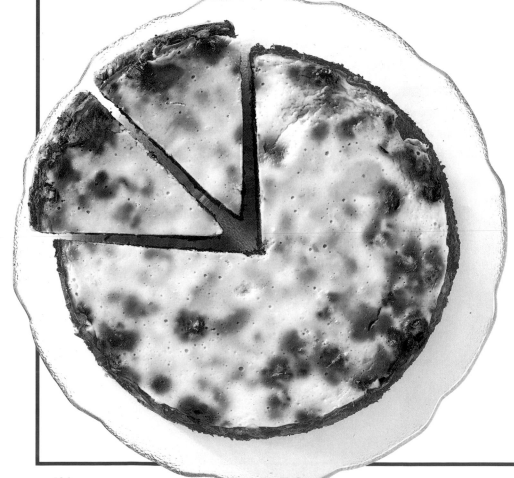

GRANNY'S ALMOND FLAN

Makes approximately 6 portions

35g/1½oz margarine
50g/2oz caster sugar
1½ tsps vanilla sugar
1 egg
2 tbsps whipping cream
75g/3oz ground almonds
1 tbsp flour
Good pinch of baking powder
1 portion shortcrust pastry
Margarine for greasing
2 tbsps apricot jam

APPLE FLAN

Makes approximately 6 portions

500g/1lb apples
1 tbsp lemon juice
1 egg, separated
50g/2oz caster sugar
1 tsp rum
1 tbsp flour
Good pinch of baking powder
100g/3½oz ground almonds
1 portion shortcrust pastry
Margarine for greasing

1 Peel, core and quarter the apples and sprinkle with lemon juice. Whisk the egg yolk, sugar and rum until light and foamy. Whisk the egg white until stiff and fold into the mixture. Sieve together the flour and baking powder, add almonds and fold into the mixture.

2 Roll out the dough and use to line a greased 18-cm/7-inch flan tin with a removable base. Bake blind for 10 minutes in a preheated oven, Gas Mark 7/ 220°C/425°F. Reduce the heat to Gas Mark 5-6/190°-200°F/375°-400°F.

3 Spread the almond mixture into the cooked flan case. Arrange the apples on top, pressing them lightly into the mixture. Return the flan to the oven for about 45 minutes.

1 Beat the margarine, sugar, vanilla sugar, egg and whipping cream until light and fluffy, then fold in the almonds. Sieve together the flour and baking powder and fold into the mixture.

2 Roll out the pastry and use to line a greased 18-cm/7-inch flan tin with a removable base. Bake blind in a preheated oven, Gas Mark 7/220°C/425°F, for 15 minutes. Reduce the heat to Gas Mark 5-6/190°-200°C/375°-400°F. Spread the apricot jam over the pastry base and pour the almond mixture on top. Return to the oven for a further 45 minutes.

WHOLEFOOD BAKING

Enjoying your food without feeling guilty is the theme of this chapter. Wholemeal flour is an important component of a healthy diet, and it is not only tasty in bread and rolls but also in a great number of delicious cakes and biscuits as the following recipes demonstrate.

PICNIC BITES

Makes approximately 24

100g/3½oz wholemeal flour
100g/3½oz stoneground flour
50g/2oz finely ground millet
2 tsps baking powder
100g/3½oz porridge oats
100g/3½oz oatflakes
150g/5oz sultanas
50g/2oz chopped almonds
250g/8oz margarine
200g/7oz caster sugar
2 tbsps clear honey
2 eggs
1 tsps vanilla essence
Margarine for greasing
4 tbsps apricot jam, warmed

1 Mix the flours, baking powder, rolled oats, oatflakes, sultanas and almonds together well.
2 Put the margarine, sugar and honey in a saucepan and heat until the sugar has dissolved, stirring continuously. Leave to cool. Add the eggs and vanilla essence and mix into the dry ingredients.
3 Spread the mixture onto a greased baking tray and bake in a preheated oven, Gas Mark 4/180°C/350°F.
4 Take out of the oven after 5 minutes and spread with the warm apricot jam. Bake for a further 5 minutes. Leave to cool, then cut into small squares.

WHOLEMEAL BISCUITS

Makes approximately 30

300g/10oz wholemeal flour
¼ tsp baking powder
½ tsp cinnamon
Pinch of salt
Grated zest of 1 lemon
150g/5oz brown sugar
100g/3½oz ground almonds
175g/6oz margarine
2 eggs
1 egg white
1 tbsp lemon juice
1 egg yolk for brushing
Brown sugar for sprinkling

1 Sieve together the flour, baking powder, cinnamon and salt, and stir in grated lemon zest. Add the remaining ingredients and work to a smooth dough.

2 Roll out the dough, cut out rounds and place on a baking tray lined with greaseproof paper.
3 Mix the egg yolk with a little water and brush over the biscuits. Sprinkle with brown sugar. Bake in a preheated oven, Gas Mark 6/200°C/400°F, for 15-20 minutes.

TIPSY ALMOND COOKIES

Makes 60–70

200g/7oz margarine
150g/5oz caster sugar
150g/5oz golden syrup
1 tsp cinnamon
1 tsp ground cloves
125g/4oz almonds, chopped
3 tbsps brandy or rum
200g/7oz porridge oats
200g/7oz stoneground flour
2 tsps baking powder
100g/3½oz wholemeal flour
Margarine for greasing

1 Beat the margarine, sugar and syrup until light and fluffy; add the cinnamon, cloves, almonds, brandy or rum, oats and the stoneground flour, sieved together with the baking powder. Knead in the wholemeal flour.
2 Form the dough into two rolls and leave overnight in the refrigerator.
3 Slice the rolls thinly and bake on a greased baking tray in a preheated oven, Gas Mark 7/220°C/425°F, for about 10 minutes.

SPICY BISCUITS

Makes approximately 30

250g/8oz golden syrup
50g/2oz caster sugar
25g/1oz margarine
Good pinch of ground cloves
Good pinch of cardamom
Good pinch of cinnamon
Good pinch of ground ginger
½ tsp grated orange zest
250g/8oz stoneground wholemeal flour
½ tsp potash
1 tbsp water
Margarine for greasing

1 Heat the syrup with the sugar until the sugar has dissolved. Leave to cool slightly. Stir in the margarine, spices and flour. Dissolve the potash in 1 tbsp water, and mix well into the mixture. Knead the mixture lightly.
2 Roll out the dough to a biscuit thickness and cut out shapes as desired.
3 Place the biscuits on a greased baking tray and bake in a preheated oven, Gas Mark 7/220°C/425°F for 10-15 minutes.

round the inside edge of the tin.
2 Bake blind in a preheated oven, Gas Mark 6/200°C/400°F, for 10 minutes. Spread the base with quince jam. Reduce the heat to Gas Mark 4/180°C/350°F.
3 Whisk the eggs and sugar until thick and foamy. Mix the desiccated coconut, breadcrumbs, cinnamon, and grated zest with the baking powder and gradually fold into the egg mixture.
4 Spread this topping over the base and return to the oven for a further 40 minutes at the reduced temperature. Dust with icing sugar before serving.

SOUR CHERRY CRUMBLE

25g/1oz fresh yeast
250 ml/8 fl oz lukewarm milk
80g/3oz caster sugar
200g/7oz stoneground flour type
200g/7oz wholemeal flour
100g/3½oz buckwheat flour
Pinch of salt
Grated lemon zest
50g/2oz margarine, melted and cooled
2 eggs, beaten
Margarine for greasing

Topping
1kg/2lb sour cherries (bottled)

BUCKWHEAT CAKE

Makes approximately 12 portions

4 egg yolks
200g/7oz caster sugar
Good pinch of ground cloves
½ tsp cinnamon
50g/2oz ground almonds
Grated zest of ½ lemon
6 egg whites
150g/5oz buckwheat flour
Margarine for greasing
Flour
Whipped cream to decorate, if desired

1 Whisk the egg yolks and sugar until light and foamy; add the spices, almonds and grated lemon zest. Whisk the egg whites until stiff and fold them into the mixture, alternating with the flour.
2 Grease a 24-cm/9½-inch cake tin with a removable base and sprinkle with flour. Turn the mixture into this. Bake in a preheated oven, Gas Mark 4/180°C/350°F, for about 60 minutes.
3 Decorate the finished caked with whipped cream, if desired.

LIGHT BREAD FLAN

Makes approximately 12 portions

Dough
100g/3½oz wholemeal flour
100g/3½oz stoneground flour
50g/2oz buckwheat flour
125g/4oz margarine
65g/2½oz caster sugar
1 egg
Margarine for greasing

Topping
100g/3½oz quince jam
3 eggs
125g/4oz caster sugar
125g/4oz desiccated coconut
125g/4oz dry white breadcrumbs
Good pinch of cinnamon
Grated orange or lemon zest
Good pinch of baking powder
Icing sugar for dusting

1 Mix the flour, margarine, sugar and egg together to make a smooth dough. Chill. Roll out two-thirds and use to line the bottom of a greased 24-cm/9½-inch cake tin with a removable base. Shape the remaining dough into a roll and press firmly

Crumble

200g/7oz stoneground flour
150g/5oz brown sugar
50g/2oz almonds, chopped
Cinnamon
125g/4oz margarine

1 Crumble the yeast into the milk and stir in a pinch of sugar and flour. Leave, covered, in a warm place for 5-10 minutes until frothy.

2 Put the flour, sugar, salt, lemon zest, the melted and cooled margarine and the beaten eggs into a mixing bowl. Add the frothy yeast, and mix everything together. Knead the dough thoroughly, using an electric mixer for preference.

Cover the dough with foil and leave in a warm place until doubled in size. Knock down the dough and use to line a greased baking tray.

3 Drain the stoned cherries well. Combine the flour, sugar, almonds, cinnamon and margarine to form a crumble mixture. Arrange the cherries and crumble mixture alternately over the dough.

4 Leave to rise in a warm place for a short time. Bake in a preheated oven, Gas Mark 6-7/200°-220°C/400°-425°F, for about 30 minutes.

Note: Fresh cherries can also be used; they should be sprinkled with sugar after baking.

MUESLI CAKE

Makes approximately 16 portions

125g/4oz margarine
125g/4oz caster sugar
3 tsps vanilla sugar
3 eggs
Pinch of salt
1 tsp cinnamon
Grated zest of 1 lemon
150g/5oz fruit muesli
150g/5oz wholemeal flour
2 tsps baking powder
125g/4oz whipping cream
Margarine for greasing

1 Cream the margarine until fluffy, gradually add the sugar, vanilla sugar and eggs and continue beating until the sugar has dissolved. Add the salt, cinnamon and lemon zest.

2 Mix together the muesli, wholemeal flour and baking powder and stir into the cake mixture alternately with the cream.

3 Pour the mixture into a greased 25-cm/10-inch loaf tin and bake in a preheated oven, Gas Mark 4/180°C/350°F for 50-60 minutes.

WHOLEMEAL CAKE WITH PEARS

Makes approximately 12 portions

4 eggs, separated
125g/4oz icing sugar
Grated zest of 1 lemon
125g/4oz wholemeal flour
1 tsp baking powder
400g/13oz pears
Margarine for greasing
Jam or whipped cream, as desired

1 Whisk the egg yolks with the icing sugar and lemon zest until light and foamy; gradually fold in the flour, sieved together with the baking powder. Whisk the egg whites until stiff and fold them into the mixture. Finally, stir in the peeled, cored and diced pears.

2 Turn the mixture into a greased 24-cm/9½-inch cake tin with a removable base and bake in a preheated oven, Gas Mark 4/180°C/350°F for abut 60 minutes.

3 Cover with apricot jam, blueberry jam or whipped cream, as desired.

CHOCOLATE AND ALMOND GATEAU

Makes approximately 12 portions

250g/8oz margarine
200g/7oz caster sugar
6 eggs, separated
125g/4oz chocolate
225g/7½oz ground almonds
6 tbsps orange juice
Grated zest of 1 orange
100g/3½oz digestive biscuits, crumbled
2½ tsps baking powder
Margarine for greasing
2 tbsps icing sugar
2 tbsps cocoa powder

1 Beat the margarine and sugar until light and fluffy. Gradually beat in the egg yolks. Cut the chocolate into small pieces and add to the mixture together with the almonds, orange juice and zest. Mix the biscuit crumbs with the baking powder and stir in. Whisk the egg whites until very stiff and fold into the mixture.
2 Turn the mixture into a greased 24-cm/9½-inch cake tin with a removable base and bake in a preheated oven, Gas Mark 4/180°C/350°F for about 60 minutes.
3 Turn out onto a cake rack to cool. Sprinkle the cake with sieved icing sugar and cocoa.

TRADITIONAL CINNAMON CAKE

Makes approximately 20 portions

125g/4oz margarine
200g/7oz caster sugar
4 eggs
200g/7oz ground almonds
100g/3½oz wholemeal flour
100g/3½oz stoneground flour
60g/2oz buckwheat flour
2-3 tsps baking powder
4 tsps cinnamon
125 ml/4 fl oz cream, whipped
15g/½oz candied ginger
75g/3oz dried figs
50g/2oz candied lemon peel

1 Beat the margarine and sugar until light and fluffy. Beat in the eggs and then the almonds. Sieve together the flour, baking powder and cinnamon and gradually fold into mixture, alternating with the whipped cream.
2 Finely cut or grate the ginger. Finely slice the figs. Fold both into the mixture together with the lemon peel.
3 Turn into a greased 25-cm/10-inch loaf tin and bake in a preheated oven, Gas Mark 6/200°C/400°F for 50 minutes. Turn off the heat and leave the cake to stand for a further 5 minutes in the oven.

PEACH LAYER CAKE

Makes approximately 12 portions

4 eggs, separated
4 tbsps warm water
200g/7oz caster sugar
Pinch of salt
50g/2oz margarine, melted and cooled
25g/1oz cocoa powder
150g/5oz buckwheat flour
3 tsps baking powder
Margarine for greasing

Filling

425g/14oz tinned peaches
6 sheets gelatine
250 ml/8 fl oz whipping cream

For Decoration

500g/1lb whipping cream
6 tsps vanilla sugar

1 Whisk the egg yolks, water, 150g/5oz of the sugar and the salt until light and foamy. Using a balloon whisk, beat the melted and cooled margarine into the egg mixture in a thin trickle. Whisk the egg whites with the remaining sugar until stiff and pile on top of the mixture. Sieve the cocoa, flour and baking powder over the egg whites. Fold everything together very carefully.

2 Turn the mixture into a greased 25-cm/10-inch cake tin with a removable base, and bake in a preheated oven, Gas Mark, 4/ 180°C/350°F, for about 30 minutes. Slice the cooled cake in half horizontally.

3 Drain the peaches, reserving the juice. Cut the fruit into small pieces and mix with 125 ml/4 fl oz of the reserved juice. Soak the gelatine, dissolve it over hot water and add to the peach mixture. Spread the half-set mixture over the bottom layer of sponge and place the second layer on top.

4 Whip the cream with the vanilla sugar until stiff and spread all over the cake, reserving some for decoration.

POPPYSEED CAKE WITH VANILLA CREAM

Makes approximately 12 portions

60g/2¼oz poppy seeds
4 eggs, separated
200g/7oz icing sugar
3 tsps vanilla sugar
60g/2¼oz stoneground flour
50g/2oz cornflour
1 tsp baking powder
Margarine for greasing

Filling

50g/2oz cornflour
500 ml/18 fl oz milk
50g/2oz margarine
1 vanilla pod
75g/3oz caster sugar
3 tsps vanilla sugar
2 eggs, separated
5 sheets gelatine

For Decoration

50g/2oz flaked almonds
Grated chocolate or chocolate flakes

1 Bring the poppy seeds and water to the boil, leave to soak for 20 minutes, then drain in a sieve. Grind very finely.

2 Whisk the egg yolks with the icing sugar and vanilla sugar

until light and fluffy. Sieve together the flour, cornflour and baking powder, mix with the ground poppy seeds and fold into the egg mixture. Whisk the egg whites until very stiff, then fold in carefully.

3 Grease a 24-cm/9½-inch cake tin with a removable base and line with greaseproof paper. Turn the mixture into it and bake immediately in a pre-heated oven, Gas Mark 6/ 200°C/400°F, for abut 45 minutes. Turn out, and remove the paper. Leave to cool, then slice in half horizontally.

4 Mix the cornflour with a little milk. Bring the remaining milk to

the boil with the margarine, vanilla, sugar and vanilla sugar and thicken with the cornflour and the egg yolks. Dissolve the soaked and well-drained gelatine in this. Whisk the egg whites until stiff and fold in.

5 When the cream is half set, use two-thirds to sandwich together the cake layers. Spread the remaining cream all over the cake. Decorate with the flaked almonds and grated chocolate. Chill in the refrigerator for a few hours before serving.

FARMHOUSE APRICOT CAKE

Makes approximately 24 portions

40g/1½oz fresh yeast
250 ml/8 fl oz lukewarm milk
125g/4oz caster sugar
Pinch of salt
200g/7oz stoneground flour
200g/7oz wholemeal flour
100g/3½oz porridge oats
100g/3½oz ground almonds
2 eggs
125g/4oz margarine, melted and cooled
Margarine for greasing

Topping

1kg/2lb apricots, halved and stoned
50g/2oz caster sugar
100g/3½oz almonds, chopped

Icing

250g/8oz icing sugar
3-4 tbsps lemon juice

1 Crumble the yeast into the lukewarm milk, stir in a pinch of sugar and a little flour, cover and leave in a warm place for 5-10 minutes until frothy. Mix together the salt, flours, oats and almonds, add the frothy yeast, eggs and margarine and knead to a smooth dough. Cover and leave in a warm place until doubled in size.

2 Knead the dough again. Roll out and use to line a greased baking tray. Arrange the halved and stoned apricots on top. Sprinkle with the sugar and chopped almonds. Bake in a preheated oven, Gas Mark 5-6/190°-200°C/375°-400°F, for approximately 25 minutes.

3 Mix the icing sugar and lemon juice and spread over the cake. Leave to harden.

CARROT CAKE

Makes approximately 12 portions

5 eggs, separated
250g/8oz caster sugar
Grated zest of 1 lemon
4 tbsps lemon juice
250g/8oz hazelnuts, ground
250g/8oz carrots, grated
80g/3oz buckwheat flour
3 tsps baking powder
Pinch of salt

Icing
200g/7oz icing sugar
2 tbsps rum
1-2 tbsps lemon juice
Marzipan carrots, to decorate

1 Whisk the egg yolks with the sugar until light and fluffy. Add, one by one, the lemon zest and juice, hazelnuts and carrots. Sieve the buckwheat flour with the baking powder and fold in. Whisk the egg whites with the salt until stiff and fold into the mixture.
2 Grease a 25-cm/10-inch cake tin with a removable base and dust it with flour. Turn mixture into this and bake in a preheated oven, Gas Mark 5-6/ 190°-200°C/375°-400°F for 50-60 minutes.
3 Combine the icing sugar, rum and lemon juice and spread over the cooled cake. Decorate with marzipan carrots.

PEAR GATEAU

Makes approximately 12 portions

100g/3½oz stoneground flour
150g/5oz wholemeal flour
2 tsps baking powder
60g/2¼oz caster sugar
3 tsps vanilla sugar
Pinch of salt
60g/2¼oz margarine
Margarine for greasing
125g/4oz low fat curd cheese, well drained
1 egg
2 tbsps milk

Topping
425g/14oz tinned pear halves
200g/7oz bottled cranberries

Crumble
100g/3½oz wholemeal flour
75g/3oz stoneground flour
75g/3oz caster sugar
Pinch of salt
3 tsps vanilla sugar
100g/3½oz margarine

1 Mix together the flour, baking powder, sugar, vanilla sugar and salt on a pastry board. Dot with the well-chilled margarine and the curd cheese and mix everything together with a palette knife. Work in the egg, beaten with the milk, and knead to a smooth dough. Chill.
2 Drain the pear halves and the cranberries. Make up a crumble mixture using the flour, sugar, salt, vanilla sugar and margarine.
3 Roll out the pastry dough and use to line a greased 25-cm/ 10-inch flan tin with a removable base. Arrange the pear halves on top, spread the cranberries over and cover with the crumble mixture. Bake in a preheated oven, Gas Mark 7/ 220°C/425°F, for approximately 60 minutes.

APPLE AND ALMOND CAKE

Makes approximately 12 portions

Mixture
200g/7oz stoneground flour
50g/2oz finely ground millet
60g/2¼oz caster sugar
Pinch of salt

125g/4oz margarine
1 egg, beaten
Margarine for greasing

Topping
3 eggs, separated
150g/5oz caster sugar
1 tbsp lemon juice
1 tbsp rum
1 large and 6 small apples, peeled
50g/2oz buckwheat flour

Good pinch of baking powder
200g/7oz ground almonds
Melted margarine
Icing sugar for dusting

1 Mix together the flour, millet and sugar on a pastry board, dot generously with cold margarine and cut in with a palette knife. Make a well in the centre and put in the beaten egg. Mix well and knead quickly to a

CRUMBLE SLICES

Makes approximately 12 slices

150g/5oz margarine
150g/5oz caster sugar
Pinch of salt
1 egg
Grated zest of 1 lemon
200g/7oz wholemeal flour
150g/5oz stoneground flour
25g/1oz buckwheat flour
3 tsps baking powder
Margarine for greasing
750g/1½lb apples
20g/3/4oz sesame seeds

75g/3oz raisins
50g/2oz almonds, chopped
50g/2oz ground almonds

1 Beat the margarine with the sugar, salt, egg and lemon juice until light and fluffy. Sieve together the flour and baking powder, and stir a few spoonfuls into the cake mixture. Sprinkle the remainder over the top and rub in with your fingertips to a crumble consistency. Divide into two portions. Turn one portion into a greased 25-cm/10-inch cake tin with a removable base.

2 Peel and slice the apples and arrange on top. Sprinkle over the raisins together with the sesame seeds.
3 Bake in a preheated oven, Gas Mark 6/200°C/400°F, for about 60 minutes. Cut into slices to serve.

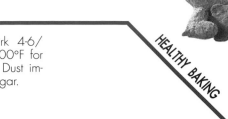

smooth dough. Chill for 30 minutes.

2 Line a deep 25-cm/10-inch flan tin with a removable base. Bake the pastry case blind in a preheated oven, Gas Mark 6-7/200°-220°C/400°-425°F, for 15 minutes.

3 Meanwhile, whisk the egg yolks with the sugar until light and fluffy. Add the lemon juice and rum and grate in the large apple.

Whisk the egg whites until stiff, and pile on top of the mixture. Sieve over the buckwheat flour, add the almonds and carefully fold everything together. Pile into the cooked pastry case.

4 Halve and core the small apples, and score them in a fan shape. Arrange the apple halves on the almond mixture, cut side down, and brush with melted margarine.

5 Bake at Gas Mark 4-6/180°-200°C/350°-400°F for a further 50 minutes. Dust immediately with icing sugar.

REDCURRANT CAKE WITH MERINGUE

Makes approximately 24 portions

25g/1oz fresh yeast
150 ml/5 fl oz lukewarm milk
50g/2oz caster sugar
100g/3½oz wholemeal flour
100g/3½oz stoneground flour
50g/2oz buckwheat flour
Pinch of salt
25g/1oz ground almonds
50g/2oz margarine, melted
Margarine for greasing

Topping
500g/1lb redcurrants

Meringue
3 egg whites
100g/3½oz icing sugar
50g/2oz ground almonds

1 Crumble the yeast into the lukewarm milk, stir in a pinch of sugar, cover and leave in a warm place for about 10 minutes until frothy. Mix together the sugar, flour, salt, almonds and melted margarine together, add the frothy yeast and knead to a smooth dough. Cover and leave in a warm place until doubled in size. Knead well and use to line a greased baking tin.

2 Meanwhile, wash and pick over the redcurrants. Spread over the dough and leave in warm place to rise again. Bake in a preheated oven, Gas Mark 7/220°C/425°F, for about 30 minutes.

3 Whisk the egg whites until stiff, then whisk in the icing sugar and almonds. Spread this meringue on the cooked cake and either pop under the grill to brown or put into the oven at Gas Mark 9/240°C/475°F for 6 minutes.

APRICOT AND WALNUT CAKE

Makes approximately 12 portions

250g/8oz margarine
200g/7oz caster sugar
3 tsps vanilla sugar
4 eggs
3 tsps cinnamon
½ tsp ground cloves
½ tsp ground ginger
100g/3½oz wholemeal flour
150g/5oz stoneground flour
1 tbsp clear honey
100g/3½oz walnut halves
100g/3½oz fresh apricots, stoned
Margarine for greasing
Milk chocolate couverture

1 Beat the margarine, sugar, vanilla sugar and eggs until light and fluffy. Sieve together the flour, baking powder, cinnamon, cloves and ginger and fold into the mixture, together with the honey. Reserve six walnut halves for decoration and roughly chop remainder. Cut the apricots into large chunks and stir them into the mixture with the chopped walnut.
2 Turn the mixture into a greased 30-cm/12-inch loaf tin and bake in a preheated oven, Gas Mark 4/180°C/350°F, for about 75 minutes.
3 Leave to cool, then coat with the melted chocolate couverture and decorate with the reserved walnut halves.

RED BERRY SAVARIN

Makes approximately 12 portions

15g/½oz fresh yeast
6 tbsps lukewarm milk
50g/2oz caster sugar
100g/3½oz stoneground flour
50g/2oz wholemeal flour
50g/2oz buckwheat flour
50g/2oz rye flour
Pinch of salt
75g/3oz margarine, melted
5 eggs, beaten
Margarine for greasing

Filling

1kg/2lb red berries (raspberries, strawberries etc), frozen
150/5oz caster sugar
Grated zest of ½ lemon
1 tbsp lemon juice
6 tbsps rum

1 Crumble the yeast into the lukewarm milk, and stir in 1 tbsp sugar and 1 tbsp flour. Cover and leave in a warm place for about 15 minutes until frothy. Put the flour, salt, sugar, margarine and beaten eggs into a bowl, and add the frothy yeast. Mix to a dough and knead thoroughly. Cover and leave to rise in a warm place. Knock down and press into a greased 25-cm/10-inch ring tin. The dough should only come half way up the sides of the tin.
2 Leave to rise again in a warm place. Bake in a preheated oven, Gas Mark 4-6/180°-200°C/350°-400°F, for about 30 minutes.
3 Meanwhile, sprinkle 100g/3½oz of the sugar over the berries. Leave to macerate. Drain, reserving the juice. Mix the juice with the remaining sugar, the lemon peel and juice and boil until the mixture is reduced to about 125 ml/4 fl oz. Add the rum. Turn the savarin out whilst still hot, slice in half horizontally and soak with the juice mixture, reserving a little.

4 Turn the berries in the reserved juice, then use to sandwich together the two savarin layers.

ALMOND AND HAZELNUT CAKE

Makes approximately 16 portions

125 g/ 4oz margarine
100g/3½oz caster sugar
1 tsp cinnamon
3 tsps vanilla sugar
2 eggs
50g/2oz hazelnuts, chopped
50g/2oz almond kernels, chopped
75g/3oz wholemeal flour
50g/2oz stoneground flour
2 tsps baking powder
100 ml/3½ fl oz whipped cream
2 tbsps rum
Margarine for greasing

1 Beat the margarine, sugar, cinnamon, vanilla sugar and eggs until light and fluffy. Fold in the nuts. Sieve the flour with the baking powder and gradually fold into the mixture, together with the cream. Stir in the rum.
2 Turn the mixture into a greased 25-cm/10-inch loaf tin and bake in a preheated oven, Gas Mark 4/180°C/350°F, for about 45 minutes.

HAZELNUT LAYER CAKE

Makes approximately 12 portions

8 eggs, separated
300g/10oz caster sugar
Pinch of salt
250g/8oz hazelnuts, ground
2 tsps baking powder
80g/3oz stoneground flour
Margarine for greasing

Filling

625 ml/generous 1 pt whipping cream
3 tbsps caster sugar
Hazelnut kernels for decoration

1 Whisk the egg yolks with the sugar until very light and foamy. Whisk the egg whites with the salt until stiff, and pile onto the beaten yolks. Sprinkle with the ground hazelnuts and sieve over the flour and the baking powder. Carefully fold everything together.
2 Grease the base of a 26-cm/10½-inch cake tin with a removable base. Turn the mixture into it and bake in a preheated oven, Gas Mark 4-6/180°-200°C/350°-400°F, for 30-35 minutes. Turn off the heat and leave to stand in the oven 5-10 minutes.
3 Carefully remove the cake from the oven and leave to cool in the tin, to avoid the risk of collapse.
4 Whip the cream with the sugar. Slice the cake horizontally into three layers and sandwich together using most of the cream. Decorate with the remaining cream and hazelnut kernels.

DRIED FRUIT CAKE

Makes approximately 16 portions

100g/3½oz prunes, stoned
100g/3½oz dried apricots
100g/3½oz dried pears
300g/10oz margarine
300g/10oz caster sugar
Pinch of salt
6 eggs
Grated zest of 1 lemon
3 tsps vanilla sugar
200g/7oz stoneground flour
50 g /2oz wholemeal flour
100g/3½oz porridge oats
3 tsps baking powder
100g/3½oz walnuts, chopped
Margarine for greasing

1 Dice the prunes, apricots and pears.
2 Beat the margarine, sugar, salt, eggs. lemon peel and vanilla sugar until light and fluffy.
3 Mix the flours with the porridge oats, and sprinkle a little over the fruit. Mix the remainder with the baking powder and stir into the cake mixture. Fold in the dried fruit and the nuts.
4 Turn into a greased 22-cm/8 ½-inch gugelhupf tin and bake in a preheated oven, Gas Mark 4/180°C/350°F for 60-70 minutes.

CHERRY CAKE

Makes approximately 16 portions

4 eggs, separated
125g/4oz caster sugar
1 tsp cinnamon
Grated zest of 1 lemon
75g/3oz wholemeal rusk
500g/1lb jar bottled sour cherries, stoned
Margarine for greasing

1 Whisk the egg yolks, sugar, cinnamon and lemon peel until light and fluffy. Whisk the egg whites until stiff and fold into the mixture. Grate the rusk and fold in, together with the drained cherries.
2 Grease and line a 25-cm/ 10-inch loaf tin, turn the mixture into it and bake in a preheated oven, Gas Mark 4/180°C/ 350°F, for 50-60 minutes.

MIXED NUT LOAF

Makes approximately 16 portions

250g/8oz margarine
250g/8oz caster sugar
4 eggs
Pinch of salt
100g/3½oz mixed nuts, ground
3 tbsps milk
Grated zest of ½ lemon
1½ tsps baking powder
250g/8oz stoneground flour

1 Beat the margarine and sugar until light and fluffy, then gradually beat in the eggs. Stir in the salt, nuts, milk and lemon peel. Sieve together the flour and baking powder and fold in.
2 Turn the mixture into a greased 25-cm/10-inch loaf tin and bake in a preheated oven, Gas Mark 4/180°C/350°F, for 50-60 minutes.

BANANA AND WALNUT CAKE

Makes approximately 12 portions

100g/3½oz stoneground flour
50g/2oz buckwheat flour
2 tsps baking powder
50g/2oz porridge oats
100g/3½oz walnuts, chopped
50g/2oz oat flakes
2 small bananas
2 eggs
100g/3½oz margarine
200g/7oz caster sugar
2 tbsps clear honey
Margarine for greasing
Icing sugar for dusting

1 Sieve the flour with the baking powder and cinnamon. Mix with the porridge oats, chopped walnuts and oat flakes.

2 Mash the bananas with a fork and mix with the eggs. Heat the margarine, sugar and honey, stirring continuously, until the sugar has dissolved. Leave to cool, then stir into the banana mixture. Beat into the flour mixture.

3 Turn into a greased 22-cm/8 ½-inch ring tin and bake in a preheated oven, Gas Mark 4/180°C/350°F, for about 50 minutes.

4 Dust the cooled cake with icing sugar.

BROWN BREAD CAKE

Makes approximately 12 portions

3 eggs, separated
65g/2½oz icing sugar,
40g/1½oz chocolate, grated
50g/2oz ground almonds
1/2 tsp cinnamon
Good pinch of ground cloves
Aniseed
Grated zest of 1 lemon
75g/3oz brown bread
125 ml/4 fl oz red wine
Margarine for greasing
4 tbsps cranberries
200 ml/7 fl oz cream, whipped

1 Whisk the egg yolks with the icing sugar until light and fluffy. Stir in the chocolate, almonds, cinnamon, cloves, aniseed and lemon peel. Whisk the egg whites until stiff and fold in carefully. Dry the brown bread out in the oven and crumble finely. Mix with the red wine and stir into the mixture.

2 Turn the mixture into a greased 26-cm/10½-inch cake tin with a removable base and bake in a preheated oven, Gas Mark 4/180°C/350°F, for about 60 minutes.

3 Fold the cranberries into the whipped cream and spread over the cake.

COFFEE IN THE AFTERNOON

For a change, serve coffee and freshly baked, delicious-smelling cakes and cookies in the afternoon, Continental style. Here are a variety of sweet temptations.

WALNUT CAKES

Makes 12

5 eggs, separated
3 tbsps warm water
225g/7½oz icing sugar
Pinch of salt
50g/2oz walnuts, ground
50g/2oz plain flour
40g/1½oz cornflour
1 tsp baking powder
Coconut oil
Sugar for dusting

Filling

250 ml/8 fl oz whipping cream
25g/1oz caster sugar
3 tsps vanilla sugar
50g/2oz walnuts, ground

Icing

100g/3½oz icing sugar
1 tbsp cocoa
2 tbsps rum
1 tbsp water
25g/1oz coconut oil

For Decoration

100g/3½oz marzipan paste

1 Whisk the egg yolks with the lukewarm water, sugar and a pinch of salt until light and fluffy. Whisk the egg whites until stiff, and pile on top of the mixture. Fold in the walnuts. Sieve over the flour, cornflour and baking powder. Using a balloon whisk, carefully fold everything together.

2 Grease and line a baking tray. Spread the mixture onto it and bake in a preheated oven, Gas Mark 6-7/200°-220°C/400°-425°F, for approximately 15 minutes.

3 Sprinkle sugar over the cooked cake. With the aid of a tea towel, turn it over, remove the paper and leave to cool. Cut into 6-cm/2½-in rounds.

4 Whip the cream with the sugar and vanilla sugar until stiff. Fold in the walnuts. Use the walnut cream to sandwich together the cake rounds in pairs.

5 Mix together the icing sugar, cocoa, rum, water and coconut oil and ice the cakes.

6 Roll out the marzipan paste, cut out shapes, and use to decorate the cakes.

ECLAIRS WITH VANILLA CREAM

Makes 10 éclairs

250 ml/8 fl oz water
Pinch of salt
3 tsps vanilla sugar
60g/2½oz margarine
125g/4oz flour
4 eggs
Margarine for greasing
Flour

Icing

125g/4oz icing sugar
2 tsps cocoa powder
2 tbsps water

Filling

250 ml/8 fl oz milk
1 vanilla pod
Pinch of salt
3 eggs, separated
100g/3½oz caster sugar
6 sheets gelatine
125 ml/4 fl oz cream, whipped

1 Bring the water, salt, vanilla sugar and margarine to the boil, remove from the heat, and add the flour. Using a wooden spoon, beat the mixture until smooth, return to the heat and continue beating until the mixture comes away from the sides of the saucepan in a ball. Beat in one egg immediately, then gradually beat in the remaining eggs.

2 Use a piping bag to pipe double finger-length strips onto a greased and floured baking tray. Bake in a preheated oven, Gas Mark 7/220°C/425°F for abut 30 minutes.

3 Mix the icing ingredients. Split the éclairs immediately and ice the tops while still warm. Leave to cool.

4 Bring the milk, vanilla pod and salt to the boil and let it cool. Remove the pod. Whisk the egg yolks and sugar until light and fluffy, then add the vanilla milk. Soak the gelatine, dissolve it over a low heat, stir into the mixture and leave until half set.

5 Whisk the egg whites until stiff, and fold into the half-set mixture, together with the whipped cream. When filling has set to a firm consistency, pipe into the bottom half of each éclair. Replace the tops.

POPPY SEED CAKE

Makes approximately 24 portions

600g/1¼lb flour
2 packets dried yeast
150g/5oz caster sugar
150g/5oz margarine, melted
200 ml/7 fl oz lukewarm milk

Filling

750 ml/1¼ pt milk
200g/7oz margarine
500g/1lb poppy seeds
200g/7oz raisins
150g/5oz semolina
1 tsp lemon juice
4 egg whites

1 Put the flour in a bowl, make a well in the centre and add the yeast, melted margarine and lukewarm milk. Mix well. Knead to a smooth dough, cover and leave in a warm place until dough has doubled in size.
2 Knead again. Roll out thinly and use to line a well greased 30-cm x 40-cm/12-inch x 16-inch baking tray.
3 Meanwhile, bring the filling milk to the boil. Stir in the sugar, margarine, poppy seeds, raisins and semolina. Allow to boil for a moment. Set aside to cool. Stir in the lemon juice; whisk the egg whites until stiff and fold in.
4 Spread the filling over the dough and bake in a preheated oven, Gas Mark 6-7/200°-220°C/400°-425°F, for about 35-40 minutes.

CRUNCHY CREAM WAFFLES

Makes approximately 12 portions

375 ml/12 fl oz whipping cream
150g/5oz flour
Pinch of salt
125 ml/4 fl oz water
50g/2oz margarine
3 tsps vanilla sugar
Margarine for greasing
Icing sugar for dusting

1 Whip the cream until stiff. Mix together the flour, salt and water. Quickly fold in the whipped cream. Chill in the refrigerator for 1 hour.
2 Melt the margarine and leave to cool. Stir into the mixture together with the vanilla sugar.
3 Brush the waffle iron with margarine. Cook the waffle mixture 2-3 tbsps at a time for about 2-3 minutes.
4 Dust the waffles with icing sugar before serving.

DECORATIVE APPLE CAKES

Makes approximately 8 portions

Mixture

150g/5oz margarine	
200g/7oz caster sugar	
3 tsps vanilla sugar	
6 eggs	
2 packets chocolate pudding mix	
100g/3½oz flour	
100g/3½oz ground almonds	
2 small apples, peeled and grated	
Margarine for greasing	
Breadcrumbs	

For Decoration

100g/3½oz marzipan paste
Food colouring
Chocolate leaves and sugar flowers

1 Cream the margarine until fluffy, beat in the sugar, vanilla sugar, eggs, chocolate pudding mix, flour and almonds. Finally, add the grated apple.

2 Grease two apple-shaped moulds or deep bun tins, and sprinkle with breadcrumbs. Turn mixture in and bake in a preheated oven, Gas Mark 4-6/180°-200°C/350°-400°F, for about 45 minutes. Leave to cool in the moulds for abut 5 minutes, then turn out.

3 Colour the marzipan paste, roll out between two sheets of foil and wrap round the cakes. Decorate with leaves and flowers.

ICED HAZELNUT TRIANGLES

Makes approximately 30 triangles

250g/8oz margarine
200g/7oz sugar
3 tbsps vanilla sugar
Pinch of salt
3 eggs
4 tbsps whipping cream
200g/7oz hazelnuts, ground
250g/8oz flour
3 tsps baking powder
Margarine for greasing

Icing

250g/8oz icing sugar
2 tsps instant coffee powder
2-3 tbsps water
30 hazelnut kernels for decoration

1 Mix together the margarine, sugar, vanilla sugar, salt, eggs, whipping cream, hazelnuts, flour and baking powder.

2 Spread the mixture onto a greased baking tray and bake in a preheated oven, Gas Mark 6/200°C/400°F, for 15-20 minutes.

3 Meanwhile, mix together the icing sugar, coffee powder and water. Cut the cake into 30 small triangular pieces, while it is still warm. Ice each triangle and decorate with a hazelnut kernel.

FRANKFURT RING LAYER CAKE

Makes approximately 20 portions

200g/7oz margarine
200g/7oz caster sugar
Pinch of salt
4 eggs
1 tsp baking powder
200g/7oz flour
Margarine for greasing

Filling
500 ml/18 fl oz milk
50g/2oz caster sugar
1 packet pastry cream, vanilla flavour
250g/8oz margarine

For Decoration
150g/5oz almonds, chopped
50g/2oz caster sugar
25g/1oz margarine
Whipped cream
10 cocktail cherries

1 Beat the margarine, sugar, salt and eggs until light and fluffy. Sieve together the flour and baking powder and fold in gradually.
2 Turn into a greased 26-cm/10½-inch ring tin and bake in a preheated oven, Gas Mark 4/180°C/350°F, for abut 60 minutes. Turn out onto a wire rack and leave to cool. Slice the ring horizontally into three.
3 Make up the vanilla pastry cream with the milk and sugar according to the packet instructions. Sandwich together the layers with half the cream. Cover the top and sides of the finished cake with the remaining cream.
4 Cook the almonds in sugar and margarine until a golden brown; remove from pan immediately. Leave to cool, then sprinkle over the cake. Decorate with piped whipped cream and cocktail cherries.

ALMOND AND CINNAMON PASTRIES

Makes approximately 20 pastries

200g/7oz well-chilled margarine
50g/2oz flour
40g/1½oz fresh yeast
200 ml/7 fl oz lukewarm milk
60g/2½oz caster sugar
500g/1lb flour
Pinch of salt
50g/2oz cinnamon sugar
25g/1oz almonds, chopped
Egg yolk

1 Cut the margarine into the flour using a palette knife. Knead quickly to a smooth dough and chill in the refrigerator.
2 Make a yeast dough from the yeast, milk, sugar, flour, salt, margarine and egg. Leave to rise in a warm place until doubled in size. Knead again, and roll out to a rectangle about 20 cm x 30 cm/8 inches x 12 inches.
3 Roll out the first dough between two sheets of grease-proof paper to a rectangle 20 cm x 15 cm/8 inches x 6 inches. Lay this over one half of the yeast dough rectangle. Fold the empty half over and roll out again to form a rectangle as

above. Fold the dough in half, short sides together. Cover and chill for about 10 minutes.
4 Turn the dough so the fold is on the right-hand side. Roll out into a rectangle and fold in half as above. Chill. Repeat the process once more. FInally, roll out the dough to a rectangle about

40 cm x 50 cm/16 inches x 20 inches, brush with milk and sprinkle with a mixture of the cinnamon sugar and almonds.
5 Roll up the dough lengthways and cut into 2-cm/¾-inch-thick slices. Line a baking tray with greaseproof paper, arrange the pastries on it and leave in a warm place to rise again. Bake in a preheated oven, Gas Mark 6/200°C/400°F, for 10-15 minutes. Mix the egg yolk with a little water and brush over the pastries shortly before the end of cooking time.

Variation:
Cut the final dough rectangle into squares of about 12 cm/4 ½in. Place a piece of marzipan in the centre of each square, and fold up like an envelope. Leave to rise, then bake.

over. Sprinkle with salt, and knead well to a smooth dough. Leave to stand in a bowl of cold water for 2-3 hours.

2 Drain the dough well and roll out on a floured pastry board to about ½ cm/⅛ inch thick. Cut out 6-cm/2½-inch rounds. Place on a greased baking tray. Preheat the oven for just the time it takes to reach Gas Mark 6-7/200°-220°C/400°-425°F and bake for 15-20 minutes.

3 Mix the icing sugar and vanilla sugar and sprinkle over the thaler while they are still warm.

YEAST THALER

Makes 30-40 cakes

40g/13oz flour
250g/8oz coconut butter
15g/½oz fresh yeast
125 ml/4 fl oz lukewarm milk
Salt
Coconut butter
100g/3½oz icing sugar
6 tsps vanilla sugar

1 Sieve the flour into a bowl. Using a kitchen knife, flake the coconut butter very finely into the flour. Crumble the yeast into the lukewarm milk and pour

Variation:
The thaler can also be coated with lemon icing, or sandwiched together with jam.

BRANDY CUP-CAKES

Makes 16 cakes

1 packet sponge mixture with nuts
100g/3½oz soft margarine
2 eggs
5 tbsps water

Filling

125g/4oz dried apricots
125 ml/4 fl oz water
8 tbsps apricot brandy
200g/7oz marzipan paste
40g/1½oz icing sugar

Icing

200g/7oz chocolate couverture
Hazelnut kernels for decoration

1 Make up the sponge mixture with the margarine, eggs and water according to the packet instructions and turn into 8-cm/3-inch paper cases. Bake in a preheated oven, Gas Mark 4/180°C/350°F, for about 20 minutes.

2 Boil the apricots with the water and 5 tbsps of the apricot brandy for about 10 minutes, then leave them to cool in the liquid. Drain and dice. Knead together the marzipan paste, icing sugar, remaining brandy and the apricots. Stir in about 3 tbsps of the apricot liquid to make a mixture of spreading consistency.

3 Slice the cup-cakes horizontally, then sandwich them together again with the marzipan mixture.

4 Melt the chocolate couverture over hot water. Ice the cupcakes and decorate with hazelnut kernels.

LEMON CREAM CAKES

Makes approximately 10 cakes

4 eggs, separated
2 tbsps lukewarm water
150g/5oz caster sugar
3 tsps vanilla sugar
Pinch of salt
75g/3oz flour
50g/2oz cornflour
Good pinch of baking powder
Margarine for greasing
Sugar for dusting

Filling

25g/1oz cornflour
250 ml/8 fl oz milk
50g/2oz caster sugar
Grated zest of 1 lemon
Pinch of salt
3 tbsps lemon juice
75g/3oz margarine

Icing

100g/3½oz icing sugar
3 tbsps lemon juice
2 tbsps coconut oil
Glacé cherries for decoration

1 Whisk the egg yolks with the lukewarm water, sugar, vanilla sugar and salt until light and fluffy. Whisk the egg whites until stiff, and pile onto the yolk mixture. Sieve over the flour, cornflour and baking powder. Using a balloon whisk, carefully fold everything together.

2 Grease a baking tray and line it with greaseproof paper. Spread in the mixture and bake in a preheated oven, Gas Mark 6-7/200°-220°C/400°-425°F for 10-15 minutes. Dust with sugar, turn out onto a wire rack, remove the paper and leave the sponge to cool. Cut into 6-cm/2½-inch rounds.

3 Mix the cornflour with a little milk. Bring the rest of the milk, the sugar, lemon zest and salt to the boil, and thicken with the cornflour. Remove from the heat, stir in the lemon juice and leave to cool. Cream the margarine until light and fluffy, then gradually stir the cornflour mixture into it. Use to sandwich the sponge rounds together in pairs.

4 Mix together the icing sugar, lemon juice and coconut oil. Use to ice the cakes, then decorate with the glacé cherries.

STRAWBERRY CREAM ROLL

Makes 16 portions

4 eggs, separated
3 tbsps warm water
125g/4oz caster sugar
3 tsps vanilla sugar
50g/2oz margarine, melted and cooled
50g/2oz flour
50g/2oz cornflour
1 tsp baking powder
20g/¾oz ground almonds
Margarine for greasing
Sugar for dusting

Filling

250g/8oz strawberries
3 tsps vanilla sugar
375 ml/12 fl oz whipping cream
40g/1½oz caster sugar
5 sheets gelatine

1 Beat the egg yolks, water, sugar and vanilla sugar to a thick, creamy consistency, then stir in the melted and cooled margarine. Whisk the egg whites until very stiff. Pile onto the yolk mixture. Sieve the flour, cornflour, baking powder and almonds, over the egg whites. Carefully fold everything together.

2 Grease a baking tray and line with greaseproof paper. Spread in the sponge mixture, and bake in a preheated oven, Gas Mark 7/220°C/425°F, for 10-12 minutes.

3 Turn the cooked sponge out onto a tea towel sprinkled with sugar, remove the paper, roll the cake up with the towel and leave to cool.

4 Wash, clean and halve the strawberries, sprinkle with vanilla sugar and leave to macerate.

5 Whip the cream with the sugar. Soak the gelatine, dissolve it over a low heat and leave to cool. Carefully fold into the whipped cream. As soon as the mixture starts to set, fold in the strawberries.

6 Unroll the sponge, spread it with the strawberry cream and roll up again. Chill until set.

FESTIVE MERINGUES

Makes 24

2 egg whites
Pinch of salt
125g/4oz caster sugar
600 ml/1 pt whipping cream
3 tsps vanilla sugar
25g/1oz cashew nuts, chopped
25g/1oz candied cherries, finely chopped

1 Whisk the egg whites with the salt until stiff, working quickly so they do not dry out. Gradually whisk in half the sugar, then carefully fold in the remainder.

2 Line a baking tray with greaseproof paper. Using two teaspoons, spoon 48 little mounds of meringue onto the tray, or pipe out rosettes of the mixture. Put in a very low oven, Gas Mark ½/130°C/250°F, for 1 hour, or until quite dry but still light in colour.

Mark 6-7/200°-220°C/400°-425°F, for 15 minutes. Reduce the heat to Gas Mark 4/180°C/350°F.

3 Meanwhile, purée the drained apricots with the jam and 25g/1oz of the almonds.

4 Stone and finely chop the dates. Whisk the egg whites until very stiff. Mix the sugar, the remaining almonds and the dates together, and fold into the egg whites. Spoon the mixture into a piping bag fitted with a plain nozzle. Pipe a strip along each long edge of the cooked cake base. Pipe a series of parallel lines every 5 cm/2 inches. Fill the gaps with the apricot mixture.

5 Return to the oven for a further 15-20 minutes. When cold, cut

between the parallel lines and then into 3-cm/2-inch-wide slices.

3 Shortly before serving, whip the cream with the vanilla sugar, and use to sandwich the meringues together in pairs. Decorate the cream filling with the nuts and cherries.

APRICOT AND DATE SLICES

Makes 35 slices

300g/10oz flour
100g/3½oz icing sugar
Pith of 2 vanilla pods
Pinch of salt
200g/7oz margarine
1 egg yolk
7 tbsps whipping cream
Margarine for greasing

Topping

200g/7oz tinned apricots
4 tbsps apricot jam
150g/5oz ground almonds
250g/8oz dates
4 egg whites
150g/5oz caster sugar

1 Mix together the flour, icing sugar, vanilla, salt, margarine, egg yolk and cream to a smooth dough. Chill.

2 Roll the dough out and use to line a greased baking tray. Bake in a preheated oven, Gas

RASPBERRY SPONGE ROLL

Makes approximately 16 portions

4 eggs, separated
3 tbsps warm water
125g/4oz caster sugar
50g/2oz flour
75g/3oz cornflour
Margarine for greasing
Sugar for dusting

Filling
250 ml/8 fl oz whipping cream
25g/1oz caster sugar
500g/1lb raspberries
50g/2oz sugar

1 Whisk the egg yolks, warm water and sugar until light and fluffy. Whisk the egg whites until stiff, and pile onto the yolk mixture. Sieve over the flour and cornflour, then carefully fold everything together.
2 Line a greased baking tray with greaseproof paper, grease the paper and spread the mixture over it. Bake in a preheated oven, Gas Mark 7/220°C/425°F, for 10-12 minutes.
3 Sprinkle sugar onto a tea towel, quickly turn the hot sponge base out onto it, remove the greaseproof paper and roll up the sponge in the tea towel.
4 Whip the cream with the sugar. Mash the raspberries with a fork, sweeten with the caster sugar and fold into the whipped cream. Unroll the sponge roll, spread with the raspberry cream, roll up again and chill.

NOUGAT ROLL

Makes approximately 16 portions

4 eggs, separated
3 tbsps warm water
125g/4oz caster sugar
Salt
50g/2oz cornflour
75g/3oz flour
Good pinch baking powder
Sugar for dusting

Filling
125 ml/4 fl oz coconut oil
100g/3½oz chocolate nougat
2 eggs
100g/3½oz icing sugar
Salt
Cinnamon
50g/2oz candied lemon peel

SWISS ROLL WITH KIRSCH

Makes approximately 20 portions

4 eggs, separated
3 tbsps warm water
125g/4oz caster sugar
3 tsps vanilla sugar
Pinch of salt
75g/3oz flour
50g/2oz cornflour
Good pinch baking powder
Margarine for greasing
Sugar for dusting

Filling
1 sheet red gelatine
5 sheets gelatine
250 ml/8 fl oz kirsch
250 ml/8 fl oz whipping cream
25g/1oz caster sugar

1 Whisk the egg yolks, water, sugar, vanilla sugar and salt until light and fluffy. Whisk the egg whites until stiff and pile onto the yolk mixture. Sieve over the flour, cornflour and baking powder and carefully fold everything together.

50g/2oz candied orange peel
50g/2oz hazelnuts
3 tbsps rum

1 Whisk the egg yolks with the water, sugar and salt until light and fluffy. Whisk the egg whites until stiff, then pile onto the yolk mixture. Sieve over the flour, cornflour and baking powder.

2 Line a greased baking tray with greaseproof paper and spread the mixture into it. Bake in a preheated oven, Gas Mark 6-7/200°-220°C/400°-425°F, for 10-12 minutes.
3 Sprinkle a tea towel with sugar and quickly turn the cooked sponge out onto it. Remove the greaseproof paper, and roll up the sponge in the tea towel. Leave to cool.
4 Soak and then dissolve the gelatine over hot water, and stir it into the kirsch. Leave to set. Whip the cream with the sugar

Using a balloon whisk, carefully fold everything together.

2 Line a baking tray with greaseproof paper, spread the mixture over it, and bake in a preheated oven, Gas Mark 6/200°C/400°F, for about 12 minutes.

3 Sprinkle sugar onto a tea towel, and turn the sponge out onto it. Remove the paper and quickly roll up the sponge in the towel. Leave to cool.

4 Melt the chocolate nougat over a pan of warm water, and stir in the coconut oil. Whisk the eggs with the icing sugar, salt and cinnamon until light and foamy. Chop the candied peel and the hazelnuts, and stir into the slightly cooled nougat mixture together with the rum. Leave in the refrigerator until it is firm enough to spread.

5 Unroll the sponge roll carefully, spread with the nougat mixture, roll up again and chill.

until thick, then carefully fold into the half-set kirsch mixture.

5 Unroll the sponge carefully, spread with the filling and roll up again. Cover and leave in the refrigerator until the filling has set.

CHOCOLATE SADDLE

Makes 16 portions

4 eggs
150g/5oz caster sugar
3 tsps vanilla sugar
Pinch of salt
2 tbsps rum
Grated zest of ½ lemon
125g/4oz margarine, melted
75g/3oz flour
100g/3½oz wheat semolina
75g/3oz cornflour
50g/2oz cocoa powder
2 tsps baking powder
Margarine for greasing
Flour

Icing
200g/7oz icing sugar
2 tbsps cocoa powder
½ tsp cinnamon
1-2 tbsps rum

1 Whisk the eggs, sugar, vanilla sugar and salt until light and fluffy. Whisk in the rum, lemon peel and margarine. Sieve together the flour and baking powder, mix with the semolina, cornflour and cocoa powder and gradually fold into the cake mixture. If the mixture is too stiff, add a little milk.

2 Grease a loaf tin and sprinkle with flour. Turn the mixture into this and bake in a preheated oven, Gas Mark 4/180°C/350°F, for abut 60 minutes. Turn out onto a wire rack and leave to cool.

3 Mix together the icing sugar, coco powder, cinnamon and rum until smooth and use to ice the cake.

MARZIPAN CAKE

Makes approximately 24 portions

40g/1½oz fresh yeast
200 ml/7 fl oz lukewarm milk
100g/3½oz caster sugar
500g/1lb flour
Pinch of salt
100g/3½oz margarine, melted and cooled
1 egg, beaten
Margarine for greasing

Filling

250g/8oz marzipan paste
1 egg white, stiffly beaten
25g/1oz caster sugar
25g/1oz margarine, melted
25g/1oz cinnamon sugar

Glaze

1 egg yolk
1 tbsp water

1 Crumble the yeast into the milk, and stir in a pinch of sugar and flour. Cover and leave in a warm place for 5-10 minutes until frothy. Put the flour, sugar, salt, margarine and beaten egg into a bowl. Mix in the frothy yeast to make a dough, knead thoroughly and leave in a warm place to rise.
2 Mix the marzipan paste, stiffly-beaten egg white and sugar to a smooth paste.
3 Knead the yeast dough again, and divide it into three

portions. Roll out one portion and use to line a greased baking tin. Spread with the marzipan mixture.

4 Roll out the second portion of dough to fit the tin, lay it on top of the marzipan, pressing

the edges together lightly.
5 Brush with the melted margarine and sprinkle with cinnamon sugar. Roll out the third portion to fit, and place it on top, pressing down lightly. Leave in a warm place to rise again. Carefully score a diamond pattern on the top. Mix the egg yolk with the water and brush over the dough, to glaze.

6 Brush lightly with the egg and water a second time, then bake in a preheated oven, Gas Mark 4/180°C/350°F, for about 30 minutes. Cut the cold cake into slices.

STRAWBERRY CREAM PUFFS

Makes approximately 10 puffs

250 ml/8 fl oz water
Pinch of salt
3 tsps vanilla sugar
60g/2¼oz margarine
125g/4oz flour
4 eggs
Margarine for greasing
Flour

Filling

500g/1lb strawberries
375g/12oz whipping cream
40g/1½oz caster sugar
Icing sugar for dusting

1 Bring the water, salt, vanilla sugar and margarine to the boil. Remove from heat, pour in all the flour, and beat with a wooden spoon until smooth. Return to the heat and continue beating until the mixture shrinks away from the sides of the pan in a ball. Beat in the eggs one by one.
2 Grease a baking tray, dust with flour and spoon about ten small dollops of mixture onto it. Bake in a preheated oven, Gas Mark 7/220°C/425°F, for about 30 minutes.
3 Cut the puffs in half immediately, then leave to cool.
4 Mash the strawberries. Whip the cream with the sugar until thick

and fold in the strawberries. Fill the bottom half of each puff with cream and replace the tops. Dust with icing sugar.

MINCE PIES

Makes approximately 20 pies

Filling

175g/6oz apples, chopped
175g/6oz sultanas
75g/3oz currants
25 g/1oz margarine
75g/3oz brown sugar
1 tsp cinnamon
½ tsp ground cloves
½ tsp nutmeg, grated
100 ml/3½ fl oz brandy
Juice and grated zest of 1 lemon

Pastry

200g/1lb flour
150g/5oz caster sugar
Pinch of salt
300g/10oz margarine
2 eggs
Margarine for greasing
Egg white
Icing sugar for dusting

1 Simmer all the filling ingredients together for about 30 minutes, uncovered, over a low heat, stirring occasionally, then leave to cool.
2 Make a dough from the pastry ingredients. Chill.
3 Roll out the dough and cut out 8-cm/3-inch rounds. Put half of these on a greased baking tray and heap a little of the filling on each one. Cut small star shapes out of the centres of the remaining rounds. Brush the outer rings with egg white and press them onto the mince pie bases. Top with the star-shaped 'lids'. Brush with egg white and bake at Gas Mark 6-7/200°-220°C/400°-425°F, for about 25 minutes until golden brown. When cool, dust with icing sugar.

ANTOINETTE SLICES

Makes approximately 48 slices

50g/2oz candied lemon peel
50g/2oz candied orange peel
100g/3½oz raisins
3 tbsps cognac, lightly heated
50g/2oz walnut kernels
50g/2oz pistachio nuts
125g/4oz margarine
100g/3⅓oz brown sugar
Pinch of salt
3 eggs
2 tsps ground cardamom
2 tsps ground red pepper
2 tsps ground cinnamon
125g/4oz clear honey
200g/7oz flour

Icing

100g/3½oz icing sugar
4 tbsps brandy
Walnut kernels, to decorate

1 Roughly chop the lemon and orange peel and the raisins. Turn them in the brandy, cover and leave to soak. Roughly chop the walnuts and pistachios.
2 Cream the margarine, sugar and salt until light and fluffy. Beat in the eggs one at a time, then the spices, honey and flour. Fold in the brandy-soaked fruit and the nuts with a spoon.
3 Line a 20-cm x 40-cm/8-inch x 6-inch baking tray with greaseproof paper. Turn the mixture into this and smooth the top. Bake in a preheated oven, Gas Mark 4-6/180°-200°C/350°-400°F for 15-20 minutes.
4 Mix together the icing sugar and brandy and use to ice the warm cake. Decorate with walnut kernels. When cold, cut into small pieces.

VICARAGE TEA PARTY STOLLEN

Makes approximately 20 portions

25g/1oz fresh yeast
200 ml/7 fl oz lukewarm milk
70g/3oz caster sugar
500g/1lb flour
½ tsp salt
100g/3½oz margarine, melted and cooled
Grated zest of 1 lemon
2 eggs, beaten
Margarine for greasing

Filling

100g/3½oz marzipan paste
100g/3½oz brown sugar
100g/3½oz hazelnuts, ground
2 egg whites
2 tbsps rum
½ tsp cinnamon
1 egg yolk
1 tbsp water

Icing

120g/4oz icing sugar
1-2 tbsps lemon juice
50g/2oz crushed cracknel

1 Crumble the yeast into the milk and stir in a pinch of sugar and flour. Leave covered in a warm place for 10-15 minutes until frothy. Mix together the flour, sugar, salt, margarine, lemon zest, eggs and frothy yeast and knead well, preferably using an electric mixer with pastry hook. Cover with foil and leave in a warm place until doubled in size.

For Soaking

125 ml/4 fl oz rum
25g/1oz ground almonds
100 ml/3½ fl oz milk

Filling

250 ml/8 fl oz whipping cream
25g/1oz caster sugar
Chopped pistachio nuts, to decorate

1 Crumble the yeast into milk, and stir in a pinch of sugar and flour. Cover and leave in a warm place for 5-10 minutes until frothy. Put the sugar, flour, salt, lemon zest, cooled margarine and the beaten eggs into a bowl, and add the frothy yeast. Mix well together and knead the dough thoroughly. Cover with foil and leave in a warm place until doubled in size.

2 Knead the risen dough again. Grease eight small ring moulds and divide the mixture between them. Bake in a preheated oven, Gas Mark 6/200°C/400°F, for 30-35 minutes.

3 Leaving the hot babas in their moulds, moisten them generously with the rum and leave to cool. Meanwhile, bring the almonds to the boil in the milk. When cold, use to moisten the babas.

4 Whip the cream with the sugar until thick. Unmould the babas, split and fill with the cream, then sprinkle with the pistachio.

2 Meanwhile, mix together the marzipan paste, sugar, hazelnuts, egg whites, rum and cinnamon. Roll out the risen yeast dough to a 45-cm/18-inch square, and spread with the filling, leaving the edges clear. Brush the edges with egg yolk mixed with water. Roll up the stollen, pressing the edges together.

3 Place on a greased baking tray and score the top of the stollen at 2½-cm/1-inch intervals. Leave to rise in a warm place for 15 minutes, then bake in a preheated oven, Gas Mark 6-7/200°-220°C/400°-425°F, for 30 minutes. Brush with beaten egg yolk 10 minutes before the end of baking time.

4 Mix together the icing sugar and lemon juice and spread over cooked stollen. Sprinkle with crushed cracknel.

RUSSIAN BABAS

Makes 8 babas

20g/¾oz fresh yeast
200 ml/7 fl oz lukewarm milk
75g/3oz caster sugar
250g/8oz flour
Pinch of salt
Grated zest of 1 lemon
100g/3½oz margarine, melted
4 eggs, beaten
Margarine for greasing

TREAT YOURSELF

A variety of cakes for different occasions: little cakes for two, fun cakes for children's parties, and quick treats for the unexpected guest.

MANDARIN CAKE

Makes approximately 6 portions

100g/3½oz margarine
100g/3½oz caster sugar
Pinch of salt
2 eggs
125g/4oz flour
1 tsp baking powder
Grated zest of 1 lemon
2 tbsps lemon juice
125g/4oz tinned mandarins
2 tbsps flour
Margarine for greasing
Breadcrumbs

Icing

75g/3oz icing sugar
3 tbsps orange liqueur or orange juice

1 Cream the margarine, sugar, salt and eggs until light and fluffy. Sieve together the flour and baking powder, and fold into the mixture. Add the lemon zest and juice. Drain the mandarins, dip the segments in flour and fold them into the mixture.
2 Grease a 15-cm/6-inch loaf tin. Sprinkle with breadcrumbs and turn the mixture into it. Bake in a preheated oven, Gas Mark 4/180°C/350°F for 45-50 minutes.
3 Mix the icing sugar with the orange liqueur and spread over the finished cake.

CREAM PUFFS

Makes 4 puffs

500g/1lb puff pastry, frozen
Sugar

Filling

250 ml/8 fl oz cream, whipped
Sugar
1-2 sheets gelatine

1 Thaw the pastry, and roll it out on a pastry board dusted with sugar. Cut out eight ovals measuring 8 cm/3 in long.
2 Rinse a baking tray with cold water, and place the pastry puffs on it, sugared side up. Prick each puff several times with a cocktail stick and leave to stand for 15 minutes. Bake in a preheated oven, Gas Mark 8-9/230°-240°C/450°-475°F, for 8-10 minutes.
3 Sweeten the cream to taste. Dissolve the gelatine and fold it into the whipped cream. Use this to sandwich together the pastry ovals in pairs.

MARBLE CAKE

Makes 6 portions

150g/5oz margarine
150g/5oz caster sugar
1½ tsps vanilla sugar
Pinch of salt
3 eggs
175g/6oz flour
1 tsp baking powder
Margarine for greasing
Breadcrumbs
15g/1½oz cocoa
2 tbsps rum

1 Cream the margarine, sugar, vanilla sugar, salt and eggs until light and fluffy. Sieve together the flour and baking powder, and fold into the mixture.

2 Grease a 16 cm/6 inch ring tin, sprinkle with breadcrumbs and turn half the mixture into it. Stir the cocoa and rum into the remaining mixture and turn into the tin. Swirl a fork through both mixtures to create a marble effect. Bake the cake in a preheated oven, Gas Mark 4/180°C/350°F, for 45-50 minutes.

LITTLE CHOCOLATE CAKES

Makes 10 cakes

Sponge Mixture

125g/4oz margarine
125g/4oz caster sugar
Pinch of salt
4 eggs
200g/7oz milk chocolate
1 tsp baking powder
125g/4oz flour
Margarine for greasing

Icing

150g/5oz icing sugar
3 tbsps lemon juice
2 tbsps rum

1 Cream the margarine, sugar salt and eggs until light and fluffy. Break up the chocolate, pour hot water over and leave to stand for a few minutes. Drain and stir the chocolate into the cake mixture. Sieve together the flour and baking powder and fold into the mixture.

2 Turn the mixture into greased bun tins. Bake in a preheated oven, Gas Mark 4/180°C/350°F, for about 20 minutes.

3 Meanwhile, mix together the icing sugar, lemon juice and rum until smooth. Spread this over the warm cakes.

147

GRAPE GATEAU

Makes approximately 6 portions

Pastry Base
65g/2½oz flour	
25g/¾oz caster sugar	
10g/½oz desiccated coconut	
40g/1½oz margarine	
Margarine for greasing	
2 tbsps apricot jam	

Sponge Mixture
2 eggs, separated	
2 tbsps warm water	
60g/2½oz caster sugar	
40g/1½oz flour	
40g/1½oz cornflour	
Good pinch of baking powder	

Topping
500g/1lb black grapes	
125 ml/4 fl oz white wine	
2 tbsps water	
2 tbsps caster sugar	
1 heaped tbsp cornflour	
250 ml/8 fl oz whipping cream	
25g/1oz caster sugar	

1 Make a pastry dough from the flour, sugar, coconut and margarine. Knead and chill for about 30 minutes. Roll out and use to line a greased 18-cm/7-inch flan tin with a removable base. Bake in a preheated oven, Gas Mark 7/220°C/425°F, for 10 minutes. Reduce the heat to Gas Mark 6/200°C/400°F.

2 Whisk the egg yolks with the water and sugar until light and fluffy. Whisk the egg whites until stiff, and fold them into the mixture. Sieve over the flour, cornflour and baking powder. Using a balloon whisk, carefully fold everything together.

3 Spread the apricot jam over the cooked pastry base, pour the sponge mixture on top and return to the oven for 25 minutes. Leave to cool, then slice through the sponge top horizontally.

4 Halve and deseed grapes and arrange them on the bottom layer of the sponge, reserving about fifteen for decoration. Put the wine, water, sugar and cornflour into a saucepan, mix well, and bring slowly to the boil, stirring continuously. Pour carefully over the grapes. Replace the second sponge layer.

5 Whip the cream with the sugar, spread it over the gâteau and decorate with the reserved grapes.

SNAIL RING

Makes approximately 8 portions

25g/1oz fresh yeast
125 ml/4 fl oz lukewarm milk
25g/1oz caster sugar
250g/8oz flour
Pinch of salt
75g/3oz margarine, melted and cooled

Filling

100g/3½oz raisins
2 tbsps rum
75g/3oz margarine
75g/3oz caster sugar
1 tsp cinnamon
25g/1oz ground almonds
25g/1oz chopped candied orange peel
25g/1oz chopped candied lemon peel
Margarine, melted
1 tbsp apricot jam

1 Crumble the yeast into the milk, adding a pinch of flour and sugar. Leave in a warm place until frothy. Put the flour, sugar, salt and margarine into a bowl, mix in the frothy yeast and knead thoroughly to a smooth dough. Set aside in a warm place to rise.

2 Soak the raisins in the rum.

3 Roll out the risen dough to a thickness of ½ cm/¼ inch. Spread with the margarine. Mix together the sugar, cinnamon, almonds, orange and lemon peel and soaked raisins and spread over the dough, pressing in lightly.

4 Cut the dough into 8-cm/3-inch-wide strips and fold each one in half lengthwise. Roll up one strip and place it in the centre of a greased 16-cm/6-inch cake tin with a removable base, open edge downwards. Curl the remaining strips around this centre, brushing the outer edge of each one with a little melted margarine, and working until the tin is full.

5 Leave to rise in a warm place for 15 minutes, then bake in a preheated oven, Gas Mark 6/200°C/400°F, for 30-35 minutes.

6 Whilst the cake is still warm, spread with the apricot jam, to glaze.

QUEEN CAKE

Makes approximately 6 portions

Sponge Mixture
100g/3½oz margarine
100g/3½oz caster sugar
1½ tsps vanilla sugar
Pinch of salt
2 eggs
100g/3½oz flour
25g/1oz cornflour
1 tsp baking powder
50g/2oz candied lemon peel
25g/1oz chopped almonds
1 tbsp rum
Margarine for greasing

Icing
75g/3oz icing sugar
1 tbsp lemon juice
25g/1oz mixed candied peel
6 glacé cherries

1 Cream together the margarine, sugar, vanilla sugar, salt and eggs until light and fluffy. Sieve together the flour and baking powder, then fold into the mixture. Stir in the finely-chopped lemon peel, the almonds and rum.
2 Turn the mixture into a greased 16-cm/6-inch cake tin with a removable base and bake in a preheated oven, Gas Mark 4/180°C/350°F, for about 40 minutes.
3 Mix together the icing sugar, lemon juice and water and spread over the warm cake. Decorate the cake with the chopped mixed peel and the glacé cherries.

JELLIED FRUIT ROUND

Makes approximately 6 portions

Pastry
75g/3oz flour
Pinch of salt
25g/1oz icing sugar
2 tsps vanilla sugar
40g/1½oz margarine
Margarine for greasing

Topping
50g/2oz marzipan paste
2 tbsps rum
350g/12oz bottled sour cherries
1 large banana
2 tbsps lemon juice
2 packets quick-setting gelatine
25g/1oz flaked almonds, toasted

1 Make the pastry dough and chill.
2 Roll the pastry out thinly and use to line a greased 16-cm/6-inch flan tin with a removable base. Bake in a preheated oven, Gas Mark 6/200°C/400°F, for about 15 minutes.
3 Mix the marzipan paste with the rum and spread over the pastry base.
4 Drain the sour cherries thoroughly, reserving the juice. Peel and slice the banana, sprinkling the slices with lemon juice. Arrange the fruit on the marzipan.
5 Make up the quick-setting gelatine according to the

packet instructions, using the reserved cherry juice and additional water as required. Pour over the fruit. Sprinkle with the toasted flaked almonds.

FRENCH WAFFLES

Makes 12 waffles

1 packet frozen puff pastry, thawed
Sugar
250 ml/8 fl oz whipping cream
Sugar to taste
1-2 sheets gelatine
60g/2¼oz raspberry jam

1 Roll the pastry out to a rectangle about 18cm x 48 cm/7 inches x 19 inches.
2 Cut out 24 6-cm/2½-inch rounds. Sprinkle the pastry board with sugar and roll out each round to an oblong shape about 10 cm/4 in long. Rinse a baking tray in cold water, and place the pastries on it, sugary side up. Prick each pastry several times with a cocktail stick and leave to stand for 15 minutes. Bake in a preheated oven, Gas Mark 8-9/230°-240°C/450°-475°F, for about 8 minutes. Leave until completely cold.
3 Whip the cream and sweeten to taste. Stir in the dissolved gelatine.

4 Spread jam on the unsugared side of each waffle and sandwich together in pairs with the whipped cream.

BUTTERFLY CAKES

Makes approximately 6 cakes

100g/3½oz margarine
100g/3½oz caster sugar
3 tsps vanilla sugar
Pinch of salt
2 eggs
200g/7oz flour
1 tsp baking powder
½ tsp cinnamon
Grated zest of 1 lemon

Filling
250 ml/8 fl oz whipping cream
25g/1oz caster sugar
50g/2oz hazelnuts, ground
Icing sugar for dusting

1 Cream together the margarine, sugar, vanilla sugar and salt until light and fluffy. Beat in the eggs, one by one. Sieve together the flour, baking powder and cinnamon. Stir in the lemon zest and fold into the cake mixture.
2 Divide between six bun tins or greaseproof paper cases and bake in a preheated oven, Gas Mark 4/180°C/350°F, for about 25 minutes. Leave to cool.
3 Whip the cream with the sugar until thick, then carefully fold in the hazelnuts. Slice the top off each cake and cut each top in half.
4 Pipe the cream onto each cake, then press the halved tops into the cream to form 'wings'. Dust with icing sugar.

RASPBERRY ECLAIRS

Makes 5 éclairs

125 ml/4 fl oz water
Pinch of salt
1½ tsps vanilla sugar
35g/1½oz margarine
75g/3oz flour
2 eggs
Margarine for greasing
Flour

Filling

250g/8oz raspberries
1½ tsps vanilla sugar
35g/1½oz caster sugar
200g/7oz whipping cream
Icing sugar for dusting

1 Bring the water, salt, vanilla sugar and margarine to the boil. Remove from heat, add the flour and beat until smooth. Return the pan to the heat and continue beating until the mixture comes away from the sides of the saucepan in a ball. Remove from the heat and beat in one egg. Beat in the remaining eggs one by one.

2 Sprinkle a greased baking tray with flour. Put the mixture into a piping bag fitted with a large nozzle and pipe five strips about 10 cm/4 in long onto the tray.

3 Bake in a preheated oven, Gas Mark 7/220°C/425°F, for about 30 minutes. Using scissors, cut the tops off the éclairs as soon as they come out of the oven. Leave to go quite cold.

4 Wash, clean and halve the raspberries, sprinkle with the vanilla sugar and 2 tsps of the caster sugar and leave to macerate. Whip the cream with the remaining sugar and spoon into a piping bag.

5 Spread the drained raspberries over the bottom half of each éclair, pipe the cream over and replace the tops.

LEMON PIE

Makes approximately 6 portions

Pastry

80g/3oz flour
Pinch of salt
50g/2oz margarine
1-2 tbsps water
Margarine for greasing

Filling

2 eggs, separated
60g/2½oz caster sugar
Grated zest of ½ lemon
6 tsps lemon juice
Icing sugar for dusting

1 Use the flour, salt, margarine and water to make a basic shortcrust pastry.
2 Roll the pastry out and use to line a 16-cm/7-inch greased pie dish. Prick the base several times with a fork and bake blind in a preheated oven, Gas Mark 6/200°C/400°F, for 25-30 minutes. Reduce the heat to Gas Mark 4/180°C/350°F.
3 Whisk the egg yolks, 50g/ 2oz of the sugar, the lemon zest and juice together in a bowl

over hot water until thick and creamy. Remove from the heat.
4 Whisk the egg whites with the remaining sugar until very stiff, then carefully fold them into the hot filling mixture.
5 Turn the filling into the hot pie base and return to the oven for a further 10 minutes. Dust with icing sugar.

NUTTY CHOCOLATE GATEAU

Makes approximately 8 portions

Sponge Mixture

100g/3½oz nougat chocolate
65g/2½oz margarine
65g/2½oz caster sugar
2 eggs, separated
40g/1½oz hazelnuts, ground
40g/1½oz flour
Good pinch of baking powder
Margarine for greasing

Filling

2 tbsps apricot jam
250g/8oz whipping cream
1 tsp vanilla sugar
10 small macaroons, to decorate

1 Melt the chocolate in a bowl over a pan of hot water. Cream 65g/2½oz of the margarine with 40g/1½oz of the sugar until light and fluffy. Add the cooled chocolate, the egg yolks and hazelnuts.
2 Whisk the egg whites with the remaining sugar until stiff and fold carefully into the chocolate mixture. Gently fold in the flour, sieved together with the baking powder.
3 Turn the mixture into a greased 18-cm/7-inch cake tin with a removable base and bake in a preheated oven, Gas Mark 4/ 180°C/350°F, for abut 30 minutes.
4 Slice the cake in half horizontally and spread each layer with apricot jam. Whip the cream with the vanilla sugar and use to sandwich together the cake layers. Decorate with the macaroons.

MOTHER'S DAY BUTTERFLY

Makes approximately 8 portions

375g/12oz flour
3 tsps baking powder
200g/7oz caster sugar
3 tsps vanilla sugar
Pinch of salt
Grated zest of 1 orange
200g/7oz margarine
4 eggs
2 tbsps lemon juice
3 tbsps orange juice
Margarine for greasing

Icing
100g/3½oz icing sugar
About 4 tbsps orange juice
Food colouring
Sugar letters
2 tbsps apricot jam

1 Sieve together the flour and baking powder, add the rest of the cake ingredients and mix to a creamy consistency, using an electric mixer. Begin mixing at a low speed, then mix at the highest speed for not more than 1 minute.
2 Turn the mixture into an ovenproof butterfly mould and bake in a preheated oven, Gas Mark 6/200°C/400°F, for about 45 minutes.
3 Turn the cooked butterfly out of the mould and leave to cool.
4 Mix together the icing sugar and orange juice and colour as desired. Spread over the cake and leave to harden. Decorate the butterfly as desired with more icing and the jam.

LOLLIPOP CAKES

Makes approximately 8 cakes

125g/4oz margarine
125g/4oz caster sugar
3 tsps vanilla sugar
250g/8oz flour
2 tsps baking powder
75g/3oz raisins
5 tbsps milk
Margarine for greasing
Icing sugar for dusting
Glacé cherries/candied angelica

1 Cream together the margarine, sugar and vanilla sugar until light and fluffy. Sieve together the flour and baking

MOTHER'S DAY HEART

Makes approximately 8 portions

200g/7oz margarine
200g/7oz caster sugar
3 tsps vanilla sugar
Pinch of salt
Grated zest of 1 orange
4 eggs
375g/12oz flour
3 tsps baking powder
2 tbsps lemon juice
100 ml/3½ fl oz orange juice
Margarine for greasing

Icing

1 egg white
200g/7oz icing sugar
Sugar flowers and leaves

1 Cream together the margarine, sugar, vanilla sugar, salt, orange zest and eggs until light and fluffy. Sieve together the flour and baking powder and gradually fold into the mixture, alternating with the lemon and orange juice.

2 Turn the mixture into a heart-shaped cake tin and bake in a preheated oven, Gas Mark 4/180°C/350°F, for about 45 minutes.

3 Whisk the egg whites until stiff, then whisk in sufficient icing sugar to achieve a piping consistency. Using a piping bag, decorate the cake with the icing as desired, finishing it off with the sugar flowers and leaves.

powder, reserving a little flour for the raisins. Fold into the cake mixture. Add the milk. Turn the raisins in the reserved flour and fold into the mixture.

2 Grease eight bun tins and divide the mixture between them. Bake in a preheated oven, Gas Mark 4/180°C/350°F for about 45 minutes.

3 Once the cakes have cooled, dust them with icing sugar and decorate with a lollipop, made from a glacé cherry and a stick of candied angelica.

Variation:
These cakes can also be iced with glacé icing.

CHILDREN'S FROGGY CAKES

Makes approximately 16

3 eggs, separated
2 tbsps water
125g/4oz sugar
Pinch of salt
150g/5oz flour
50g/2oz cornflour
3 tsps baking powder

Filling and Topping

1 packet blancmange mix, vanilla flavour
Green food colouring
25g/¾oz cocoa powder
2-3 tbsps water
2 tbsps coconut oil
Smarties, to decorate

1 Whisk the egg yolks with the water, sugar and salt until light and foamy. Whisk the egg whites until stiff and pile them onto the yolk mixture. Sieve over the flour, cornflour and baking powder. Using a balloon whisk, carefully fold everything together.

2 Spoon the mixture into a piping bag fitted with a large, round nozzle and pipe into paper cases about 6 cm/2½ inches in diameter. Bake in a preheated oven, Gas Mark 4/ 180°C/350°F for 15-20 minutes. Once cooled, slice each cake in half horizontally.

3 Make up the blancmange according to the instructions and colour with green food colouring. When almost set, spoon onto the cake bases.

4 Mix together the icing sugar, cocoa powder, water and coconut oil until smooth and use to ice the tops. Add Smarties for eyes, pressing them into the soft icing. Replace the tops at an angle on top of the cream.

CARNIVAL MASKS

Makes approximately 15 biscuits

Pastry
300g/10oz flour
200g/7oz ground almonds
125g/4oz caster sugar
6 tsps vanilla sugar
1 level tsp cinnamon
1 egg
1 egg yolk
200g/7oz margarine, chilled

Icing
1 egg white
200g/7oz icing sugar
Food colouring
Chocolate couverture

1 Sieve the flour onto a pastry board and add the almonds, sugar, vanilla sugar and cinnamon. Make a well in the centre and put in the egg and egg yolk. Dot with the chilled margarine and mix quickly to a dough. Knead, wrap in foil and chill in the refrigerator for at least 1 hour.

2 Cut out cardboard patterns for the mask. Roll out the dough on a floured board to a thickness of about 5 mm/¼ inch. Place the cardboard patterns on top, and cut out the masks.

3 Arrange the masks on a baking tray lined with greaseproof paper and bake in a preheated oven, Gas Mark 6/200°C/400°F, for 10-15 minutes. Leave to cool on a wire rack.

4 Whisk the egg whites until stiff, then stir in the icing sugar. Colour the icing as desired. Melt the chocolate couverture in a bowl over a pan of hot water. Draw fun faces on the masks with the icing and melted chocolate.

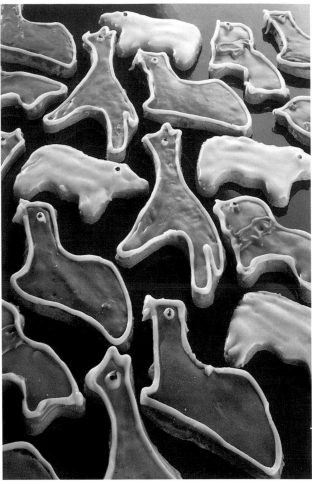

LEMON COCONUT ICE CAKE

Makes approximately 20 portions

250g/8oz coconut butter
150g/5oz icing sugar
2 eggs
2 tbsps lemon juice
Grated zest of 1 lemon
150g/5oz desiccated coconut
250g/8oz ready-made chocolate cake, cut into about 30 squares
Jellied fruit, to decorate

1 Cream the coconut butter with the icing sugar, eggs, lemon juice, lemon zest and desiccated coconut.

2 Line a 20-cm/8-inch loaf tin with greaseproof paper and fill with alternate layers of the coconut mixture and chocolate cake, ending with

a layer of the coconut mixture.
3 Chill in the refrigerator. Decorate with jellied fruit before serving.

ANIMAL SHAPES

Makes approximately 30 biscuits

250g/8oz flour
Good pinch baking powder
65g/2½oz caster sugar
Pinch of salt
125g/4oz margarine
1 egg
Margarine for greasing

Icing

1 egg white
200g/7oz icing sugar
Food colouring

1 Mix together the flour, baking powder, sugar and salt on a pastry board. Dot with flakes of cold margarine and cut in with a

palette knife. Add the egg and mix quickly to a smooth dough. Set aside in a cool place.
2 Roll out the pastry, cut out animal shapes and bake on a greased baking tray at Gas Mark 7/220°C/425°F for about 5 minutes. Leave to cool.
3 Beat the egg white until stiff, and stir in the icing sugar. Divide into portions, colour and use to decorate the baked animal shapes.

CARAMEL CREAMS

Makes approximately 30 creams

125g/4oz caster sugar
250 ml/8 fl oz whipping cream
25g/1oz margarine
1 tsp clear honey
3 tsps vanilla sugar
1 tbsp cocoa powder
Vegetable oil for greasing

1 Melt the sugar in saucepan, stirring continuously, until the sugar has dissolved, but not coloured. Add the whipping cream, bring to the boil, stirring continuously, and continue boiling for about 10 minutes until the mixture starts to thicken.

2 Add the margarine, honey, vanilla sugar and cocoa and continue boiling for a further 8-10 minutes until the mixture starts to shrink away from the bottom of the saucepan. Quickly pour into an oiled 20-cm/8-inch loaf tin.
3 When the mixture is half set, cut it into small squares using a knife dipped in cold water.

PARTY CAKES

Makes approximately 16 cakes

200g/7oz margarine
200g/7oz caster sugar
4 eggs
400g/13oz flour
3 tsps baking powder
10 tbsps milk
200g/7oz chocolate buttons
Margarine for greasing

Icing

300g/10oz chocolate icing
Smarties, to decorate

1 Cream together the margarine, sugar and eggs until light and fluffy. Sieve together the flour and baking powder and fold it in alternately with the milk. Fold in the chocolate buttons.
2 Grease 16 small bun tins, fill them with the mixture and bake in a preheated oven, Gas Mark 4/180°C/350°F, for 30-40 minutes. Turn out and leave to cool.
3 Make up the chocolate icing and use to ice the cakes. Decorate with Smarties, and more icing, if desired.

FLOWERPOTS

Makes 4 pots

300g/10oz flour
1 packet dried yeast
50g/2oz caster sugar
½ tsp salt
75g/3oz softened margarine
1 egg
125 ml/4 fl oz lukewarm milk
Jam
100g/3½oz marzipan
125g/4oz icing sugar
Food colouring
Cake decorations, e.g. sugar flowers, leaves and letters

1 Mix together the flour and dried yeast in a bowl, add the remaining ingredients and mix everything together thoroughly until you have a soft smooth dough. Knead and leave to prove in a warm place for about 1 hour.

2 Grease four clean 8-cm/3-inch earthenware flowerpots and line with greaseproof paper, or substitute similar-sized ramekins. Fill each pot three-quarters full with the yeast mixture. Leave to rise in a warm place for a short while, brush with milk if desired, and bake in a preheated oven, Gas Mark 6/200°C/400°F, for about 20 minutes. Turn out and leave to cool.

3 Spread the jam all round the sides of each cake. Knead together the marzipan and icing sugar and colour as desired. Roll it out and cut into four wide strips. Press the strips around the outsides of the flowerpot cakes to form a decorative cover. Fold the upper edge of the paste slightly over the top of each cake and press down. Decorate with sugar flowers and leaves or sugar letters.

Note: If you find the marzipan pot covers too much work, use crêpe or tissue paper instead.

BACK-TO-SCHOOL GOODIES

Makes approximately 15 biscuits

500g/1lb flour
250g/8oz margarine
2 small eggs
2 egg yolks
125g/4oz caster sugar
6 tsps vanilla sugar

Decoration

2 egg whites
400g/13oz icing sugar
Food colouring

1 Make a firm dough from the first six ingredients and chill for about 30 minutes.
2 Cut out cardboard patterns of various school items, e.g. exercise book, pencils, fountain pen, ruler, etc.
3 Roll out the dough to a thickness of ½ cm-1 cm/¼ inch-½ inch. Cut shapes out of the dough using the cardboard patterns. Line a baking tray with grease-proof paper, put the shapes on this and bake in a preheated oven, Gas Mark 6/200°C/400°F, for about 15 minutes. Place on a wire rack to cool.
4 Whisk the egg whites until stiff, mix with the icing sugar and divide into portions, colouring each portion differently as desired. To pipe, pack each portion into a freezer bag with a small bit cut off one corner. Decorate the shapes as imaginatively as possible.

POPCORN LOLLIES

Makes 8 lollies

125g/4oz popcorn
125g/4oz caster sugar
125 ml/4 fl oz water
2 tbsps whipping cream
75g/3oz chocolate
2 tbsps coconut oil

1 Put the popcorn in a bowl. Heat the sugar in a saucepan until it has lightly caramelized. Carefully stir the water into the caramel. Add the cream and stir until the mixture drops thickly off a spoon. Pour this over the popcorn, stir in well, then leave for a short while.
2 Shape into the mixture into balls with damp hands, spearing a few at a time onto long kebab sticks. Leave to harden for a few hours in a tall container, such as a spaghetti jar.
3 Melt the chocolate, add the coconut oil and dip the lollipops in this to cover. Leave to harden.

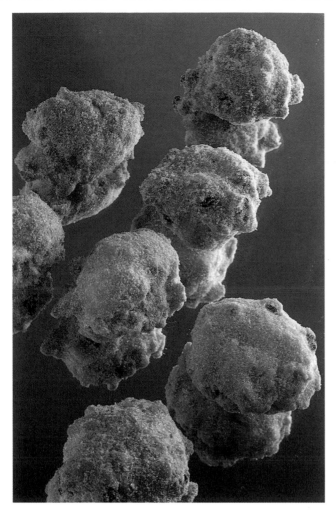

QUICK DOUGHNUTS

Makes approximately 18 doughnuts

100g/3½oz margarine
50g/2oz caster sugar
3 eggs
Pinch of salt
2 tsps baking powder
350g/12oz flour
125 ml/4 fl oz water
75g/3oz raisins
Vegetable oil for deep-frying
Cinnamon sugar for dredging

1 Cream together the margarine, sugar, eggs and salt until light and fluffy. Sieve together the flour and baking powder and fold in alternately with the water. Fold in the raisins.
2 Use a tablespoon to cut out doughnuts and deep-fry in small batches in the hot vegetable oil, 180°C/350°F, for 5-6 minutes. Drain and dredge with the cinnamon sugar.

DAMSON PARCELS

Makes approximately 10 parcels

250g/8oz frozen puff pastry, thawed
100g/3½oz damson or plum jam
50g-65g/2oz-2½oz icing sugar
1-2 tbsps lemon juice

1 Roll out the pastry and cut into about ten rectangles. Put 1 tsp damson or plum jam in the middle of each. Dampen the edges, fold two sides inwards, overlapping them slightly, and press the ends together tightly to seal.
2 Rinse a baking tray in cold water and arrange the parcels on it. Prick each one several times with a cocktail stick and leave to stand for 15 minutes. Bake in a preheated oven, Gas Mark 8-9/230°-240°C/450°-475°F, for 20-25 minutes.
3 Mix the icing sugar with the lemon juice and use to ice the damson parcels.

WALNUT BALLS

Makes approximately 35 pieces

200g/7oz white chocolate
100g/3½oz icing sugar
6 tbsps kirsch, lightly warmed
200g/7oz walnut halves

1 Melt the chocolate in a bowl over a pan of hot water. Use a hand-held electric mixer to work in the sieved icing sugar and the lightly-warmed kirsch.
2 Leave the mixture to cool, then shape into nut-sized balls.

3 Use these to sandwich together the walnut halves. Put into paper cases before serving.

CURD CHEESE FRITTERS

Makes 12 fritters

25 g/1oz margarine
50g/2oz caster sugar
3 tsps vanilla sugar
1 egg
Grated zest of 1 lemon
½ tsp salt
250g/8oz low fat curd cheese
2 level tsps baking powder
125g/4oz flour
Vegetable oil for deep-frying
Cinnamon sugar for dusting

1 Cream together the margarine, sugar, vanilla sugar and egg until light and fluffy. Add the lemon zest, salt and low fat curd cheese. Sieve together the flour and baking powder and fold in.
2 Using two tablespoons, scoop 12 portions out of the mixture and deep-fry in the hot vegetable oil, 180°C/350°F, for about 5 minutes.
3 Sprinkle with cinnamon sugar and serve immediately.

JAM ROSETTES

Makes approximately 12 portions

150g/5oz margarine
100g/3.5oz caster sugar
2 eggs
1 egg yolk
50g/2oz ground almonds
1 tsps cinnamon
125 ml/4 fl oz whipping cream
500g/1lb flour

Finishing

1 egg white
Vegetable oil for deep-frying
Various jams
Icing sugar for dusting

1 Cream the margarine and sugar until light and fluffy. Beat in the eggs and egg yolk, the almonds, cinnamon, cream and a little of the flour. Fold in the remaining flour and chill for 1 hour.

2 Roll the dough out to a thickness of 2 mm/⅛ inch. Cut out rounds with a fluted 6-cm/2½-inch pastry cutter. Brush the pastry rounds with egg white and stick together in threes, to form rosette shapes. Press down in the middle to make a hollow.

3 Deep-fry the rosettes in hot fat, 180°C/350°F, for 2-3 minutes on each side.

4 When cold, dust with icing sugar and fill the centres with different kinds of jam.

APPLE PASTRIES

Makes 10

| 250g/8oz frozen puff pastry, thawed |
| 200g/7oz apples, peeled and cored |
| Sugar |
| 25g/¾oz almonds, chopped |
| 1 tbsp raisins |
| 2 tbsps rum |
| Water |
| 1 egg yolk |
| Sugar for dusting |

1 Stew the peeled and cored apples with sugar to taste, the raisins, rum and a little water, if necessary. When just cooked but not disintegrated, set aside to cool.

2 Roll out the pastry and cut out ten squares. Spread a little of the apple mixture onto the centre of each square. Dampen the pastry edges with water, fold them over, and press the ends to seal. Place the parcels, seam side up, on a baking tray which has been rinsed in cold water. Score each pastry three times with a sharp knife.

3 Prick each pastry several times, brush with beaten egg

yolk and leave to stand for 15 minutes. Sprinkle with sugar and bake in a preheated oven, Gas Mark 8-9/230°-240°C/450°-475°F, for about 20 minutes.

ORANGE DUMPLINGS

Makes 4 dumplings

| 250g/8oz frozen puff pastry, thawed |
| 4 small oranges |
| 60g/2½oz sultanas |
| 25g/1oz pistachios, peeled |
| 25/1oz flaked almonds |
| 4 tbsps honey, |
| 2 tbsps Grand Marnier |
| 2 egg yolks |
| 2 tbsps ground almonds |

1 Peel the oranges carefully.

2 Mix the sultanas with the coarsely-chopped pistachios, flaked almonds, honey and Grand Marnier.

3 Roll out the puff pastry into four 18-cm/7-inch squares. Beat the egg yolk with 1 tbsp water, roll the oranges in it and then in the ground almonds and place one in the centre of each pastry square. Spread the sultana mixture over the oranges.

4 Fold up the corners of the pastry squares over the oranges and press together to seal. Cut out decorative shapes from the pastry trimmings and stick onto the dumplings.

5 Brush the pastry with egg yolk and arrange on a foil-lined baking tin; the foil is important as a lot of fruit juice escapes during cooking. Bake in a preheated oven, Gas Mark 8-9/220°-250°C/450°-475°F, for about 20 minutes. Serve hot or cold.

LIGHTNING CRANBERRY GATEAU

Makes 12 portions

150g/5oz icing sugar
4 eggs, separated
200g/7oz ground almonds
Margarine for greasing

Topping
500g/1lb whipping cream
120g/7oz bottled cranberries
Chocolate flakes, to decorate

1 Whisk the icing sugar and egg yolks until light and fluffy, stir in the almonds. Whisk the egg whites until stiff and fold in.
2 Grease the base of a 26-cm/10-inch cake tin with a removable base. Turn the mixture into this and bake in a pre-heated oven, Gas Mark 4/180°C/350°F, for about 30 minutes. Turn out and leave to cool.
3 Whip the cream with the vanilla sugar. Reserve a little of the cream, and fold the cranberries into the remainder. Spread the cranberry cream over the cooled base. Decorate with the reserved cream and the chocolate flakes. Serve cold.

ICED JAM PUFFS

Makes 5 puffs

250g/8oz frozen puff pastry, thawed
50g/2oz jam
50g/2oz icing sugar
1 tbsp water

1 Roll out the pastry and cut into five rectangles. Put 2 tsps of jam in the centre of each. Dampen the edges and fold them over lengthways. Press edges together to seal and make five cuts on the closed side of each puff.
2 Prick each puff several times with a cocktail stick. Rinse a baking tray in cold water and place the jam puffs on it. Leave to stand for 15 minutes. Bake in a preheated oven, Gas Mark 7-8/220°-250°C/450°-475°F, for 20-25 minutes.
3 Mix the icing sugar with the water and ice the jam puffs whilst they are still warm.

Note: If you would prefer to have ten small jam puffs, simply halve the pastry rectangles and fill each with 1 tsp jam or marzipan.

MARZIPAN POCKETS

Makes 15 portions

500g/1lb frozen puff pastry, thawed
200g/7oz marzipan paste
50g/2oz icing sugar
4 tbsps kirsch
1 egg, separated
1 tbsp water

1 Blend the marzipan paste with the kirsch and the icing sugar.
2 Roll out the pastry and cut out fifteen 12-cm/4½-inch rounds. Heap a little of the marzipan filling onto one half of each pastry round, brush the pastry edges with egg white, fold the empty half over and press the edges together firmly to seal.
3 Mix the egg yolk with the water and brush over the pastries to glaze. Decorate with pastry shapes made from the trimmings and glazed with egg and water. Rinse a baking tray in cold water, arrange the pastries on it and bake in a preheated oven, Gas Mark 6-7/ 200°-220°C/400°-425°F, for 20-25 minutes until golden brown.

Note: The pastry pockets may be filled with a variety of sweet or savoury fillings.

CHEESY CUSHIONS

Makes 10

500g/1lb frozen puff pastry, thawed
250g/8oz low fat curd cheese
Grated zest of 1 lemon
1 tbsp lemon juice
50g/2oz caster sugar
25g/1oz hazelnut kernels, ground
50g/2oz raisins
Egg white
Vegetable oil for deep-frying
Icing sugar

1 Mix together the curd cheese, lemon zest, lemon juice, sugar, nuts and raisins.
2 Roll out the pastry and cut out ten rectangles 12 cm x 15cm/4 ½ inches x 6 inches. Heap a little curd cheese mixture onto one half of each rectangle, brush the edges of the pastry with egg white, fold the empty pastry half over and press the edges together well to seal.
3 Deep-fry in hot vegetable oil, 180°C/350°F, for 10-15 minutes. Drain and dust with icing sugar.

Note: These pastries should be eaten the day they are made.

TIRAMISU

Makes approximately 6 portions

2 tsps espresso coffee powder
125 ml/4 fl oz water, boiling
6 egg yolks
150g/5oz caster sugar
400g/13oz full fat cream cheese
100g/3½oz low fat curd cheese
5 tbsps coffee liqueur
150g/5oz sponge fingers
Cocoa powder

1 Dissolve the espresso coffee in the boiling water and leave to cool. Whisk the egg yolks with the sugar over a pan of hot water until thick and creamy. Add the cheeses, stirring in alternate tablespoonfuls of cream cheese and curd cheese. Mix the espresso with the coffee liqueur.

2 Line a rectangular dish with sponge fingers, sprinkle with the coffee and cover with a layer of the cream cheese mixture, followed by another layer of sponge fingers sprinkled with coffee. Repeat the layers until all the sponge fingers and cheese mixture have been used up. Finish with a layer of the cheese mixture. Leave overnight to set.

3 Before serving, dust the Tiramisu with cocoa powder.

CURD CHEESE CAKE

Makes approximately 12 portions

250g/8oz margarine
300g/10oz caster sugar
6 egg yolks
1kg/2lb low fat curd cheese
Juice and grated zest of 1 lemon
2 packets vanilla-flavour blancmange
50g/2oz chopped pistachios
5 egg whites
Margarine for greasing
5-6 tbsps grated rusk
1 egg yolk
1-2 tbsps condensed milk

1 Beat the margarine, sugar and egg yolks until thick and creamy. Stir in the curd cheese, lemon juice and zest, blancmange and pistachios. Whisk the egg whites until stiff and fold into the mixture.

2 Grease the base of a 26-cm/10-inch cake tin with a removable base and sprinkle thickly with the grated rusk. Turn the cheese mixture into this.

3 Mix the egg yolk with the condensed milk and brush over the top. Bake in a preheated oven, Gas Mark 2/150°C/ 300°F, for 75-80 minutes.

NUTTY CHEESECAKE

Makes approximately 20 portions

150g/5oz margarine
250g/8oz caster sugar
Pinch of salt
5 eggs
250g/8oz curd cheese
200g/7oz chocolate nougat
200g/7oz hazelnuts, ground
100g/3½oz hazelnuts, chopped
200g/7oz flour
2 tsps baking powder
Margarine for greasing
Fine breadcrumbs
Icing sugar for dusting

1 Beat the margarine, sugar and salt until light and fluffy, then beat in the eggs one by one. Melt the nougat, drain the curd cheese, mix them together, then fold into the cheesecake mixture. Fold in the hazelnuts and the flour, sieved together with the baking powder.
2 Grease a 22-cm/9-inch cake tin with a removable base and sprinkle with breadcrumbs. Turn the mixture into this. Bake in a preheated oven, Gas Mark 4/180°C/350°/°F, for 60-70 minutes.
3 Leave to cool, then dust with icing sugar.

CREAMY LEMON CHEESECAKE

Makes approximately 12 portions

200g/7oz sponge fingers
4 rusks
150g/5oz margarine
1 packet (135g/4½oz) lemon jelly
250 ml/8 fl oz boiling water
400g/13oz cream cheese
500g/1lb low fat curd cheese
200g/7oz caster sugar
6 tsps vanilla sugar
2 tbsps orange liqueur
500 ml/18 fl oz whipping cream
Grated chocolate

1 Crumble the sponge fingers and rusks finely. Slightly warm the margarine and mix it well with the sponge and rusks. Turn two-thirds of this mixture into a flan tin with a removable base, pressing it down well to line the bottom of the tin.
2 Melt the jelly in the boiling water and leave until it is beginning to set. Mix the cream cheese, curd cheese, sugar, vanilla sugar and liqueur and stir into the jelly. Whip the cream until stiff and fold it in.
3 Sprinkle the top of the cheesecake with the remaining sponge and rusk and finish with grated chocolate.

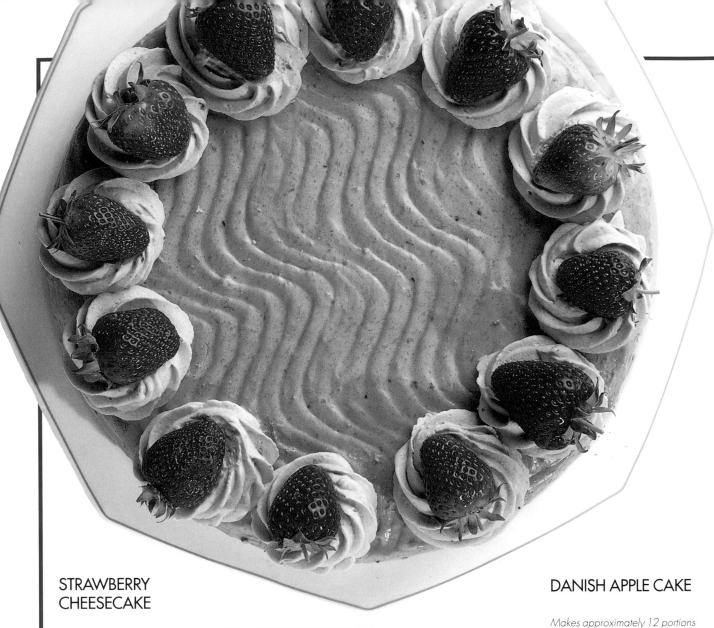

STRAWBERRY CHEESECAKE

Makes approximately 12 portions

150g/5oz margarine
150g/5oz caster sugar
3 tsps vanilla sugar
Grated zest of ½ lemon
3 eggs
150g/5oz flour
½ tsp baking powder
Margarine for greasing

Topping

300g/10oz frozen strawberries, thawed
750g/1½lb low fat curd cheese
225g/7½oz caster sugar
3 tsps vanilla sugar
Grated zest of 1 lemon
125 ml/4 fl oz lemon juice

12 sheets gelatine
2 sheets red gelatine
375 ml/12 fl oz cream, whipped
6 tbsps kirsch

1 Cream together the margarine, sugar, vanilla sugar, salt, lemon zest and eggs until light and fluffy. Sieve together the flour and baking powder and fold it gradually into the mixture.
2 Turn the mixture into a greased 24-cm/9½-inch flan tin with a removable base and bake in a preheated oven, Gas Mark 4/180°C/350°F for about 45 minutes. Turn the cake out and leave to cool.

3 Mash the strawberries and mix them into the curd cheese, with the sugar, vanilla sugar, lemon juice and zest.
4 Soak the gelatine, dissolve it over a low heat, then stir it into the strawberry mixture. Set aside to cool. When half set, fold it into the whipped cream.
5 Slice the cooled cake in half horizontally and sprinkle kirsch over each layer. Sandwich the layers together with half of the strawberry cheese mixture. Spread the rest over the top and sides of the cake. Decorate as desired.

DANISH APPLE CAKE

Makes approximately 12 portions

1½kg/3lb cooking apples
125 ml/4 fl oz white wine
2 tbsps lemon juice
Grated zest of ½ lemon
250g/8oz caster sugar
100g/3½oz currants
275g/9oz rusks
6 tsps vanilla sugar
100g/3½oz margarine
Margarine for greasing
125 ml/4 fl oz cream, whipped

1 Peel and core the apples and cut them into medium-sized wedges. Bring the wine to the boil with the lemon juice and zest and 150g/5oz of the caster sugar. Stew the apples in this over a low heat until they are soft but retain their shape. Carefully fold in the currants and leave to cool.

2 Crush the rusks with a rolling pin. Mix them with the vanilla sugar, the remaining caster sugar and the margarine. In two batches, spread the mixture onto a baking sheet and toast lightly. Leave to cool.

3 Grease a 24-cm/9½-inch flan tin with a removable base. Fill with alternate layers of toasted rusk and apple, starting and finishing with a layer of rusk. Press each layer down with a spatula. Leave to macerate for several hours.

4 Turn out the apple cake and decorate with whipped cream.

APRICOT CHEESECAKE

Makes approximately 12 portions

250g/8oz flour
Good pinch of baking powder
125g/4oz margarine
65g/2½oz caster sugar
1 egg
Margarine for greasing

Topping

25 g/¾oz ground almonds
425g/14oz tinned apricots
75g/3oz margarine
200g/7oz caster sugar
3 eggs
750g/1½lb low fat curd cheese
1 packet vanilla blancmange
1 tsp lemon juice
1 egg yolk
Water

1 Mix the flour, baking powder, margarine, sugar and egg to a smooth dough.

2 Roll out a generous half of the dough and use to line a greased 24-cm/9½-inch flan tin with a removable base. Sprinkle over the ground almonds.

3 Drain the apricots. Beat together the margarine, sugar, eggs, curd cheese, blancmange and lemon juice.

4 Spread the apricots over the pastry base and pile the cheese mixture on top, smoothing it over evenly.

5 Roll out the remaining dough and use a pastry wheel to cut it into 1-cm/½-inch-wide strips. Weave the strips into a lattice over the top of the cheesecake. Bake the cheesecake in a pre-heated, oven Gas Mark 4-6/ 180°-200°C/350°-400°F for 60-70 minutes. Beat the egg yolk with the water and brush this over the cheesecake after 50 minutes. Finish baking.

6 Leave the cheesecake to cool in the tin and turn out when cold.

SUMMER CHEESECAKE

Makes approximately 12 portions

150g/5oz flour
75g/2½oz margarine
25g/1oz caster sugar
Pinch of salt
1 egg yolk
1 tbsp milk
Margarine for greasing

Topping

3 egg yolks
150g/5oz caster sugar
3 tsps vanilla sugar
500g/1lb curd cheese
Juice from 1 lemon
8 sheets gelatine
4 egg whites
250 ml/8 fl oz whipping cream
750g/1½lb fresh strawberries, washed and picked over

1 Make a shortcrust pastry dough using the flour, margarine, sugar, salt, egg yolk and milk. Mix well, then knead and chill for several hours. Roll out the pastry and use to line a greased 24-cm/9½-inch flan tin with a removable base. Bake in a preheated oven, Gas Mark 6-7/200°-220°C/400°-425°F, for about 20 minutes. Leave to cool.

2 Turn the cooled pastry base out onto a cake dish and replace the ring part of the tin over it.

3 Whisk the egg yolks, sugar and vanilla sugar until light and fluffy, then add the curd cheese and lemon juice. Soak the gelatine, dissolve it over low heat and mix it into the cheese mixture.

4 Whisk the egg whites until stiff and whip the cream until thick. Fold them into the half-set cheese mixture. Spread the base of the cake with the strawberries, reserving some for decoration. Pour the cheese mixture over and leave overnight in the refrigerator to set. Decorate with the reserved strawberries.

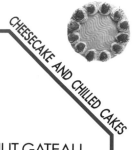

BISCUIT LAYER CAKE

Makes approximately 20 portions

175g/6oz coconut butter
2 eggs
150g/5oz icing sugar
Pinch of salt
40g/1½oz cocoa powder
1 tsp instant coffee
1 tsp hot water
40g/1½oz ground almonds
25 plain biscuits
Jellied fruit, almonds, etc., to decorate

1 Melt the coconut butter and leave to cool. Whisk the eggs, icing sugar, salt and cocoa powder until light and fluffy. Mix the coffee with the hot water and add to the mixture together with the almonds. Mix in the coconut butter.

2 Line a 20-cm/8-inch loaf tin with greaseproof paper. Fill with alternate layers of chocolate mixture and biscuits, beginning and ending with a chocolate layer.

3 Before the top layer of chocolate mixture has hardened, decorate as desired, then chill before serving.

COCONUT GATEAU

Makes approximately 12 portions

500g/1lb coconut butter
4 eggs
300g/10oz icing sugar
4 tbsps lemon juice
300g/10oz desiccated coconut
2 packets sponge fingers
Jellied fruit, to decorate

1 Melt the coconut butter and leave to cool. Whisk the eggs and icing sugar until light and fluffy, add the lemon juice and desiccated coconut and slowly stir in the coconut butter.

2 Line a greased 22-cm/8½ -inch cake tin with greaseproof paper and fill with alternate layers of coconut mixture and sponge fingers arranged in a star pattern. Finish with a layer of coconut mixture.

3 Decorate the gâteau with sponge fingers and jellied fruit. Chill for at least half a day before serving.

BAKING FOR FESTIVE OCCASIONS

Here are some original ideas and some old favourites for Christmas, Easter and many other festive occasions.

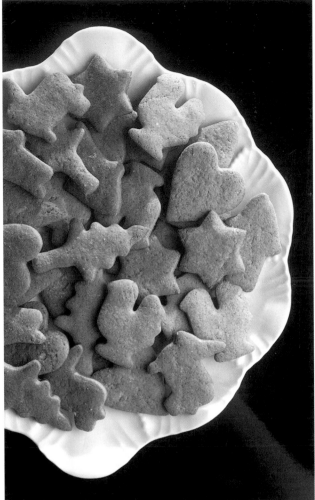

ADVENT ROSES

Makes 20 biscuits

250g/8oz flour
Pinch of salt
75g/3oz icing sugar
200g/7oz margarine
Margarine for greasing

Topping

1 egg yolk
40g/1½oz flaked almonds
100g/3½oz orange jam

1 Mix the flour, salt, icing sugar and margarine to a dough. Chill.
2 Roll the dough out and cut out round flower shapes.
3 Mix the egg yolk with a little water and brush over half the pastry flowers. Press the egged surface onto the flaked almonds. Turn right side up and arrange the flowers on a greased baking tray, setting aside the plain pastry flowers. Bake in a preheated oven, Gas Mark 6/ 200°C/400°F, for about 10 minutes.
4 Bake the plain pastry flowers in the same way. Leave to cool.
5 Sandwich the plain and almond-decorated flowers together with a little jam.

GOLDEN SYRUP COOKIES

Makes approximately 80 cookies

125g/4oz golden syrup
125g/4oz caster sugar
125g/4oz margarine
375g/12oz flour
1 level tsp baking powder
Good pinch ground cloves
2 tsps cardamom
2 tsps cinnamon
Grated zest of ½ lemon
2-3 tbsps water
Margarine for greasing

1 Heat the syrup, sugar and margarine until the sugar has dissolved.
2 Sieve together the flour, baking powder, cloves, cardamom and cinnamon. Add the lemon zest and the cooled syrup mixture and mix together well, adding a little water if necessary. Leave until cold.
3 Roll the dough out. Cut out into hearts, stars, animal shapes, etc. Arrange on a greased baking tray and bake in a preheated oven, Gas Mark 7/220°C/425°F for 10 minutes.

PEANUT BISCUITS

Makes approximately 70 biscuits

125g/4oz margarine

175g/6oz caster sugar

3 tsps vanilla sugar

1 egg

100g/3½oz unsalted peanuts, ground

1 tsp baking powder

175g/6oz flour

Peanuts, to decorate

Margarine for greasing

1 Cream the margarine until light, then gradually beat in the sugar, vanilla sugar and egg, followed by the ground peanuts and the flour, sieved with baking powder.

2 Chill for about 60 minutes in the refrigerator. Shape into hazelnut-sized balls. Decorate with halved peanuts and place on a greased baking tray, leaving space between.

3 Bake in a preheated oven, Gas Mark 6/200°C/400°F, for about 30 minutes.

SPECULOOS

Makes approximately 100 biscuits

500g/1lb flour

2 tsps cinnamon

1 tsp ground cloves

1 tsp cardamom

Good pinch of ground ginger

Good pinch of grated zest of orange

150g/5oz margarine, cut into small pieces

300g/7oz caster sugar

6 tsps vanilla sugar

1 egg

7 tbsps whipping cream

1 tsp bicarbonate of soda

Margarine for greasing

1 Sieve the flour and spices onto a pastry board. Make a well in the middle and put in the margarine, sugar, vanilla sugar and egg. Add the cream with the bicarbonate of soda dissolved in it. Mix everything together to a smooth dough and chill.

2 Roll the dough out and cut into character shapes, e.g. Father Christmas, gnomes, fairies, nursery-rhyme characters, etc.

3 Place on a greased baking tray and bake in a preheated oven, Gas Mark 6-7/200°-220°C/400°-425°F, for 8-10 minutes.

177

BROWN AND WHITE COOKIES

Makes approximately 80 cookies

250g/8oz margarine	
250g/4oz caster sugar	
Pinch of salt	
Pith of 1 vanilla pod	
Good pinch of bicarbonate of soda	
1 tsp water	
375g/12oz flour	
25g/1oz flour	
Margarine for greasing	
100g/3½oz hazelnut kernels	
25g/3/4oz cocoa powder	

1 Cream together the margarine, sugar, salt and vanilla until light and fluffy. Dissolve the bicarbonate of soda in the water and stir it into the mixture together with the flour.

2 Divide the dough into two portions. Knead the additional 25g/1oz of flour into one portion, shape into a roll and cut into about 40 slices. Roll these into balls and place on a greased baking tray. Make a slight hollow in the centre of each with your thumb and put a hazelnut kernel in each hollow.

3 Mix the cocoa powder into the remaining dough, then proceed as before.

4 Bake the cookies in a preheated oven, Gas Mark 4-6/ 180°-200°C/350°-400°F for 12-15 minutes. Make sure the light-coloured cookies do not brown.

CONTINENTAL CHRISTMAS GATEAU

Makes approximately 12 portions

125g/4oz flour
40g/1½oz caster sugar
25g/¾oz desiccated coconut
75g/3oz margarine
50g/2oz apricot jam

Sponge Mixture

2 eggs, separated
2 tbsps water
65g/2½oz caster sugar
50g/2oz flour
25g/1oz cornflour

Topping

500g/1lb apples
250 ml/8 fl oz white wine
40g/1½oz caster sugar
Grated zest of 1 lemon
375g/12oz seedless white grapes
425g/14oz tinned mandarins
2 tbsps lemon juice
125 ml/4 fl oz white wine
50g/2oz caster sugar
3 packets quick-setting gelatine
250 ml/8 fl oz cream, whipped

1 Make a pastry dough from the flour, sugar, desiccated coconut and margarine. Knead, roll out and use to line a 24-cm/9½-inch cake tin with a removable base. Prick the pastry base in several places with a fork and bake in a preheated oven, Gas Mark 7/ 220°C/ 425°F, for about 15 minutes.

2 Meanwhile, whisk the egg yolks, water and sugar until thick and creamy. Whisk the egg whites until stiff, and pile on top of the mixture. Sieve the flour and cornflour over the egg whites and carefully fold everything together.

3 If the apricot jam is quite firm, mix it with a little water, then spread it over the hot pastry base. Turn the sponge mixture into the tin. Bake for a further 12-15 minutes. Leave to cool.

4 Peel and core the apples and cut each one into eight pieces. Put them into a saucepan with the white wine, sugar and lemon zest and simmer gently for about 5 minutes. Leave to drain in a colander.

5 Wash and peel the grapes and leave them to drain. Drain the mandarins and reserve the juice.

6 Make up the juice from the apples, grapes and mandarins to 500 ml/18 fl oz with the lemon juice and white wine and sweeten to taste with sugar. Using this liquid, make up the quick-setting gelatine, according to the packet instructions.

7 Place the ring part of the cake tin over the gâteau. Fold the fruit carefully into the gelatine and spread over the gâteau. When partly set, decorate with the whipped cream.

TREE TOPS

Makes approximately 70 portions

250g/8oz margarine
250g/8oz caster sugar
6 tsps vanilla sugar
5 eggs
100g/3½oz flour
100g/3½oz cornflour
100g/3½oz ground almonds
Good pinch of cardamon
Good pinch of cinnamon
400g/13oz chocolate couverture

1 Cream together the margarine, sugar, vanilla sugar and eggs until light and fluffy. Mix together the flour, cornflour, almonds and spices and fold into the mixture.

2 Line a large rectangular baking tin with greaseproof paper. Spread one-sixth of the mixture into the tin and either put under a preheated grill or into the oven, Gas Mark 8-9/230°-240°C/450°-475°F, for about 2 minutes.

3 Spread a second layer of mixture on top and cook in the same way. Repeat for the remaining four layers.

4 Turn out the cake and cut into triangles whilst still warm. To cut triangles, first cut the cake into pieces 4-cm/1½-inch square, then halve these diagonally. Leave to cool.

5 Melt the chocolate couverture. Use a fork to dip each tree top into the chocolate. Leave on a wire rack to harden.

Note: Don't put the baking tray too close to the direct heat of the grill.

DATE COOKIES

Makes approximately 75 cookies

125g/4oz margarine
125g/4oz caster sugar
1 egg
2 tbsps lemon juice
Grated zest of ½ lemon
250g/8oz flour
Good pinch of baking powder
200g/7oz dates
100g/3½oz almonds, chopped
Margarine for greasing

1 Cream the margarine until light. Beat in, one by one, the sugar, egg, lemon juice and zest. Gradually fold in the flour, sieving the baking powder in with the last portion of flour.

2 Stone and chop dates. Add the chopped almonds and dates to the cookie mixture and drop in teaspoonfuls onto a greased baking tray.

3 Bake the cookies in a preheated oven, Gas Mark 7/220°C/425°F for about 15 minutes until they are golden brown.

FRUIT AND SPICE COOKIES

Makes approximately 24 cookies

4 eggs
250g/8oz caster sugar
Pinch of salt
3 tsps mixed spice
100g/3½oz candied lemon and orange peel
250g/8oz flour
1 tsp baking powder
100g/3½oz flaked almonds
Rice papers, 6 cm-7 cm/2½ in-3 in in diameter
50g/2oz icing sugar
Grated zest of 1 orange
1 tbsp orange juice

1 Whisk the eggs, sugar, salt and spices until thick and foamy. Finely chop the lemon and orange peel. Sieve together the flour and baking powder, mix with the peel and fold into the egg mixture, together with the flaked almonds. Leave to stand for 1 hour.

2 Put a heaped tablespoonful of the mixture on each round of rice paper and leave to dry overnight. The following day, bake the cookies in a preheated oven, Gas Mark 4/180°C/350°F for about 25 minutes.

3 Mix together the icing sugar, orange zest and juice. Ice half the cookies whilst they are still warm and leave the remainder plain.

PEAR TREATS

Makes approximately 15 portions

75g/3oz dried pears
4 tbsps water
6 tbsps pear liqueur
6 tbsps vanilla sugar
2 tbsps single cream
200g/7oz white chocolate
25 g/1oz coconut butter

1 Dice the pears, and simmer them in the water for 5 minutes. Add half the pear liqueur and the vanilla sugar and stir to a paste.

2 Bring the cream to the boil and melt the chocolate and coconut butter in it. Remove from the heat and beat in the remaining pear liqueur. Leave to cool, stirring occasionally, until the mixture has thickened enough for piping.

3 Using a piping bag, pipe a little of the chocolate mixture into small paper cases, spoon a little pear paste on top and finish with a little more of the chocolate mixture.

CHOCOLATE MARZIPAN PIES

Makes approximately 30 pies

200g/7oz flour
75g/3oz icing sugar
100g/3½oz margarine
3 egg yolks
Margarine for greasing

Filling

10g/½oz crystallized ginger
1 tbsp ginger syrup
100g/3½oz marzipan paste

Icing and Decoration

Egg white
100g/3½oz chocolate couverture, melted
Strips of crystallized ginger, or crystallized violets

1 Sieve the flour and icing sugar onto a board, cut in the margarine with a palette knife. Make a well in the centre, add the egg yolks and work the ingredients quickly to a dough, kneading lightly. Chill for about 2 hours in the refrigerator.

2 Grate the ginger and blend into the marzipan paste with the ginger syrup.

3 Roll out the pastry dough and cut out 5-cm/2-inch rounds. Place half the rounds on a greased baking tray and top with a little marzipan filling, leaving the edges clear. Brush these with egg white. Cover with the remaining rounds, pressing the edges together firmly to seal. Bake in a preheated oven, Gas Mark 7/ 220°C/425°F, for about 10 minutes.

4 Coat the finished cakes with the melted chocolate couverture and decorate with strips of crystallized ginger or crystallized violets.

RICH FRUIT CAKE

Makes approximately 12 portions

350g/12oz margarine
350g/12oz caster sugar
6 eggs
450g/15oz flour
4 tbsps milk or brandy
1 tsp cinnamon
½ tsp ground cloves
½ tsp ground ginger
450g/15oz raisins or sultanas
Grated zest of 1 orange
Grated zest of 1 lemon
100g/3½oz mixed candied peel

125g/4oz glacé cherries, halved and dipped in flour
250g/8oz almonds, chopped
50g/2oz crystallized ginger, chopped
Margarine for greasing
Fruit and nuts, to decorate
4 tbsps apricot jam

1 Cream together the margarine, sugar and eggs until light and fluffy. Add the flour, brandy and spices in that order.

Fold in the raisins, grated orange and lemon zest, chopped candied peel, cherries, almonds and ginger.

2 Grease a 26-cm/10½-inch cake tin with a removable base and line with greaseproof paper. The strip around the sides should be at least 8 cm/3 inches high. Turn the mixture into this and arrange the fruit and nut decoration on top, without pressing in.

3 Bake the cake in a preheated oven, Gas Mark 1/140°C/275°F for about 3 hours. After 1½ hours, cover the cake with greaseproof paper. Leave to cool in the tin.

4 Warm the jam, strain through a sieve and spread over the cake, whilst this is still warm.

Note: This cake tastes best when it is at least one week old. Ideally it should be baked a few weeks in advance and stored either in a tin or wrapped in foil.

CHOCOLATE FRUIT BOMBS

Makes 24 small cakes

300g/10oz clear honey
200g/7oz caster sugar
125g/4oz margarine
25g/1oz cocoa powder
3 eggs
Grated zest of 1 orange
2 tbsps orange juice
2 tsps cinnamon
2 tsps ground cloves
1 tsp cardamom
400g/13oz flour
3 tsps baking powder
100g/3½oz candied lemon peel
100g/3½oz almonds, chopped
Margarine for greasing

Filling

200g/7oz marzipan paste
100g/3½oz candied cherries
100g/3½oz candied orange peel
1 tsp rosewater

Icing

200g/7oz apricot jam
2 tbsps water
300g/10oz chocolate couverture

1 Put the honey, sugar and margarine in a saucepan and heat, stirring continuously, until the sugar has dissolved. Leave to cool. Stir in the cocoa, eggs, orange zest and juice and spices. Mix together the flour, baking powder, candied lemon peel and almonds, then mix into the honey mixture to make a smooth dough.

2 Make 5-cm/2-inch-round moulds from extra-strong aluminium foil doubled and pinched together with paper clips. The moulds should also be 5 cm/2 inches deep. Place them on a greased and lined baking tray and put in a layer of the cake mixture.

3 Mix together the marzipan, halved cherries, diced orange peel and rosewater and put a little into each ring.

4 Add a second layer of the cake mixture and bake in a preheated oven, Gas Mark 4/180°C/350°F, for about 20 minutes. Remove the foil and leave to cool.

5 Strain the jam through a sieve and heat in a saucepan with the water. Brush this over the cakes. Melt the chocolate couverture and use to coat the cooled cakes.

ALMOND LOG

Makes approximately 30 portions

60g/2½oz fresh yeast
125 ml/4 fl oz lukewarm milk
200g/7oz flour
1 tsp salt
250g/8oz soft margarine

Filling
50g/2oz each of candied
orange and lemon peel
100g/3½oz glacé cherries,
halved
2 tbsps rum
350g/12oz almonds, chopped
200g/7oz marzipan paste
Margarine for greasing

To Finish
100g/3½oz margarine, melted
3 tsps vanilla sugar
50g/2oz icing sugar

1 Crumble the yeast into the lukewarm milk. Add a pinch of sugar and leave in a warm place for about 10 minutes, until frothy. Mix together the flour, sugar and salt, dot with the margarine cut in pieces, add the frothy yeast, and knead to a smooth dough.
2 Soak the lemon and orange peel and the halved cherries in the rum for about 30 minutes. Knead into the dough, together with the almonds. Cover and leave to rise in a warm place, until doubled in size. Knead again and roll out into a 30-cm/12-inch circle. Make a hollow down the centre of the dough and brush with a little water.
3 Shape the marzipan into a long roll, place it in the hollow, fold the dough over and press the edges lightly together.

4 Place the log on a greased baking tray and leave to rise in a warm place for about 20 minutes. Brush the log with water and bake in a preheated oven, Gas Mark 4/180°C/350°F, for about 60 minutes.
5 Brush the finished almond log with the melted margarine and sprinkle with the vanilla sugar. Leave to cool. Dust with the icing sugar.

SPICY CHRISTMAS RING CAKE

Makes approximately 20 portions

250g/8oz margarine
250g/8oz caster sugar
Salt
6 eggs
2 tsps cinnamon
1 tsp ground cloves
½ tsps ground cardamom
1 tsp ground ginger
1 tsp grated zest of orange
75g/3oz almonds, chopped
100g/3½oz plain chocolate
300g/10oz flour
100g/3½oz cornflour
3 tsps baking powder
2 tbsps rum
Margarine for greasing
Icing sugar for dusting

Grated zest of ½ lemon

Pinch of salt

2 tbsps rum flavouring

1 tbsp bitter almond flavouring

1 tbsp lemon flavouring

1 egg

1 packet vanilla pudding mix

150g/5oz margarine

250g/8oz curd cheese

150g/5oz raisins

125g/4oz almonds, chopped

100g/3½oz candied orange peel

To Finish

Flour for dusting

Melted margarine

Chocolate flakes

Icing sugar

1 Gradually work all the ingredients to a dough. Roll the dough into a log shape. Dust well with flour and sprinkle a baking tray generously with flour to prevent the dough spreading.

2 Bake in the centre of a preheated oven, Gas Mark 4-6/ 180°-200°C/350° 400°F for about 60 minutes.

3 Whilst still hot, brush the fruit log with melted margarine. Leave to go cold. Decorate with chocolate flakes and dust with icing sugar.

1 Beat the margarine until smooth. Gradually beat in the sugar, salt and eggs and continue beating until the sugar has dissolved. Stir in the spices, orange zest and almonds.

2 Break chocolate into small pieces, put into a small bowl and cover with hot water. Leave to melt, then drain and add the chocolate to the mixture.

3 Sieve together the flour, cornflour and baking powder and fold into the mixture, together with the rum.

4 Turn the mixture into a greased 22-cm/8½-inch ring tin. Bake in a preheated oven, Gas Mark 4/180°C/350°F, for 50-60 minutes. Dust with icing sugar before serving.

LIGHT FRUIT LOG

Makes approximately 20 portions

Mixture

500g/1lb flour

3 tsps baking powder

150g/5oz caster sugar

3 tsps vanilla sugar

VANILLA PAISLEYS

Makes approximately 50 cookies

200g/7oz flour
Pith of 1 vanilla pod
Pinch of salt
125g/4oz ground almonds
150g/5oz margarine
1 egg yolk
75g/3oz caster sugar
Margarine for greasing
25g/1oz icing sugar
3 tsps vanilla sugar

1 Make a smooth dough with the flour, vanilla, salt, almonds, margarine, egg yolk and sugar and chill it in the refrigerator for about 1 hour.

2 Shape the dough into rolls the thickness of a finger, then cut into strips 5 cm/2 inches long. Bend and flatten each strip slightly to make paisley shapes.

3 Arrange on a greased baking tray and bake in a preheated oven, Gas Mark 4-6/ 180°-200°C/350°-400°F for about 13 minutes.

4 Mix the icing sugar with the vanilla sugar and press the warm paisleys in this to coat.

MACAROON HATS

Makes approximately 40 portions

225g/7½oz flour
100g/3½oz icing sugar
100g/3½oz margarine
Pith of 1 vanilla pod
3 egg yolks
Margarine for greasing

Macaroon Mixture

3 egg whites
150g/5oz caster sugar
175g/6oz ground almonds
1 heaped tsp cinnamon

1 Make a shortcrust pastry dough using the flour, icing sugar, margarine, vanilla and egg yolks. Chill.

2 Whisk the egg whites until stiff. Whisk in the sugar, then fold in the almonds and cinnamon.

3 Roll out the pastry to a rectangle the thickness of the back of a knife. Cut this into strips 4 cm/1½ inches wide, then cut these into elongated diamond shapes. Arrange on a greased baking tray and pipe a blob of the macaroon mixture on top of each diamond.

4 Bake in a preheated oven, Gas Mark 4-6/ 180°-200°C/350°-400°F for about 20 minutes.

HAZELNUT FINGERS

Makes approximately 60 biscuits

250g/8oz margarine
200g/7oz caster sugar
3 tsps vanilla sugar
2 egg yolks
150g/5oz flour
½ level tsp baking powder
200g/7oz ground almonds
Margarine for greasing
150g/5oz chocolate couverture

1 Cream the margarine until light, then beat in the sugar, vanilla sugar and egg yolks and continue beating until the sugar has dissolved. Sieve together the flour and baking powder and fold into the mixture, together with the hazelnuts.
2 Spoon the mixture into a piping bag fitted with a medium nozzle and pipe out 5-cm/2-inch-long strips onto a greased baking tray. Bake at Gas Mark 6/200°C/400°F for 10-15 minutes. Leave to cool.
3 Melt the chocolate couverture over a pan of hot water and use to decorate the hazelnut fingers.

GINGER SNAPS

Makes approximately 30 biscuits

75g/3oz margarine
100g/3½oz caster sugar
100g/3½oz golden syrup
3 tsps vanilla sugar
25 g/1oz crystallized ginger, finely chopped
2 tbsps ginger syrup
125g/4oz flour
Margarine for greasing

Icing

100g/3½oz icing sugar
1 tbsp cocoa powder
1 tbsp ginger syrup
1-2 tbsps water
2 tbsps coconut oil

1 Cream together the margarine, sugar, syrup and vanilla sugar until light and fluffy. Fold in the ginger, ginger syrup and flour. Drop teaspoonfuls of the mixture onto a greased baking tray, leaving large gaps between. Dip a knife in cold water and flatten the uncooked snaps.
2 Bake in a preheated oven, Gas Mark 6-7/200°-220°C/400°-425°F, for 3-5 minutes.
3 Leave to cool slightly, then, whilst still warm, carefully remove each snap and bend round a roll of foil or a rolling pin.
4 Mix together the icing ingredients and use to coat half of each snap.

EASTER BUNS

Makes 16 buns

25g/1oz fresh yeast
250 ml/8 fl oz lukewarm milk
Pinch of salt
500g/1lb flour
75g/3oz sugar
Pinch of salt
100g/3½oz margarine, melted and cooled
1 egg
Margarine for greasing

Filling

100g/3½oz whipping cream
100g/3½oz caster sugar
100g/3½oz flaked almonds
100g/3½oz raisins

To Finish

50g/2oz margarine
Icing sugar

1 Crumble the yeast into the lukewarm milk, stir in a little sugar and leave in a warm place for about 15 minutes, until frothy. Mix together the flour, sugar and salt in a bowl, then stir in the melted and cooled margarine, the egg and the frothy yeast. Knead continuously until the dough shrinks away from the sides of the bowl and is no longer sticky. Leave to rise in a warm place for another 30 minutes.

2 Meanwhile, mix together the cream, sugar, flaked almonds and raisins and set aside until the liquid has been almost absorbed.

3 Knead the dough again, roll into a rectangle about 1 cm/½ inch thick. Spread with the filling mixture and roll up.

4 Cut into sixteen equal slices and place on a greased baking tray. Leave to rise in a warm place, then bake in a preheated oven, Gas Mark 6/ 200°C/ 400°F, for about 20 minutes. During the last ten minutes of baking time, brush the buns several times with melted margarine. When cold, dust the buns with icing sugar.

EASTER BUNNIES

Makes 2 large, or about 10 small, rabbits

35g/1½oz fresh yeast
175g/6oz single cream, lukewarm
175g/6oz caster sugar
375g/12oz flour
Grated zest of 1 lemon
Pith of 1 vanilla pod
150g/5oz melted margarine
3 eggs, beaten
50g/2oz almonds, chopped
Margarine for greasing

1 Crumble the yeast into the lukewarm cream and stir in a pinch of sugar and flour. Cover and leave in a warm place for 5-10 minutes until frothy.

2 Mix together the flour, sugar, salt, lemon zest, vanilla, cooled margarine and beaten eggs in a bowl. Add the frothy yeast and the almonds, mix to a dough and knead thoroughly. Cover with foil and leave in a warm place until doubled in volume.

3 Knock down, put into greased rabbit-shaped moulds as desired, cover and leave in a warm place to rise again. Bake in a preheated oven, Gas Mark 4/180°C/350°F, for about 30 minutes.

EASTER NESTS

Makes approximately 12 nests

250 ml/8 fl oz water
Pinch of salt
1 tsp sugar
3 tsps vanilla sugar
100g/3½oz margarine
125g/4oz flour
4 eggs
Margarine for greasing
Flour

Filling

250 ml/8 fl oz milk
Pith from 1 ½ vanilla pods
Pinch of salt
4 egg yolks
100g/3½oz caster sugar
6 sheets gelatine
250g/8 fl oz cream, whipped
4 egg whites
Icing sugar
Easter chicks and eggs

1 Bring the water, salt, sugar, vanilla sugar and margarine to the boil. Pour all the flour in and beat the mixture over a low heat until it comes away from the sides of the saucepan in a ball. Remove from the heat and beat in one of the eggs. Leave to cool slightly, then beat in the remaining eggs one at a time.

2 Spoon the mixture into a piping bag with a large, serrated nozzle and pipe out rings about 7 cm/2½ inches in diameter onto a greased and floured baking tray. Bake in a preheated oven, Gas Mark 4-6/ 180°-200°C/350°-400°F, for about 30 minutes. Use scissors to cut the rings in half as soon as they are removed from the oven, then leave to cool.

3 Bring the milk to the boil with the vanilla and salt. Leave to cool. Whisk the egg yolks with the sugar until light and foamy. Soak the gelatine, dissolve it over a low heat, and stir it into the yolk mixture, together with the cooled milk. Set aside to cool.

4 When the mixture is half set, fold in the whipped cream. Whisk the egg whites until stiff and fold in. When almost set, spoon the cream mixture into a piping bag and use to sandwich the nest rings together. Dust the nests with icing sugar and fill with little sugar Easter eggs and chicks.

EASTER ALMOND RING

Makes approximately 16 portions

250g/8oz margarine
250g/8oz caster sugar
Pinch of salt
6 eggs
150g/5oz flour
2 tsps baking powder
250g/8oz ground almonds
100g/3½oz plain chocolate flakes
2 tbsps brandy
Margarine for greasing
Fine breadcrumbs

1 Beat the margarine, sugar and salt until light and fluffy. Beat in the eggs one at a time. Sieve together the flour and baking powder, and fold into the mixture together with the almonds, chocolate flakes and brandy.

2 Grease a fluted 26-cm/10½-inch ring tin and sprinkle with breadcrumbs. Turn the mixture into this and bake in a preheated oven, Gas Mark 4/180°C/350°F, for 60-70 minutes.

PLAITED EASTER RINGS

Makes 8 rings

25g/1oz fresh yeast
250 ml/8 fl oz lukewarm milk
500g/1lb flour
Pinch of salt
75g/3oz caster sugar
75g/3oz margarine, melted and cooled
1 egg
100g/3½oz raisins
3 tbsps rum
80g/3oz candied orange and lemon peel
Margarine for greasing

To Finish

8 boiled eggs
1 egg white
Harlequin sugar for dusting

1 Crumble the yeast into the lukewarm milk, add a pinch of sugar and flour and leave in a warm place for about 15 minutes until frothy. Mix together the flour, salt and sugar, then stir in the melted and cooled margarine, the egg and the frothy yeast. Mix to a dough and knead until smooth. Leave to rise for about 30 minutes in a warm place.

2 Soak the raisins in the rum before kneading them into the risen dough, together with the orange and lemon peel.

3 Divide the dough into eight equal portions. Make three rolls of equal length from each portion and plait them together. Bend each plait into a ring.

4 Arrange the rings on a greased baking tray and place a boiled egg in the centre of each ring, pointed end up.

5 Leave the rings in a warm place to rise, then bake in a preheated oven, Gas Mark 6/200°C/400°F, for about 20 minutes. Whilst still hot, brush the rings with lightly-beaten egg white and sprinkle with harlequin sugar.

PANNETONE

Makes approximately 12 portions

50g/2oz fresh yeast
250 ml/8 fl oz lukewarm milk
150g/5oz caster sugar
650g/1¼lb flour
200g/7oz margarine, melted and cooled
1 egg
4 egg yolks
1 tsp salt
Grated zest of 1 lemon
50g/2oz almonds, chopped
200g/7oz candied orange and lemon peel
150g/5oz raisins
Margarine for greasing
Egg yolk

1 Crumble the yeast into the lukewarm milk, add a pinch of sugar and leave in a warm place for 10 minutes, until frothy. Mix together the flour, sugar, margarine, egg, egg yolk, salt, lemon zest and frothy yeast to a dough. Knead until smooth, using the pastry hook on an electric mixer, if possible. Knead in the almonds, candied peel and raisins. Cover and leave in a warm place until doubled in volume.

2 Meanwhile, grease a soufflé dish 12 cm/4½ inches deep, and line with greaseproof paper. Knead the dough again, put it into the soufflé dish and leave to rise in a warm place for another 20 minutes.

3 Brush the dough with egg yolk and make two criss-cross slashes in the top. Bake in a preheated oven, Gas Mark 4/180°C/350°F, for about 90 minutes.

EASTER PLAIT

Makes approximately 20 portions

40g/1½oz fresh yeast
250 ml/8 fl oz lukewarm milk
150g/5oz margarine
600g/1½lb flour
Pinch of salt
75g/3oz caster sugar
1 egg
Margarine for greasing
Milk for brushing
1 egg yolk
1 tbsp milk
25g/1oz coarse sugar
25g/1oz flaked almonds

1 Crumble the yeast into the lukewarm milk, add a pinch of sugar, cover and leave in a warm place, until frothy. Meanwhile, melt the margarine. Put the flour into a bowl, and add the salt, sugar, egg, egg yolk, cooled margarine and frothy yeast. Mix to a dough and knead until smooth. Cover and leave to rise in a warm place.
2 With floured hands, use three-quarters of the dough to form three equal rolls. Plait the rolls together and place the plait on a greased baking tray. Make a thinner plait with the remaining dough. Brush the surface of the larger plait with milk. Lay the smaller plait on top, pressing it down lightly and leave to rise in a warm place for 10 minutes.
3 Bake in a preheated oven, Gas Mark 6-7/200°-220°C/400°-425°F for 30-35 min-

utes. Beat the egg yolk with the milk, brush over the plait 10 minutes before the end of

baking time and sprinkle with the coarse sugar and flaked almonds.

EASTER BUNNIES

Makes 3 bunnies

125g/4oz margarine
125g/4oz caster sugar
Pinch of salt
1 egg
200g/7oz low fat curd cheese
375g/12oz flour
3 tsps baking powder
Egg yolk
Mini sugar eggs
Icing sugar

1 Cream together the margarine, sugar, salt and egg until light and fluffy. Beat in the curd cheese. Sieve together the flour and baking powder, and fold half into the mixture. Knead in the remainder. Cover and chill for about 30 minutes.
2 Meanwhile, cut out a cardboard pattern for an Easter bunny.
3 Roll out the dough to a thickness of 1 cm/½ inch and, using the pattern, cut out three Easter bunnies. Beat the egg yolk with water and brush over the bunnies. Roll out the remaining

has melted, then drain. Mix the melted nougat into the egg mixture. Whisk the egg whites stiffly and pile onto the mixture. Sieve over the flour, cornflour and baking powder. Carefully fold everything together.

2 Line a baking tray about 30 cm x 40 cm/12 inches x 16 inches with greaseproof paper, grease it and spread the mixture over. Bake in a preheated oven, Gas Mark 4/180°C/350°F, for about 15 minutes.

3 Turn out onto a wire rack, and quickly remove the greaseproof paper. Leave to cool. Cut out twenty equal-sized ovals to make the eggs. Whip the cream with the sugar and vanilla sugar until stiff. Soak the gelatine, dissolve it over a low heat, then fold it thoroughly into the cream.

4 Pipe the mixture onto ten of the ovals and top with the remaining ten, to make filled eggs.

5 Melt the chocolate nougat with the coconut butter and use to ice eggs. Decorate with the chopped pistachios.

dough to a thickness of ½ cm/ ¼ inch, cut out ears, paws, and an eye for each of the bunnies and attach them. To make the basket, make thin rolls of dough, plait them, make them into a basket shape and attach to the bunnies.

4 Brush the bunnies again with egg yolk and bake in a preheated oven Gas Mark 4-6/ 175°-200°C/350°-400°F for 10-12 minutes. Mix a little icing sugar with a little water and use to stick mini eggs onto the basket.

NOUGAT EGGS

Makes 10 eggs

4 eggs, separated
4 tbsps warm water
125g/4oz caster sugar
Pinch of salt
50g/2oz margarine, melted and cooled
125g/4oz chocolate nougat
75g/3oz flour
50g/2oz cornflour
1 tsp baking powder

Filling

250 ml/8 fl oz whipping cream
25g/1oz sugar
3 tsps vanilla sugar
2 sheets gelatine

Topping

75g/3oz chocolate nougat
25g/1oz coconut butter
25g/1oz pistachios, chopped

1 Whisk the egg yolks, water, sugar and salt until thick and foamy, then whisk in the melted and cooled margarine. Pour hot water over the chocolate nougat, leave until the nougat

CRUSTY HOME-MADE BREAD

Home-made breads made with wholemeal flour or with savoury fillings are simply the best.
This section's delicious recipes are for interesting breakfast and brunch breads: tasty croissants, brioches or crusty loaves of bread, which get the day off to a good start.

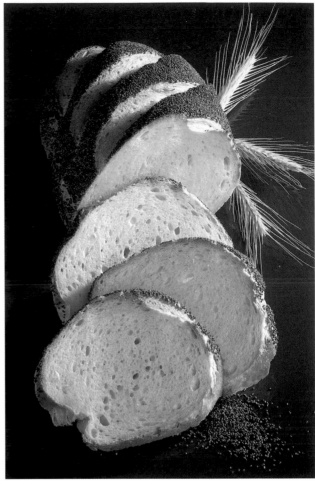

NUT AND MUSHROOM LOAF

Makes approximately 10 slices

25g/1oz fresh yeast
½ tsp sugar
150 ml/5 fl oz lukewarm milk
25g/1oz flat mushrooms, dried
250g/8oz strong flour
½ tsp salt
Pinch of cinnamon
25g/1oz soft margarine
100g/3½oz hazelnut kernels
Milk to glaze

1 Crumble the yeast into the lukewarm milk. Cover and leave in a warm place for about 10 minutes until frothy. Soak the mushrooms in water, then allow to drain. Put the flour, salt, cinnamon, margarine, hazelnuts and mushrooms into a bowl. Add the frothy yeast mixture, mix it all together well, then knead until you have a smooth, elastic dough. Cover and leave in a warm place to rise, until doubled in volume.

2 Knead again, form into a long loaf shape and set aside on a sheet of baking paper in a warm place to prove. Brush with milk and score a pattern of diamond shapes on top of the loaf with a sharp knife.

3 Bake in a preheated oven, Gas Mark 6/200°C/400°F for 45 minutes.

POPPYSEED BREAD

Makes approximately 15 slices

25g/1oz fresh yeast
250 ml/8 fl oz lukewarm water
½ tsp sugar
350g/12oz strong flour
1 tsp vinegar
1 tsp salt
40g/1½oz margarine, melted
Poppy seeds

1 Crumble the yeast into the lukewarm water, stir in the sugar and set aside in a warm place for 10 minutes, until frothy. Mix together the flour, vinegar, margarine and frothy yeast. Work into a smooth dough, knead, cover and leave to rise until doubled in volume.

2 Knock the dough down, form into a long loaf shape and leave to prove on a sheet of baking paper in a warm place. Brush with water and sprinkle generously with poppy seeds. Using a sharp knife, make two or three diagonal cuts across the top of the loaf.

3 Bake for about 60 minutes in a preheated oven, Gas Mark 6/200°C/400°F.

COUNTRY BREAD

Makes approximately 25 slices

750g/1½lb coarse rye flour
250g/8oz strong flour
50g/2oz sourdough
400 ml/14 fl oz lukewarm buttermilk
Salt
Caraway seeds
Margarine for greasing

1 Mix the flours together. Mix the sourdough with 200 ml/7 fl oz of the buttermilk and 100g/3½oz of the flours. Cover and leave to work for 4 hours in a warm place. Knead in the remaining buttermilk and a further 400g/13oz of the flours. Cover and leave to stand overnight.

2 Next day, knead the dough until firm, adding remaining flour, salt and caraway seeds.
3 Place the dough in a greased loaf tin and allow to prove for 45-50 minutes. Bake at Gas Mark 9/240°C/475°F for ten minutes. Lower the heat to Gas Mark 7/220°C/425°F and bake for further 60 minutes.

PROVENCAL BREAD

Makes approximately 14 slices

1 small onion, chopped
25g/1oz margarine
15g/½oz fresh yeast
½ tsp sugar
125 ml/4 fl oz buttermilk
200g/7oz strong flour
50g/2oz wholemeal oat flakes
1 tsp salt
100g/3½ oz cottage cheese
2 tbsps fresh mixed herbs, finely chopped
Milk to glaze

1 Lightly fry the onion in the margarine. Leave to cool. Mix the yeast, buttermilk and sugar together. Put flour, oat flakes, salt and cottage cheese into a bowl. Pour over the yeast and milk mixture and work the ingredients together until you have a smooth dough. Add the onion and herbs and knead them well in. Cover and leave to stand in a warm place to rise. Knead again.
2 Grease and line a 20-cm/8-inch loaf tin. Put in the dough and leave in a warm place to prove. Brush the dough with milk.
3 Bake in a preheated oven Gas Mark 6/200°C/400°F for about 45 minutes.

BREAD HEART

Makes approximately 8 portions

250g/8oz strong white flour	
250g/8oz rye flour	
40g/1½oz fresh yeast	
250 ml/8 fl oz lukewarm water	
40g/1½oz melted margarine	
1 egg	
Salt	
Margarine for greasing	
Lentils, rice or beans for baking blind	

Filling

1 large onion
1 small red pepper
1 small leek
1 small fresh chilli
1 carrot
2 small pickled gherkins
2 eggs

500g/1lb mixed beef and pork, minced
Seasoning
Paprika
Egg white to glaze

1 Mix together the flours and sieve them into a bowl. Make a well in the centre and crumble the yeast into it. Add a little of the water and flour and mix to a thickish paste. Leave to work for 15 minutes in a warm place. Add the remaining water, the margarine, egg and salt. Mix the ingredients to a dough and knead thoroughly. Cover and leave in a warm place to rise until doubled in volume, about 30 minutes.

2 Meanwhile, peel the onions, and wash and trim the pepper, leek and chilli; peel and blanch the carrots. Dice the onions, pepper and pickled gherkins and finely chop the chilli. Slice the leek into thin rings and dice the carrot. Mix the vegetables with the eggs and meat. Season to taste with salt, pepper and paprika.

3 Roll out two-thirds of the dough to a thickness of 2 cm/ ¾ inch and use to line a large, well-greased heart-shaped baking tin. Cover the dough with greaseproof paper, spread lentils, rice or beans over and bake blind at Gas Mark 6/200°C/400°F for 10 minutes.

4 Remove the lentils, rice or beans and the greaseproof paper and spread the meat mixture over the dough. Return to the oven for about 40 minutes.

5 Roll out the remaining third of the dough to a thickness of about 1 cm/½ inch. Cut out a heart shape to fit the tin. Lay over the cooked meat mixture and press firmly down. Use any dough trimmings to make decorations and stick on the heart with egg white. Return to the oven for about 15-20 minutes. The loaf can be served hot or cold.

SUNFLOWER

Makes 8 rolls

250g/8oz wholemeal flour
250g/8oz strong white flour
25g/1oz fresh yeast
2 tsps sugar
300 ml/10 fl oz lukewarm water
50g/2oz margarine
1 tsp salt
2 tsps white vinegar
Margarine for greasing
Poppy seeds, sesame seeds or sunflower seeds for sprinkling

1 Put the flours in a bowl, make a hollow in the centre and crumble the yeast into it. Stir in the sugar and some of the lukewarm water. Allow this work for about 15 minutes in a warm place. Add the margarine, vinegar, salt and the rest of the water. Work to a smooth dough and leave to rise in a warm place for another 30 minutes.

2 Shape the dough into a roll and cut this into eight equal pieces. Form each piece into a ball and arrange them on a greased baking tray in a circle, with one roll in the centre, all touching each other. Leave in a warm place to prove. Brush with water and sprinkle with poppy, sesame or sunflower seeds.

3 Bake in a preheated oven, Gas Mark 6-7/200°-220°C/ 400°-425°F for 25-30 minutes.

CRUSTY HERB STICKS

Makes 6 medium French sticks

80g/3oz margarine
250 ml/8 fl oz lukewarm water
40g/1½oz fresh yeast
300g/10oz rye flour
300g/10oz stoneground flour
1 tsp salt
1 pinch sugar
1 tbsp fresh, mixed herbs, chopped
4 tbsps parsley, chopped
Margarine for greasing

1 Melt the margarine in the water, crumble in the yeast and mix well. Mix the rye flour with half of the stoneground flour and stir into the yeast mixture. Beat the mixture thoroughly. Cover and set aside in a warm place for 30 minutes. Knead the remaining flour, the salt, sugar, parsley and mixed herbs into the dough.

2 Divide into six portions and shape them into French sticks. Grease two long loaf tins, patterned if possible, and press three sticks into each. Leave in a warm place to prove.

3 Bake in a preheated oven, Gas Mark 7/220°C/425°F for 20-30 minutes. Shortly before the end of baking time turn out, brush the patterned side

with a little water and put back in oven, patterned side up, to finish baking the crust.

ONION BREAD

Makes approximately 16 slices

125g/4oz rye flour
250g/8oz stoneground flour
25g/1oz fresh yeast
½ tsp sugar
250 ml/8 fl oz lukewarm water
75g/3oz sourdough
1-2 tsps salt
40g/1½oz fried onions, dried
Black pepper, ground coriander and cardamom
Margarine for greasing

1 Put the flour into a large bowl, and make a well in the centre. Into this put the yeast, mixed with the sugar and 2-4 tbsps of the lukewarm water. Cover the bowl with a cloth and leave to work in a warm place for 15 minutes. Add the remaining flour, the sourdough, salt and spices and mix together well.
2 Knead the dough thoroughly until smooth and no longer sticky. Set aside in a warm place to rise until doubled in volume.
3 Knead the onions into the dough. Shape into an oblong loaf. Place on greaseproof paper and leave in a warm place to prove. Brush the bread with warm water and score the top several times with a sharp knife.
4 Bake on a greased baking tray in a preheated oven, Gas Mark 7/220°C/425°F for about 50 minutes.

FRIESLAND BLACK BREAD

Makes approximately 18 slices

750g/1½lb finely-milled rye flour
250g/8oz strong white flour
50g/2oz sourdough
750 ml/1¼ pt lukewarm water
1 tsp salt
Margarine for greasing

1 Put half the quantity of each flour into a bowl and warm it. Make a well in the centre. In a second bowl, mix the sourdough with 500 ml/18 fl oz of the lukewarm water and pour into the well. Stir in slowly to make a thickish paste. Cover the bowl and leave overnight in a warm place.
2 Add the remaining water and the salt. Slowly stir in the remaining flours. Knead the dough lightly until just firm. Shape into a ball, place in a warm, floured bowl, cover and leave to stand for 3 hours.
3 Shape the dough into a round, flattish loaf. Place on a greased baking tray and leave to prove for 1½ to 2 hours.
4 Bake in a preheated oven, Gas Mark 9/240°C/475°F for 10 minutes. Reduce the heat to Gas Mark 6/200°C/400°F and bake for further 60-70 minutes.

1 Mix the yeast with 2 tbsps of the lukewarm water, stir in the remaining water, the salt and spices. Knead to a smooth dough with the flour, cover and leave to rise in a warm place for about 45 minutes.

2 Thoroughly knead again. Divide the dough into five portions and roll out each one very thinly. Cut into rectangles 10 cm x 5 cm/4 inches x 2 inches, put on a greased and floured baking tray and prick each one several times with a fork.

3 Bake in a preheated oven, Gas Mark 9/240°C/475°F for 5-7 minutes.

SWEDISH CRISPBREADS

Makes 40-50 crispbreads

15g/½oz fresh yeast
200 ml/7 fl oz lukewarm water
1 tsp salt
1 tsp caraway seeds, ground
1 tsp fennel seeds, ground
250g/8oz wholemeal rye flour
Margarine for greasing
Flour

2 Thoroughly knead the dough again. Divide into four equal portions and roll each one into a flattish round loaf. Brush with water, sprinkle with sesame seeds and leave to rise in a warm place for another 5-10 minutes.

FLAT LOAF

Makes approximately 24 slices

1kg/2lb strong white flour
80g/3oz fresh yeast
1 tbsp sugar
1-2 tsps salt
200 ml/7 fl oz vegetable oil
500 ml/18 fl oz lukewarm water
80g/3oz sesame seeds for sprinkling
Margarine for greasing

1 Sieve the flour into a bowl, and crumble in the yeast. Add the sugar, salt and oil. Stir in the lukewarm water, working from the centre out. Mix well and knead thoroughly. Cover and leave in a warm place to rise for 25-30 minutes.

3 Place the loaves on a greased baking tray and bake in a preheated oven, Gas Mark 7/220°C/425°F for 20-25 minutes.

SESAME BREAD

Makes approximately 15 slices

60g/2½oz fresh yeast
500 ml/18 fl oz lukewarm milk
60g/2½oz caster sugar
300g/10oz strong white flour
250g/8oz rye flour
200g/7oz wholemeal flour
Pinch of salt
100g/3½oz margarine, melted and cooled
100g/3½oz sesame seeds
Margarine
1 egg, separated
Sesame seeds

1 Crumble the yeast into the lukewarm milk, reserving 3 tbsps of the milk. Mix in a little sugar and flour and leave in a warm place for about 15 minutes until frothy. Put sugar, flour, salt, margarine and sesame seeds into a bowl. Add the frothy yeast and knead all the ingredients to a smooth, elastic dough. Cover and leave to rise in a warm place, until doubled in volume.
2 Thoroughly knead a second time and divide the dough into three portions, each one smaller than the last. Roll each portion with three equal lengths and plait them together. Place the largest plait on a greased baking tray; brush the bottom of the second-largest with egg white and stick onto the first. Using the same method, top with the smallest dough plait.
3 Leave to prove in a warm place, brush with melted margarine and bake in a preheated oven, Gas Mark 6/200°C/400°F for about 45 minutes.
4 Mix egg yolk with milk. After 20 minutes baking time brush over the loaf and sprinkle with sesame seeds.

SUNFLOWER SEED BREAD

Makes approximately 25 slices

50g/2oz wheat grains
800g/1½lb coarse rye flour
200g/7oz strong wholemeal flour
1 tbsp salt
60g/2½oz fresh yeast
600 ml/1 pt lukewarm water
50g/2oz margarine, melted and cooled
50g/2oz sunflower seeds
Margarine for greasing
Milk
Sunflower seeds

1 Pour hot water over the wheat grains and leave overnight to swell. Drain well in a colander. Knead the flour, salt, crumbled yeast, lukewarm water and margarine to a smooth dough. Cover and leave to rise in a warm place, until doubled in volume. Mix together the sunflower seeds and wheat grains and knead into the dough.

2 Reserving a little dough for decoration, shape the rest into a loaf. Place on a greased baking tray and brush with milk. Roll the reserved dough into three lengths, plait them together and press onto the top of the loaf. Cover and leave to prove in a warm place.

3 Brush the loaf with milk and bake in a preheated oven, Gas Mark 4-6/180°-200°C/350°-400°F for about 50 minutes. Ten minutes before the end of baking time, sprinkle the loaf with sunflower seeds.

SWEDISH RINGS

Makes approximately 20 rings

60g/2½oz fresh yeast
500 ml/18 fl oz lukewarm milk
1 tbsp caster sugar
750g/1½lb rye flour
150g/5oz strong white flour
25g/1oz margarine, melted and cooled
2 tsps salt
75g/3oz golden syrup
Grated zest of orange, grated fennel and/or powdered aniseed

1 Crumble the yeast into the lukewarm milk and add the sugar and a little flour. Cover and leave for 5-10 minutes in a warm place, until frothy. Put the flours into a bowl and add the margarine, salt, syrup and frothy yeast. Mix in the orange zest, fennel and/or aniseed according to taste. Mix together thoroughly. Knead, cover and leave to rise in a warm place, until doubled in volume.
2 Knock back and knead again. If necessary, add a little milk, as the dough must not be too firm. Roll out five circles, 20 cm/8 inches in diameter and cut a hole in the centre of each one.
3 Prick the dough several times with a fork. Place on a greased baking tray, brush with water, leave to prove in a warm place for a short while and bake in a preheated oven, Gas Mark 6-7/200°-220°C/400°-425°F for 10-15 minutes.

Note: This dough also makes good rolls. Bake them for 20-25 minutes.

STUFFED BREAD

Makes approximately 10 slices

250g/8oz strong white flour
250g/8oz rye flour
25g/1oz fresh yeast
Pinch of sugar
250 ml/8 fl oz lukewarm water
35g/1¼oz margarine, melted and cooled
1 egg yolk
Salt

Stuffing
200g/7oz mushrooms
1 small leek
50g/2oz margarine
375g/12oz veal, cooked and cut into julienne strips
Seasoning
Egg yolk

1 Sieve the flours together into a bowl. Make a well in the centre and crumble in the yeast. Mix this to a thickish paste with the sugar, and a little of the water and flour. Leave to work in a warm place for 15 minutes. Add the remaining water, the margarine, egg yolk and salt. Mix everything together well and knead the dough thoroughly. Cover and leave in a warm place until doubled in volume.
2 Wash and dice the mushrooms. Wash the leek and cut it into thin rings. Sauté the mushrooms and leek in the margarine and leave to cool. Mix with the veal and season to taste.
3 On a floured board, roll out the dough to a rectangle about 2 cm/¾ inch thick. Spread the stuffing mixture over the dough and roll the dough up in the shape of a loaf. Prick several holes in the top of the bread. Make a few decorative rounds from dough trimmings and fix to the bread with egg yolk.
4 Bake in a preheated oven, Gas Mark 6-7/200°-220°C/400°-425°F, for 40-50 minutes.

TURKISH SESAME RINGS

Makes about 20 rings

25g/1oz fresh yeast
1 tsp sugar
250 ml/8 fl oz lukewarm milk
200g/7oz strong white flour
200g/7oz stoneground flour
150g/5oz rolled oats
25g/1oz sesame seeds
1-2 tsps salt
Milk
Sesame seeds
Margarine for greasing

1 Crumble the yeast into the lukewarm milk with the sugar. Sieve the flours together and stir 200g/7oz of this into the yeast mixture. Leave to work in a warm place for 15 minutes. Sieve the remaining flour over, add the oats, sesame seeds and salt and mix everything together. Knead to a smooth dough. Cover and leave to rise in a warm place for 30 minutes.
2 On a floured board, roll out the dough to a rectangle. Use a pastry wheel to cut the rectangle into strips 2 cm/¾ inch wide. Twist the strips, and join the ends to make a circle. Brush with milk and sprinkle with sesame seeds.
3 Place on a greased baking tray, cover with a tea towel and leave to prove in a warm place for 20 minutes. Bake in a preheated oven, Gas Mark 7/220°C/425°F, for 20-25 minutes.

ROLLS WITH BACON

Makes 10 rolls

225g/7½oz smoked belly of pork, diced
150g/5oz wholemeal flour
225g/7½oz strong white flour
25g/1oz fresh yeast
Pinch of sugar
150 ml/5 fl oz lukewarm water
100 ml/3½ fl oz lukewarm buttermilk
2-3 tsps salt

1 Sauté the belly of pork, drain in a colander and leave to cool.
2 Sieve the flours into a bowl, make a well in the centre and crumble in the yeast. Stir in a little of the water, the sugar and a little of the flour and leave in a warm place for about 15 minutes, until frothy. Gradually work in the remaining water, the buttermilk and salt. Thoroughly knead the dough.
3 Mix the pork into the dough. Cover and leave for about 30 minutes in a warm place, until doubled in volume.
4 Thoroughly knead the dough a second time. Shape into small oval rolls. Place on a greased and lined baking tray and leave in a warm place to prove. Brush with water and bake in a preheated oven, Gas Mark 6/200°C/400°F, for 25-30 minutes.

SPICED BREAD

Makes approximately 18 slices

300g/10oz coarse rye flour
300g/10oz wholemeal flour
1 tsp salt
350 ml/12 fl oz water
25g/1oz fresh yeast
50g/2oz margarine, melted and cooled
2 tbsps sesame seeds
3 tbsps mixed spicy herbs
Good pinch of black pepper
Margarine for greasing
Milk

1 Mix the flours, salt, lukewarm water, crumbled yeast, and margarine together and knead to a smooth dough. Cover and leave in a warm place until doubled in volume. Knead in the remaining ingredients.
2 Put a good three-quarters of the dough into a greased 25-cm/10-inch loaf tin. Brush the dough with milk. Roll the remaining dough into two equal strips, twist them round each other and press the twist lightly onto the top of the loaf.
3 Leave the bread in a warm place to prove, brush with milk

and bake in a preheated oven, Gas Mark 6/200°C/400°F, for about 40 minutes.

Note: A small, ovenproof container filled with water should also be placed in the oven during baking.

HERB LOAF

Makes approximately 16 slices

250g/8oz strong white flour
250g/8oz rye flour
25g/1oz fresh yeast
Pinch of sugar
250 ml/8 fl oz lukewarm water
35g/1¼oz margarine, melted
and cooled
1 egg yolk
Salt
1 bunch parsley
1 bunch dill
1 sprig basil
1 sprig marjoram
½ tsp caraway seeds
Seasoning
Margarine for greasing

1 Sieve the flours into a bowl, make a well in the centre and crumble in the yeast. Mix to a thickish paste with the sugar, and a little of the water and flour. Leave to work in a warm place for about 15 minutes. Mix in the remaining water, margarine, egg yolk and salt to make a dough. Thoroughly knead the dough. Cover and leave in a warm place for about 30 minutes, until doubled in volume.

2 Finely chop the parsley, dill, basil and marjoram and mix with the caraway seeds. Add a little seasoning and knead them well into the dough.

3 Shape the dough into a loaf, put on a greased baking tray and bake in a preheated oven, Gas Mark 6-7/200°-220°C/ 400°-425°F, for 30-40 minutes.

FRUIT AND NUT LOAF

Makes approximately 20 slices

375g/12oz dried pears
50g/2oz dried bananas
50g/2oz prunes
40g/1½oz candied lemon peel
50g/2oz dried apricots
150g/5oz stoneground
wholemeal flour
250g/8oz strong white flour
100g/3½oz rolled oats
250 ml/8 fl oz lukewarm milk
25g/1oz fresh yeast
Pinch of sugar
1 tsp salt

200g/7oz whipping cream, warmed

25g/1oz margarine, melted

50g/2oz raisins

50g/2oz caster sugar

Grated zest of half a lemon

Good pinch of ground cloves

Good pinch each of ground ginger, cinnamon and cardamom

1 tbsp kirsch

75g/3oz hazelnut kernels, chopped

Margarine for greasing

1 egg yolk

1 Finely dice the pears, bananas, prunes, lemon peel and apricots. Put the flours and oats into a bowl, make a well in the centre and pour in the lukewarm water. Crumble in the yeast with the sugar and a little flour. Leave in a warm place for about 10 minutes, until frothy. Add the salt, lukewarm whipping cream and margarine. Mix all the ingredients to a smooth dough and knead thoroughly.

2 Mix together the raisins, sugar, lemon zest, cloves, ginger, cinnamon, cardamom, kirsch, diced fruit and chopped nuts.

3 Roll out the dough, place the fruit mixture on top and wrap the dough around this, to form a loaf. Place the loaf on a greased baking tray, prick the dough several times with a cocktail stick and leave to prove in a warm place for 20 minutes.

4 Bake in a preheated oven, Gas Mark 4/180°C/350°F, for about 60 minutes. After 45 minutes, mix the egg yolk with a little water and brush over the loaf.

CROISSANTS

Makes 15 croissants

25g/1oz fresh yeast
Scant 250 ml/8 fl oz whipping cream, warmed
50g/2oz caster sugar
400g/7oz flour
Pinch of salt
200g/7½oz margarine, melted and cooled
2 eggs
Margarine for greasing

1 Crumble the yeast into the whipping cream and blend with a pinch of sugar and flour. Cover and leave in a warm place for 5-10 minutes, until frothy. Put the sugar, flour, salt, margarine and egg yolks into a bowl, then add the frothy yeast. Mix to a smooth dough, and knead thoroughly.

2 Cover with foil and leave in a warm place for about 20 minutes, until doubled in volume. Knead thoroughly for a second time. Divide the dough into three portions. Roll out each portion into a circle about ½ cm/ ¼ inch thick.

3 Using a pastry wheel or knife, each circle into five triangles. Starting at the broad edge, roll the dough loosely up towards the point. Bend into a crescent shape and place on a greased baking tray. Leave to prove in a warm place for a short while, then bake in a preheated oven, Gas Mark 6/200°C/400°F, for about 30 minutes.

PIROZHKI

Makes approximately 10 portions

40g/1½oz fresh yeast
250 ml/8 fl oz lukewarm milk
Pinch of sugar
500g/1lb flour
½ tsp salt
100g/3½oz margarine, melted and cooled
1 egg, beaten
Margarine for greasing

Stuffing

200g/7oz streaky bacon
200g/7oz leeks
1 large clove of garlic
Salt
100g/3½oz mushrooms
3 hard-boiled eggs
200g/3½oz pickled gherkins
1 bunch dill
2 small onions
750g/1½lb minced pork
Salt and pepper
1 egg yolk
2 tbsps milk

1 Crumble the yeast into the lukewarm milk, add a pinch of sugar and flour, cover and leave in a warm place for 5-10 minutes, until frothy. Put the flour, salt, margarine and egg into a bowl, then add the frothy yeast. Mix everything to a smooth dough and knead thoroughly. Cover with foil and leave to rise in a warm place until doubled in volume. Knead again and set aside to prove.

2 Dice the bacon and soften in a frying pan. Wash and halve the leeks, cut them into thin strips and sauté in the bacon fat. Crush the garlic with a little salt. Wash and thinly slice the mushrooms, then add them to the leeks together with the garlic. Using an egg slicer, slice the eggs first lengthwise and then diagonally. Dice the gherkins, finely chop the dill and dice the onions. Mix all the foregoing ingredients together with the minced pork and season with salt and pepper. Knead the dough again and roll it out into a rectangle 30 cm x 40 cm/12

inches x 16 inches. Spread the meat and vegetable mixture over the dough, leaving a 3-cm/1¼-inch edge clear all round. Mix the egg yolk with the milk, and brush around the edges. Carefully roll up the dough and press the edges together to seal.

3 Shape the roll into a semicircle. Place on a greased baking tray. Score the top of the roll with the back of a knife. Leave to prove in a warm place. Brush the remaining egg yolk mixture over the pirozhki. Bake in a preheated oven, Gas Mark 6/ 200°C/400°F, for about 45-50 minutes. If necessary, cover the loaf with foil to prevent the crust burning.

SCONE TRIANGLES

Makes 6 triangles

250g/8oz flour
Pinch of salt
2 tsps baking powder
75g/3oz margarine
1 egg
6 tbsps milk
Margarine for greasing

1 Make a smooth dough with the flour, salt, baking powder, margarine, egg and milk. Roll out into a circle about 24 cm/ 9½ inches in diameter. Cut into six triangular wedges.
2 Place on a greased baking tray and bake in a preheated oven, Gas Mark 6/200°C/ 400°F, for about 15 minutes. Serve warm.

Note: The scones are delicious spread with butter, jam and clotted cream.

SESAME SEED PRETZELS

Makes 6 pretzels

15 g/½oz fresh yeast
4 tbsps lukewarm milk
250g/8oz flour
40g/1½oz margarine
1 egg
½ tsp salt
1 tsp caster sugar
1 egg yolk
Sesame seeds

1 Crumble the yeast into the lukewarm milk. Put the flour, margarine, egg, salt and sugar into a bowl, add the yeasted milk and knead all the ingredients to a smooth dough.
2 Cover with foil and leave the dough to rise in a warm place. Knead the dough a second time, shape it into a long roll and cut it into six portions. Roll each portion out to a long length and twist this into traditional pretzel forms.
3 Place the pretzels on greased and lined baking tray, and leave them in a warm place to prove. Brush with egg yolk and sprinkle with sesame seeds. Bake in a preheated oven, Gas Mark 7/220°C/425°F, for about 15 minutes.

SUNDAY LOAF

Makes approximately 15 slices

40g/1½oz fresh yeast
2 tbsps caster sugar
500 ml/18 fl oz milk
1kg/2lb flour
250g/8oz margarine, melted and cooled
Grated zest of 1 lemon
1 egg
Margarine for greasing

1 Stir the yeast and sugar into the lukewarm milk and leave covered for about 10 minutes, until frothy. Sieve the flour into a bowl. Mix in the margarine, lemon zest and egg. Add the frothy yeast and mix well. Knead to a smooth dough.

2 Leave to rise in a warm place, until doubled in volume. Put into a greased 35-cm/13½ -inch loaf tin and bake in a pre-heated oven, Gas Mark 4/ 180°C/350°F, for about 25 minutes.

RAISIN BUNS

Makes 10 buns

250g/8oz flour
25g/1oz fresh yeast
25g/1oz caster sugar
125 ml/4 fl oz lukewarm milk
60g/2½oz margarine
250g/8oz raisins

1 Make a smooth dough mixture with the flour, yeast, sugar, salt, milk and margarine. Add the raisins. Knead the dough thoroughly, then leave to rise in a warm place.

2 Shape the dough into ten rolls and place on a greased and lined baking tray. Leave in a warm place to prove. Bake in a preheated oven, Gas Mark 6/ 200°C/400°F, for 15-20 minutes.

HERB ROLL

Makes approximately 8 slices

Stuffing

1 bunch each chives, parsley, dill
1 small onion
2 cloves garlic

Dough

100g/3½oz quark
1 tsp salt
2 small eggs
2 tbsps margarine, melted
200g/7oz flour
1 ½ tsps baking powder
Margarine

1 Wash and finely chop the herbs. Finely dice the onions and crush the garlic. Mix these ingredients together.
2 Make a smooth dough from the dough ingredients and roll out into a rectangle 16 cm x 40 cm/6 inches x 16 inches. Spread the dough very thinly with the melted margarine and sprinkle generously with the stuffing.
3 Roll the dough up from the short side and put into a well greased loaf tin. Score the surface of the roll, decorate with shapes made from the dough trimmings and bake in the centre of a preheated oven, Gas Mark 4/180°C/350°F, for about 40 minutes.

BACON LOAVES

Makes 2 loaves

40g/1½oz fresh yeast
250 ml/8 fl oz lukewarm milk
Pinch of sugar
300g/10oz smoked bacon, in one piece
1 large bunch parsley, chopped
500g/1lb flour
1 tsp salt
50g/2oz margarine, melted
Margarine for greasing
Egg yolk

1 Crumble the yeast into the lukewarm milk, and stir in a pinch of sugar and a little flour. Cover and leave in a warm place for 10 minutes, until frothy.
2 Meanwhile, dice the bacon and sauté until transparent. Stir in the chopped parsley and leave to cool.
3 Put the flour, salt and margarine into a bowl, and add the frothy yeast. Mix and knead to a smooth dough. Cover the dough and leave in a warm place, until doubled in volume. Knead in the bacon mixture and shape the dough into two elongated loaves.
4 Place on a greased baking tray and leave to prove in a warm place for 20 minutes.

Score the top of each loaf diagonally two or three times, brush with egg yolk and bake in a preheated oven, Gas Mark 6/200°C/400°F, for 30-35 minutes.

BRIOCHE RING

Makes approximately 8 portions

500g/1lb flour
25g/1oz fresh yeast
Scant 125 ml/4 fl oz lukewarm milk
150g/5oz margarine
60g/2½oz caster sugar
1 heaped tsp salt
1 egg
5 egg yolks
Grated zest of half a lemon
Margarine for greasing

1 Make a dough from the flour, yeast, lukewarm milk, margarine, sugar, salt, egg, 4 of the egg yolks and the lemon zest. Knead everything thoroughly to a smooth dough. Leave in a warm place until doubled in volume.
2 Shape the dough into a ball. Place on a greased baking tray and press the dough down in the centre to form a ring. Place a small cake tin in the hole to prevent the dough from closing up during cooking.
3 Brush the brioche with egg

yolk. Leave briefly in a warm place to prove, then bake in a preheated oven, Gas Mark 7/220°C/425°F, for about 30 minutes.

Note: The brioche is delicious with butter and jam.

SWISS BREAKFAST BREAD

Makes 8 slices

25g/1oz fresh yeast
Scant 375 ml/12 fl oz lukewarm milk
Pinch of sugar
500g/1lb strong flour
½ tsps salt
60g/2½oz margarine, melted and cooled
Margarine
1 egg yolk
25g/1oz Emmenthal cheese, grated

1 Make a yeast dough from the yeast, lukewarm milk (reserving 3 tbsps), sugar, flour, salt and margrine. Leave to rise in a warm place.
2 Grease a wide loaf tin. Fill with the dough to a depth of about 1 cm/½ inch. Shape the remaining dough into eight rolls and place on top of the bread in a double line. Press lightly on, cover and leave to prove in a warm place.

3 Brush the dough with melted margarine and bake in a preheated oven, Gas Mark 6/200°C/400°F, for about 40 minutes.
4 Mix the egg yolk with the reserved milk and brush over the rolls after 15 minutes. Sprinkle the rolls with the cheese after a further 15 minutes.

STUFFED ALMOND AND CHERRY SLICE

Makes 16 portions

25g/1oz fresh yeast
125 ml/4 fl oz lukewarm milk
1 tbsp caster sugar
375g/12oz flour
75g/3oz caster sugar
Pinch of salt
80g/3oz margarine, melted and cooled
1 egg
Margarine for greasing

WEEKEND BREAD

Makes approximately 16 slices

500g/1lb flour
40g/1½oz fresh yeast
250 ml/8 fl oz lukewarm milk
50g/2oz caster sugar
1 egg
1 egg white
1 tsp salt
Juice of half a lemon
2 tbsps raisins
100g/3½oz almonds, chopped
Margarine for greasing
1 egg yolk

1 Sieve the flour into a bowl. Make a well in the centre and crumble in the yeast. Add a little of the lukewarm milk and a good pinch of sugar and mix together with a little flour to a thick paste. Leave to rise until the yeast mixture has doubled in volume. Dot the margarine over the flour, add the remaining milk, egg and egg white and mix together thoroughly. Add the salt, lemon juice, raisins and almonds. Mix and knead thoroughly to a smooth dough and leave covered in a warm place until doubled in volume.

2 Shape the dough into a thick roll, reserving a little for decoration. Put into a greased 25-cm/10-inch loaf tin and leave in a warm place to prove. Cut decorative shapes from the reserved dough and stick them onto the loaf with beaten egg yolk. Brush the whole loaf with egg yolk.

3 Bake in a preheated oven, Gas Mark 6/200°C/400°F, for 40-50 minutes. After about 30 minutes, cover the loaf with foil to prevent the crust burning.

Filling

250g/8oz ground almonds

50g/2oz caster sugar

1 egg

100 ml/3½ fl oz whipping cream

1 apple

125g/4oz morello cherry jam

Icing

1 egg yolk

50g/2oz icing sugar

2 tbsps water

1 Crumble the yeast into the lukewarm milk, add the sugar and leave in a warm place until frothy. Put the flour, sugar, salt, margarine and egg into a bowl. Add the frothy yeast and mix everything together well. Knead the dough thoroughly, cover with foil and leave in a warm place until doubled in volume.
2 Mix together the almonds, sugar, egg and whipping cream. Peel and core the apples, grate them and stir into the mixture together with cherry jam.

3 Roll the dough out to a thickness of about 1 cm/½ inch, to fit a 35-cm/13½-inch loaf tin. Mark the dough into three equal sections. Spread the filling over the middle section. Cut the two outer sections into strips 2 cm/¾ inch wide and turn into decorative edges, slightly overlapping the filling.

4 Carefully place the slice in the loaf tin and leave in a warm place to prove. Brush the slice with egg yolk and bake in a preheated oven, Gas Mark 4-6/180°-225°C/350°-400°F, for about 30 minutes.
5 Mix together the icing sugar and water and thinly coat the almond and cherry slice with this.

SWEDISH YEAST ROUND

Makes approximately 16 portions

25g/1oz fresh yeast
Scant 375 ml/12 fl oz lukewarm milk
Pinch of sugar
500g/1lb flour
40g/1½oz caster sugar
Pinch of salt
60g/2½oz margarine, melted and cooled
200g/7oz white marzipan paste
1 egg yolk
25g/1oz icing sugar
Margarine for greasing
1 egg yolk

1 Crumble the yeast into the lukewarm milk, reserving 3 tbsps. Add a pinch of sugar and leave in a warm place until frothy. Put the flour, sugar, salt and margarine into a bowl, add the frothy yeast and knead the dough well. Leave in a warm place until doubled in volume.
2 Grease a 24-cm/9½-inch tin with a removable base and line with dough to a depth of about 1 cm/½ inch.
3 Knead together the marzipan paste, egg yolk and icing sugar. Roll it out and lay it over the dough. Make a thick coil with half the remaining dough and arrange it around the outside edge of the marzipan, like a frame.
4 Shape the remaining dough into eight rolls and place these inside the dough frame. With kitchen scissors, make a few nicks or swirls on top of the rolls. Cover and leave in a warm place for 15 minutes to prove.

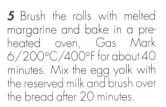

5 Brush the rolls with melted margarine and bake in a pre-heated oven, Gas Mark 6/200°C/400°F for about 40 minutes. Mix the egg yolk with the reserved milk and brush over the bread after 20 minutes.

STUFFED BUN PLAIT

Makes approximately 15 slices

25g/1oz fresh yeast
125 ml/4 fl oz lukewarm milk
375g/12oz flour
80g/3oz caster sugar
40g/1½oz margarine, melted and cooled
Margarine for greasing
Pinch of salt

Filling

125g/4oz ground almonds
250g/8oz raisins
50g/2oz currants
75g/3oz caster sugar
8 tbsps brandy

Icing

125g/4oz icing sugar
1 tbsp lemon juice
1 tbsp water

1 Crumble the yeast into the lukewarm milk, stir in a pinch of sugar, cover and leave in a warm place until frothy. Put the flour, sugar, margarine, egg

BULLAR

Makes approximately 40 pieces

150g/5oz margarine
500 ml/18 fl oz milk
40g/1½oz fresh yeast
150g/5oz caster sugar
1kg/2lb flour
½ tsp salt
6 tbsps caster sugar
2 tsps cinnamon
Margarine for greasing
2 egg yolks
Coarse sugar, desiccated coconut or flaked almonds

1 Melt the margarine, add the milk and crumble the yeast into it. Stir in the sugar and leave for 5-10 minutes until frothy. Gradually beat in the flour and salt. Knead the dough well, cover and leave in a warm place for about 40 minutes.
2 Mix together the sugar and cinnamon and knead them into the dough.
3 Form the dough into two equal rolls and slice these into 2-cm/¾-inch-thick rounds. Place on a greased baking tray and leave to prove for about 30 minutes.

4 Brush the rounds with egg yolk and sprinkle with coarse sugar, coconut or flaked almonds. Bake in a preheated oven, Gas Mark 7/220°C/425°F, for about 10 minutes.

and salt into a bowl, mix in the frothy yeast and knead the dough thoroughly. Cover and leave in a warm place until doubled in volume.
2 Roll out the dough to a rectangle 25 cm x 60 cm/10 inches x 23½ inches and cut into three equal pieces.
3 Mix the almonds with the raisins, currants, sugar and brandy and spread evenly over each piece of dough. Roll up each piece beginning with the long side. Plait the three rolls together into a round (see illustration) and

put into a greased 22-cm/8½-inch tin with a removable base.

4 Bake in a preheated oven, Gas Mark 6/200°C/400°F, for abut 30 minutes.
5 Mix the icing sugar with the lemon juice and water and spread over the hot bun plait.

SAVOURY SNACKS

Pizzas, quiches and flans can be made in a hundred different ways. This chapter gathers together a few of the most delicious versions from Italy, France and Germany, together with irresistible savoury pies, choux, rolls and party snacks.

SALMON QUICHE

Makes approximately 4 portions

200g/7oz plain flour
100g/3½oz margarine
3 tbsps water
½ tsp salt
Margarine for greasing

Filling

3 eggs
150g/5oz soft cheese with herbs
250 ml/8 fl oz single cream
Freshly ground black pepper
Salt
250g/8oz broccoli florets, cooked and drained
150-200g/5-7oz cooked salmon

1 Make a smooth dough from the flour, margarine, water and salt. Chill.

2 Whisk the eggs with the soft cheese and cream and season with pepper and salt.

3 Roll out the pastry and use to line a 26-cm/10-inch flan dish, pressing it in firmly. Prick the pastry several times with a fork and bake it blind in a preheated oven, Gas Mark 6/200°C/400°F, for 10 minutes.

4 Fill the flan case with the salmon and broccoli and pour in the cheese mixture. Return the quiche to the oven for a further 30 minutes.

MUSHROOM PIE

Makes 4-6 portions

Pastry

400g/13oz flour	
175g/6oz margarine	
Scant 125 ml/4 fl oz milk	
1 egg	
1 egg white	
Pinch of salt	
Pinch of sugar	
Margarine for greasing	

Filling

100g/3½oz smoked bacon	
150g/5oz onions	
1kg/2lb mushrooms	
1 heaped tbsp flour	
150g/5oz crème fraîche	
2 eggs	
Salt, pepper	
1 bunch parsley	
1 egg yolk	
1 tbsp milk for brushing	

1 Working quickly, mix together the pastry ingredients and knead to a smooth dough. Chill.

2 Dice the bacon and sauté lightly. Dice the onions and colour them in the bacon fat. Slice the mushrooms, add them to the pan and cook gently until almost all the liquid has evaporated. Sprinkle over the flour and leave the mixture to cool. Whisk the crème fraîche with the eggs, season and pour over the mushroom and bacon mixture. Wash the parsley, chop and add to the mixture.

3 Roll out a good half of the dough and use to line a well greased 30-cm/12-inch pie dish, allowing pastry to overlap the rim slightly. Fill evenly with the mushroom and bacon mixture.

4 Roll out the remaining dough to cover the pie. Dampen the pastry edges and press them together firmly to seal. Trim and make two diagonal cuts in the top of the pie, folding the pastry back slightly, to show the filling.

5 Cut out decorative mushroom shapes from the pastry trimmings. Mix the egg yolk with the milk, brush a little onto the base of the pastry mushrooms and stick them onto the pie. Brush the pie with the egg yolk and milk.

6 Bake in the centre of a preheated oven, Gas Mark 6/ 200°C/400°F, for about 40 minutes.

Note: This pie may be served hot or cold.

QUICHE RAMEE

Makes approximately 4 portions

200g/7oz flour
200g/7oz margarine
Pinch of salt
1 egg

Filling

150g/5oz crème fraîche
2 eggs
Pinch of pepper
100g/3½oz smoked ham, diced
100g/3½oz soft cheese with mushrooms, crumbled

1 Make a smooth dough from the pastry ingredients and set aside in the refrigerator to chill.
2 Reserving a little for decoration, use the pastry to line a greased 26-cm/10½-inch flan dish, pinching it up well round the edge. Bake blind in a preheated oven, Gas Mark 6-7/200°-220°C/400°-425°F, for about 15 minutes.
3 Thoroughly mix together the crème fraîche, eggs and pepper and pour into the flan case. Spread the diced ham and the crumbled cheese evenly over.
4 Cut four decorative rounds from the reserved pastry and arrange them attractively on top.
5 Return the quiche to the oven for a further 15 minutes.

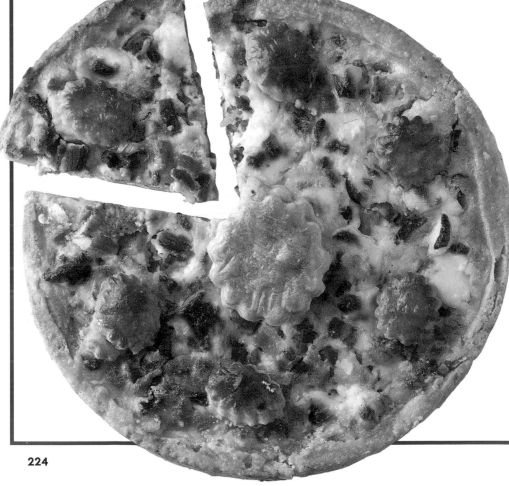

ASPARAGUS QUICHE

Makes 4-6 portions

750g/1½lb asparagus
Salt, Pinch of sugar

Flan Case

225g/7½oz flour
½ tsp salt
½ tsp mixed herbs
125g/4oz margarine
1 egg yolk
3 tbsps water
Margarine for greasing

Filling

250g/8oz quark or curd cheese
3 eggs, 1 egg white
125 ml/4 fl oz whipping cream
Salt, pepper
100g/3½oz prawns or shrimps

QUICHE LORRAINE

Makes approximately 2 portions

180g/6oz frozen puff pastry, thawed

2 tbsps golden breadcrumbs

200g/7oz Gouda cheese, sliced

200g/7oz smoked ham

125 ml/4 fl oz soured cream

4 eggs

3 tbsps parsley, chopped

1 tsp mild paprika pepper

1 Roll out the pastry and use to line a 20-cm/8-inch flan tin. Pinch up an edge 3-cm/1¼-inch high. Sprinkle the base with the breadcrumbs.

2 Cut the cheese into strips, dice the ham and mix with the cream, eggs, parsley and paprika. Turn the mixture into the uncooked flan case.

3 Bake the quiche in a preheated oven, Gas Mark 7/220°C/425°F, for about 45 minutes. Serve hot.

1 Peel the asparagus and cook in salted water with a pinch of sugar for about 10 minutes, until tender.

2 Knead the flour, salt, herbs, margarine, egg yolk and water to a smooth dough. Roll out the dough and use to line a 26-cm/10-inch flan tin.

3 Bake the case blind in a preheated oven, Gas Mark 6/200°C/400°F, for about 10-15 minutes. Turn the drained asparagus into the pastry case.

4 Mix together the quark, eggs, additional egg white, cream, salt and pepper. Stir in the prawns and pour this over the asparagus.

5 Bake the quiche in a preheated oven, Gas Mark 6/200°C/400°F, for 10-15 minutes, then reduce the heat to Gas Mark 4/180°C/350°F for a further 10-15 minutes.

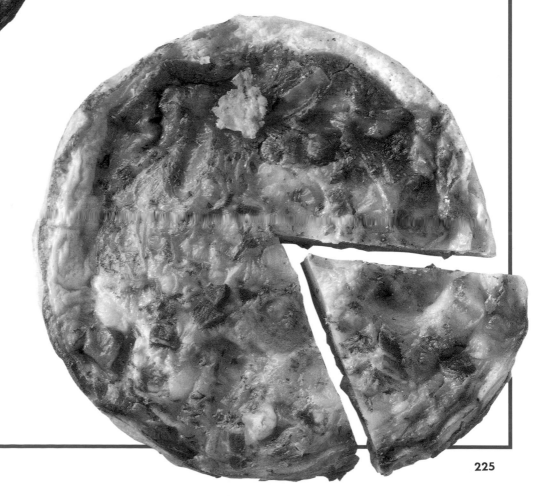

MINI PIZZA WITH CREAM CHEESE

Makes approximately 4 portions

125g/4oz pizza dough mix
10 small tomatoes
100g/3½oz mushrooms
½ each red, yellow and green peppers
12 olives
1 chilli pepper
1 tbsp vegetable oil
Salt, pepper

Oregano
150g/5oz cream cheese with herbs
Fresh marjoram

1 Make up the pizza dough mixture according to the packet instructions. Scald, skin and slice the tomatoes. Wash and slice the mushrooms. Deseed, trim and dice the pepper halves. Slice the olives and the chilli pepper.
2 Sauté the mushrooms and peppers in hot oil for 5 minutes.

Season with salt, pepper and oregano.
3 Divide the dough into four portions and roll it out into thin rounds. Spread the sautéed vegetables over the dough together with the chilli and olives. Decorate with the tomatoes and leave to rise in a warm place for a short while.
4 Bake in a preheated oven, Gas Mark 6/200°C/400°F, for 10-15 minutes. Top with dollops of cream cheese, sprinkle with marjoram and bake for a further 5 minutes.

HAM AND VEGETABLE PIZZA

Makes 3-4 portions

200g/7oz green and red peppers
1 onion
2 tbsps vegetable oil
125g/4oz courgettes
Salt, pepper
250g/8oz pizza dough mix
125g/4oz tomatoes, sliced
25g/1oz sliced salami
10 black olives
60g/2½oz cooked ham
1 tsp oregano
75g/3oz mozzarella cheese
80g/3oz Gouda, grated
20g/3/4oz Parmesan, grated

1 Cut the peppers into strips and the onions into rings and sauté for 10 minutes in the hot oil. Add the sliced courgettes, season with salt and pepper and sauté for a further 5 minutes.

2 Make up the pizza dough mix according to the instructions on the packet and work to a smooth dough.

3 Knead the dough well with floured hands, roll it out and use to line a greased 24-cm/9½-inch pizza dish or flan ring, pinching up a good edge.

4 Spread the vegetable mixture over the dough, arrange the tomato slices on top. Twist the salami into little cones and top with an olive. Arrange the ham in a fan shape on the tomatoes and decorate with the salami. Season with pepper, salt and oregano. Slice the mozzarella cheese and arrange over everything. Sprinkle the pizza with the grated Gouda and Parmesan.

5 Bake in a preheated oven, Gas Mark 6/200°C/400/F, for about 30 minutes, then increase the heat to Gas Mark 7/220°C/425°F for a further 10 minutes.

4 Using a balloon whisk, beat together the eggs, cream, 75g/3oz of the cream cheese, salt, pepper, nutmeg and marjoram and pour this over the vegetable mixture.

5 Bake in a preheated oven, Gas Mark 4/180°C/350°F, for about 80 minutes.

6 Mix the remaining cheese with the egg yolk and spread over the quiche after 1 hour.

Note: The final cheese and egg yolk mixture may be heated and served separately with the hot quiche.

1 Roll the pastry out and use to line a greased 35-cm/13-inch flan tin. Prick the pastry several times with a fork.

2 Cut the peppers into quarters, trim, deseed, wash and dice. Cut the leeks in half lengthways, wash and slice. Chop the onions. Cut the pork and ham into thin strips.

3 Blanch the peppers and leek in boiling salted water for 1 minute. Soften the belly of pork in a saucepan over a high heat. Add the ham, peppers, leek and onions and sauté for 5 minutes. Fill the flan case with this mixture to 2 cm/3/4 inch below the top.

HERB QUICHE

Makes 4-6 portions

300g/10oz frozen puff pastry, thawed
Margarine for greasing
1 each red, green and yellow peppers
5 thin leeks
5 medium onions
250g/8oz smoked belly of pork
250g/8oz cooked ham
6 eggs
250 ml/8 fl oz whipping cream
150g/5oz cream cheese with mixed herbs
Salt, pepper
Nutmeg
Marjoram
1 egg yolk

PARTY PIZZA

Makes approximately 12 portions

500g/1lb flour
250g/8oz margarine
Scant 250 ml/8 fl oz water
2 tsps vinegar
2 tsps salt
Margarine for greasing

Topping

375g/12oz tomatoes
125g/4oz onions
1 green and 1 red pepper, trimmed and deseeded
230g/7½oz tinned mushrooms
4 small salami sausages
200g/7oz Gouda, thinly sliced
Tomato ketchup
Thyme, mixed herbs, oregano
Salt, paprika
100g/3½oz salami, sliced
100g/3½oz cheese, grated

1 Knead the flour, margarine, water, vinegar and salt to a smooth dough and chill for 1 hour.

2 Slice the onions and tomatoes, and cut the peppers into thin strips. Drain the mushrooms and cut in half if necessary. Slice the whole salami. Cut the Gouda slices into triangles.

3 Roll out the dough to a thickness of about ½ cm/¼ inch and cut into rectangles 6 cm x 10 cm/2½ inches x 4 inches. Place these on a greased baking tray. Prick each one several times with a fork, spread them thickly with tomato ketchup and sprinkle with herbs.

4 Top with different combinations of the tomato, onion, salami, peppers and mushrooms. Season. Top with the Gouda triangles, or sprinkle with the grated cheese.

5 Bake in a preheated oven, Gas Mark 6-7/200°- 220°C/ 400°-425°F, for about 20 minutes. Serve immediately.

TOMATO FLAN

Makes 3-4 portions

Pastry
250g/8oz flour
125g/4oz margarine
1 egg
Salt, pepper, oregano

Topping
750g/1½lb small tomatoes
Salt, pepper, oregano
1 small onion
1 triangle cheese spread
7 tbsps milk
4 eggs
1 tbsp paprika
Sugar

1 Quickly knead the pastry ingredients together, and chill for about 30 minutes. Roll out thickly and use to line a lightly-greased 22-cm/8½-inch flan tin. Press the edge up well, then trim neatly to 4 cm/1½ inches high. Bake the pastry blind in a preheated oven, Gas Mark 7/220°C/425°F, for about 15-20 minutes.

2 Scald and skin the tomatoes and arrange them on the pastry case. Season well with salt, pepper and oregano. Finely chop the onions and sprinkle them between the tomato slices.

3 Over a low heat, mix the cheese spread with 3 tbsps of the milk, add the remaining milk and the eggs. Whisk together well. Season with the paprika, salt, pepper, sugar and a little oregano and pour the mixture into the flan.

4 Return to the oven for 30-40 minutes. Turn off the heat and leave the flan in the oven for a further 5 minutes. Take out and leave to stand for 10 minutes before serving.

PRAWN AND ASPARAGUS ENVELOPES

Makes approximately 10 portions

300g/10oz frozen puff pastry, thawed
200g/7oz prawns
100g/3½oz tinned asparagus
50g/2oz almonds, chopped
150g/5oz soft cheese with herbs
1 tbsp fine breadcrumbs
Salt, pepper
1 tbsp chopped fresh dill
1 tbsp water
1 egg yolk, beaten

1 Roll out the pastry and cut into 15-cm/6-inch squares.

2 Carefully mix the prawns with the asparagus, almonds, cheese and breadcrumbs. Season with salt, pepper and the dill.

3 Divide the mixture between the pastry squares. Brush the pastry edges with the water and fold the squares into triangles. Press the edges together firmly to seal.

4 Place the triangles on a baking tray, brush with the beaten

egg yolk and bake in a pre-heated oven, Gas Mark 6/ 200°C/400°F, for about 20 minutes.

SMOKED SALMON PASTRIES

Makes 10 portions

300g/10oz frozen puff pastry, thawed
50g/2oz smoked salmon
1 large onion
100g/3½oz cucumber
2 tsps capers
1 tsp horseradish
1 egg yolk

1 Chop the smoked salmon, dice the onion and cucumber and mix with the capers and horseradish.

2 Roll out the pastry and use a pastry wheel to cut out ten 11-cm/4-inch squares.

3 Place a little of the filling in the centre of each square. Dampen the pastry edges with water and fold the squares into envelopes. Press the edges firmly together to seal. Rinse a baking tray in cold water and arrange the pastries on it.

4 Mix the egg yolk with a dash of water and brush this over the pastries. Bake in a preheated oven, Gas Mark 7/220°C/425°F, for 10-15 minutes.

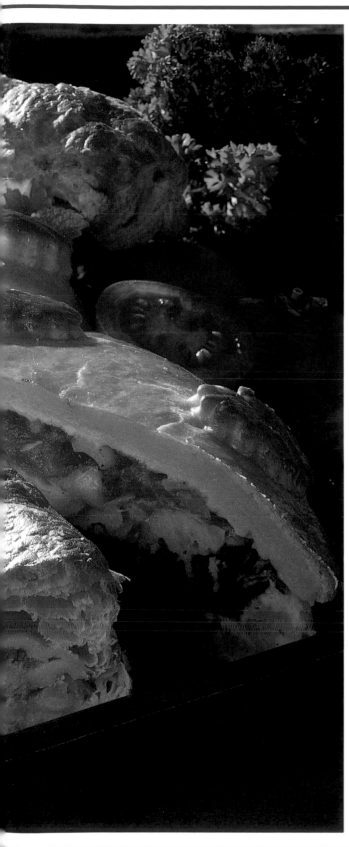

TRIESTE FISH PIE

Makes approximately 4 portions

Pastry

250g/8oz flour
Pinch of salt
80g/3oz margarine
1 egg
3-4 tbsps water

Filling

4 tomatoes
1 onion
1 clove of garlic
½ fresh chilli pepper
6 anchovy fillets
Mixed dried herbs
Oregano
450g/15oz frozen spinach
Salt, pepper
Margarine for greasing
400g/13oz fish fillets, fresh or frozen
Vinegar
1 egg yolk, beaten

1 Working quickly, make a smooth dough from the pastry ingredients. Knead lightly and chill for at least 1 hour.

2 Scald, skin, deseed and chop the tomatoes. Chop the onions, garlic, chilli pepper and anchovy fillets. Sauté these ingredients in margarine until any liquid has almost evaporated. Season with the dried herbs and oregano. Leave to cool.

3 Cook the spinach according to the instructions on the packet, allowing any liquid to evaporate completely, then season with dried herbs, salt and pepper. Grease a 26-cm/10-inch round or oval ovenproof dish and turn in the spinach.

4 Sprinkle the fish fillets with vinegar, season with salt and pepper and lay them on top of the spinach. Spread the savoury tomato mixture over the fish.

5 Roll out the pastry to a thickness of about 3 mm/⅛ inch and use to top the pie, pressing the pastry down well onto the rim of the dish to seal. Brush with the egg yolk and prick the pastry several times with a fork. Cut out decorative shapes from the pastry trimmings and use to decorate the pie. Bake in a preheated oven, Gas Mark 7/220°C/425°F, for about 40 minutes.

EMMENTHAL SLICES

Makes 4-6 portions

300g/10oz flour
20g/¾oz fresh yeast
125 ml/4 fl oz lukewarm milk
Pinch of sugar
25g/1oz margarine, melted and cooled
Pinch of salt
Margarine for greasing
German mustard
250g/8oz Emmenthal cheese, cut into 12 slices
125g/4oz streaky bacon, diced and cooked

1 Sieve the flour into a bowl, make a well in the middle and crumble in the yeast. Mix with a little of the lukewarm milk and a pinch of sugar and flour. Leave in a warm place until frothy. Add the remaining milk, the margarine and a little salt. Mix well and knead to a smooth dough. Leave in a warm place until doubled in volume. Roll out the dough and use to line a greased baking tray.

2 Spread mustard thinly over the dough, cover with the sliced cheese and sprinkle with the bacon.

3 Leave in a warm place to prove. Bake in a preheated oven, Gas Mark 7/220°C/425°F, for about 30 minutes. Cut into slices to serve.

ONION FLAN

Makes approximately 4 portions

Pastry

250g/8oz flour
125g/4oz margarine
1 egg
Pinch of baking powder
Pinch of salt
Margarine for greasing

Topping

150g/5oz smoked bacon, diced
50g/2oz margarine
1kg/2lb onions, finely chopped
250 ml/8 fl oz soured cream
2 eggs
2 tbsps flour
Salt
Caraway seeds

1 Make a shortcrust dough from the pastry ingredients and use to line a greased 26-cm/10-inch flan tin. Pinch the edge up well.

2 Colour the diced bacon in the margarine; add the finely chopped onions and sauté.

3 Whisk together the soured cream, eggs, flour, salt and caraway seeds to taste. Add the onions and pour the mixture into the uncooked flan case. Bake in a preheated oven, Gas Mark 4/180°C/350°F, for about 60 minutes.

SALAMI ROLL

Makes approximately 4 portions

20g/¾oz fresh yeast
125 ml/4 fl oz milk
Pinch of sugar
250g/9oz flour
Salt
40g/1½oz margarine, melted and cooled
200g/7oz salami, skinned and thinly sliced
1 egg, separated
Margarine for greasing

1 Make a yeast dough from the yeast, lukewarm milk, sugar, flour, salt and margarine. Leave in a warm place until well risen.
2 Roll out the dough to a rectangle. Cover it with thin slices of salami, then sprinkle with oregano. Brush the dough edges with the egg white, roll up the dough and place on a greased baking tray. Leave in a warm place to prove.
3 Mix the egg yolk with a little water and brush over the salami roll. Score the top of the roll with a sharp knife. Bake in a preheated oven, Gas Mark 6/200°C/400°F, for about 40 minutes.

HERRING AND MUSHROOM FLAN

Makes 2 portions

Dough

125g/4oz flour
5g/¼oz fresh yeast
Salt
2 tbsps lukewarm milk
25g/1oz margarine, melted and cooled
1 egg

Filling

80g/3oz tinned pickled herrings
115g/4oz tinned mushrooms
1 onion
50g/2oz red pepper, skinned
Pepper
75g/3oz Gouda cheese
Chives

1 Make a yeast dough from the dough ingredients. Leave in a warm place until well risen. Roll out the dough and use to line a greased 20-cm/8-inch flan tin.
2 Drain the herrings, slice the mushrooms, and cut the onions into rings and the pepper into thin strips. Arrange these ingredients attractively over the flan base. Sprinkle with freshly ground black pepper and grate the cheese over. Leave in a warm place to prove.
3 Bake in a preheated oven, Gas Mark 7/220°C/425°F, for 25-30 minutes. Sprinkle with chopped chives and serve hot.

DECORATIVE VEGETABLE FLAN

Makes approximately 6 portions

Pastry
200g/7oz plain flour
1 egg
100g/3½oz margarine
4 tbsps cold water
Pinch of salt

Filling
750g/1½lb leeks
4-5 medium tomatoes
250g/8oz courgettes
1 small cauliflower
50g/2oz margarine
½lb pork sausagemeat
3 tbsps soured cream
Pepper
Nutmeg
Salt
3 eggs
200 ml/7 fl oz soured cream
1 tbsp cornflour
50g/2oz Emmenthal cheese

1 Make a dough from the pastry ingredients and knead until smooth. Chill for 30 minutes. Roll out the pastry and use to line a 23-cm/9-inch flan dish.
2 Bake the pastry case blind in a preheated oven, Gas Mark 6/200°C/400°F, for 20-25 minutes. Leave to cool.
3 Meanwhile, wash and trim the vegetables. Slice the tomatoes and courgettes, cut the cauliflower into florets and finely chop the leeks. Lightly sauté the vegetables in the margarine until just soft.

4 Mix the sausagemeat with the 3 tbsps soured cream. Season with pepper, salt and nutmeg to taste. Spread this over the flan base and arrange the vegetables decoratively on top.
5 Whisk the eggs with the 200 ml/7 fl oz soured cream. Stir in the cornflour and season with nutmeg, salt and pepper. Pour this mixture over the vegetables and bake in a preheated oven, Gas Mark 6/200°C/400°F, for 25-30 minutes.
6 Grate the Emmenthal and sprinkle it over the flan. Return it to the oven for a further 5 minutes and serve hot.

CHINESE CABBAGE FLAN

Makes approximately 8 portions

250g/8oz plain flour

Pinch of salt

Pinch of baking powder

250g/8oz margarine

250g/8oz cottage cheese

Margarine for greasing

Filling

400g/13oz soft cheese

75g/3oz Stilton cheese

3 tbsps chopped fresh herbs

75 ml/3 fl oz soured cream

Pinch of gelatine dissolved in
150 ml/5 fl oz water

½ tsp salt

Pepper

6 leaves of Chinese cabbage

Meat stock

75g/3oz Gouda cheese, cut into
3 slices

3 slices cooked ham

Tomatoes, to decorate

1 Mix the flour, salt, baking powder, margarine and cottage cheese to a smooth dough. Knead and chill. Roll out the dough into a square, fold it over and roll out again. Repeat this process three times. Use the dough to line a greased 26-cm/10-inch spring-release tin and bake blind in a preheated oven, Gas Mark 6/200°C/400°F, for 10 minutes.

2 Mix together the soft cheese, Stilton, herbs, soured cream, gelatine, salt and pepper and spread this over the cooked flan base.

3 Wash the Chinese cabbage leaves and blanch them in meat stock. Drain in a colander. Place two leaves together, overlapping them slightly, and put a slice of Gouda cheese and a slice of ham on top. Roll up tightly. Repeat, to make three rolls in total.

4 Cut the rolls into 3-cm/1-inch thick slices and arrange these over the cheese mixture in the flan. Decorate with tomato slices. Return to the oven for a further 15-20 minutes.

FESTIVE PORK PIE

Makes approximately 8 portions

750g/1½lb smoked pork
375g/12oz flour
½ tsp salt
5 tbsps iced water
1 white bread roll
6 tbsps hot milk
1 onion
1 tbsp chopped fresh parsley
125 ml/4 fl oz single cream
Salt, pepper, cayenne pepper
Dried basil
Margarine for greasing
1 egg yolk

1 Put the meat into boiling water to just cover. Cook for 45 minutes until tender. Leave to cool in the broth.

2 Using a hand-held electric mixer with a pastry hook and working quickly, make a smooth dough from the flour, salt, margarine and iced water. Chill.

3 Mince the meat. Cut the bread roll into cubes, pour the hot milk over and leave to soak. Mix the meat, bread, onion, parsley, cream, basil and seasonings together well.

4 Roll out two-thirds of the dough and use to line a greased 26-cm/10-inch flan tin. Prick the base several times with a fork. Spread the filling evenly over. Roll out the remaining dough and use to top the pie, pressing the edges together well. Prick the top with a fork several times. Cut a 1 cm/½ inch hole in the centre.

5 Mix the egg yolk with a little water and brush over the pie to glaze. Cut a few decorative shapes from the pastry trimmings, attach and brush with egg yolk.

6 Bake in a preheated oven, Gas Mark 6/200°C/400°F, for about 60 minutes. Serve hot.

Note: This pie is also good cold, jellied. Dissolve 6 sheets of gelatine in 250 ml/8 fl oz of the cooking liquid from the meat. Pour into the cold pie through the hole and leave to set.

LEEK FLAN

Makes approximately 6-8 portions

Pastry

300g/10oz flour
Salt
150g/5oz margarine
1 egg

Filling

2 ½kg/5lb leeks

PARTY PIES

Makes approximately 16 pies

250g/8oz flour
250g/8oz margarine
250g/8oz low fat quark or curd cheese
Salt

Filling

200g/7oz mixed minced beef and pork
1 slice white bread
1 small green pepper, chopped
100g/3½oz Emmenthal cheese, diced
1 egg, separated
Pepper
2 tbsps water

1 Put the flour, salt, margarine and quark or curd cheese on a pastry board. Mix the ingredients with a palette knife and knead quickly to a smooth dough. Chill.
2 Mix together the meat, white bread, chopped pepper, diced cheese and egg white and season with pepper and salt.
3 Roll out the dough and cut into 12-cm/4½-inch rounds. Put one tablespoonful of the filling on half of each pastry round. Mix the egg yolk and water, brush this over the pastry edges and fold the pies up. Press the edges together with a fork to seal.
4 Arrange on a baking tray, brush with egg yolk and bake in a preheated oven, Gas Mark 6-7/200°-220°C/400°-425°F, for about 20 minutes.

50g/2oz margarine
Salt
200g/7oz smoked ham
200g/7oz crème fraîche
4 eggs
100g/3½oz grated cheese
Pepper, nutmeg
Margarine

1 Make a shortcrust dough from the pastry ingredients. Knead and chill for 30 minutes.

2 Meanwhile, wash and drain the leeks and slice them into rings. Gently sauté them in 25g/1oz of the margarine for 15 minutes. Season with salt, and drain again.
3 Roll out the pastry and use to line a 30-cm/12-inch flan tin, pinching up an edge of 3 cm/1 inch. Bake the pastry case blind in a preheated oven, Gas Mark 6/200°C/400°F, for about 20 minutes.

4 Dice the ham, and lightly brown in the remaining margarine. Spread the ham over the flan case and place the leeks on top. Beat together the crème fraîche, eggs and cheese, season with salt, pepper and nutmeg and pour over the leeks.
5 Dot the flan with the extra margarine and return to the oven for about 30 minutes.

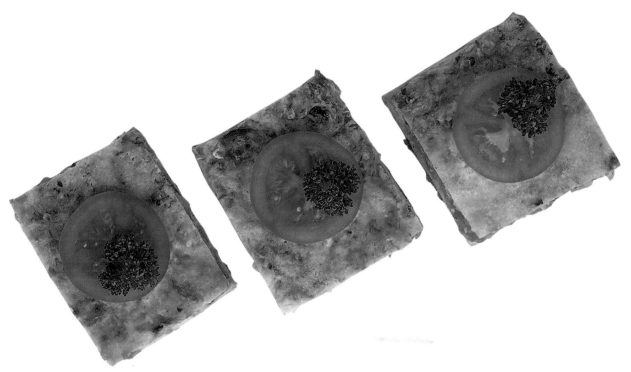

TOMATO AND ONION FLAN

Makes approximately 6 portions

15g/½oz fresh yeast
4 fl oz lukewarm milk
1 tsp sugar
250g/8oz flour
Pinch of salt
100g/3½oz margarine, melted and cooled
Margarine for greasing

Topping

1 ½kg/3lb tomatoes
500g/1lb onions
50g/2oz margarine
1 sprig each fresh basil, parsley, oregano, or 1 tsp dried herbs
Salt, pepper
3 eggs
250 ml/8 fl oz single cream
100g/3½oz Emmenthal cheese, grated

1 Crumble the yeast into the milk, add a pinch of sugar and leave, covered, in a warm place until frothy. Mix together the flour, sugar, salt and melted margarine, add the frothy yeast, mix together well and knead to a smooth dough. Cover and leave in a warm place until doubled in volume. Knead again.

2 Roll out the dough on a floured board and put into a greased baking tray, pressing the edges well into the sides. Leave in a warm place to prove.

3 Scald, peel and deseed the tomatoes. Reserve 1 or 2 for decoration and cut the rest into quarters or eighths. Slice the onions thinly and sauté them in the margarine. Chop the herbs, add them to the onions and season with salt and pepper.

4 Arrange the tomatoes over the pastry base. Spread with the cooled onion mixture. Whisk the eggs and cream together and pour evenly into the flan.

5 Bake in a preheated oven, Gas Mark 6/220°C/400°F, for 25 minutes, placing the flan on a low shelf for the first 15 minutes. Remove the flan, sprinkle with cheese and replace in the centre of the oven, cooking for a further 10 minutes.

6 Decorate with the reserved tomatoes, sliced, and a little chopped parsley and serve hot or cold.

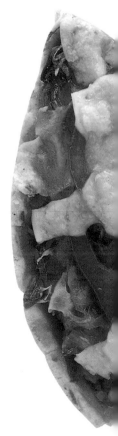

GENTLEMAN'S SAVOURY FLAN

Makes approximately 4 portions

Pastry

250g/8oz flour
125g/4oz margarine
½ tsp salt
1 egg
Margarine for greasing

Topping

2 onions
1 tbsp margarine
230g/7½oz tinned mushrooms, drained
Curry powder
Fresh parsley, to taste
2 tbsps fine breadcrumbs
375g/12oz sausagemeat
125g/4oz thin slices of ham
250g/8oz tomatoes
250g/8oz peppers
Oregano
250g/8oz Gouda cheese, sliced and cut into strips

1 Make a shortcust dough from the pastry ingredients. Chill.

2 Meanwhile, slice onions into rings and sauté in the margarine. Add the mushrooms and sauté until tender, then season to taste with curry powder. Chop the parsley and add it to the pan.

3 Grease a 26-cm/10½-inch flan tin. Roll out the pastry and use to line the tin. Sprinkle the breadcrumbs over the pastry case, spread with the sausagemeat, and top with the onion and mushroom mixture and the sliced ham. Wash the tomatoes and peppers, slice thinly and arrange on the flan. Sprinkle with oregano.

4 Bake the flan in a preheated oven, Gas Mark 7/220°C/425°F, for 10 minutes. Decorate with a lattice of cheese strips and bake for a further 15 minutes.

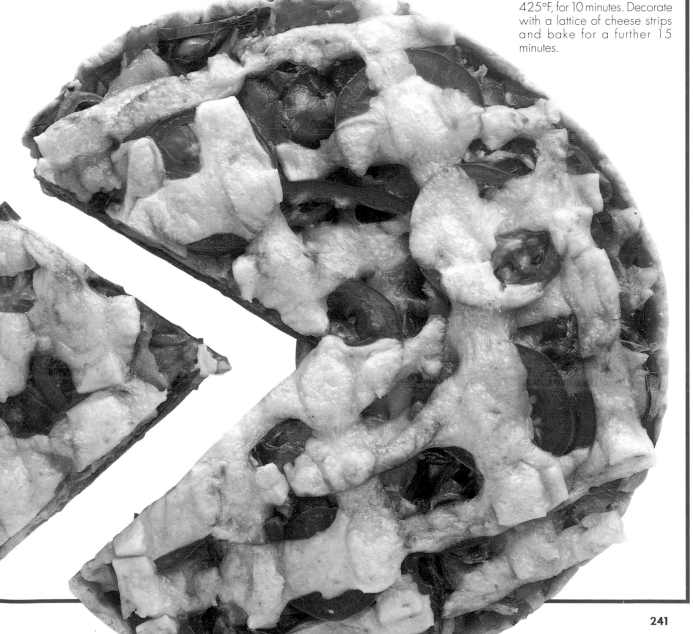

CHEESE PUFFS

Makes approximately 4 portions

250g/8oz flour
2 good pinches of baking powder
250g/8oz well-chilled margarine
250g/8oz low fat quark
Pinch of salt
200g/7oz Gouda cheese, coarsely grated
1 egg yolk, beaten

1 Sieve the flour with the baking powder, and dot with flakes of margarine. Add the drained quark and knead quickly to a smooth dough. Chill for at least 30 minutes.
2 Roll out the dough into a long, narrow strip, fold the short sides into the middle and roll out the pastry again, towards the open side. Repeat this process 3-4 times, chilling for 15 minutes between each stage.
3 Roll out the dough for the final time and cut into eight squares. Pile the cheese onto four of the

squares. Cut out a flower shape from the centre of each of the other four squares. Top the cheese squares with these decorative squares, pressing the outer edges together firmly, to seal.
4 Brush with the beaten egg yolk and bake in a preheated oven, Gas Mark 7/220°C/425°F, for about 20 minutes.

PUFF PASTRY PIROSHKI

Makes 10 portions

300g/10oz frozen puff pastry, thawed
1 onion, chopped
Margarine
125g/4oz tinned mushrooms, drained and sliced
Salt, pepper
Fresh parsley, chopped
1 egg yolk, beaten

1 Soften the chopped onions in the margarine, add the mushrooms and sauté briefly. Season with salt and pepper and add the parsley. Remove from the heat and add a little of the egg yolk.

2 Roll out the puff pastry, cut it into squares and spread these with the mushroom mixture. Fold the pastry diagonally to form triangles. Brush the edges with water and press together firmly, to seal.

3 Place the triangles on a baking tray rinsed in cold water, and prick each one several times. Brush with the remaining egg yolk and bake in a preheated oven, Gas Mark 7/220°C/425°F, for 20 minutes.

243

CHICKEN AND TURKEY LIVER TERRINE

Makes 12-16 portions

1 onion
1 apple
60g/2½oz margarine
400g/13oz turkey liver
150g/5oz cooked chicken
75g/3oz streaky bacon
1 egg yolk
6 tbsps single cream
3 tbsps cognac
2-3 tsps salt
Freshly ground black pepper
Pinch of ground cloves
Mixed herbs
10 pistachios
Meat extract
4 tbsps Madeira
3 sheets gelatine
Bay leaves and green peppercorns, to decorate

1 Chop the onion, grate the apple and sauté both in the margarine. Leave to cool. Put 300g/10oz of the turkey liver, the chicken and bacon through the mincer twice. Mix this with the egg yolk, cream and cognac and season with salt, spices and herbs. Dice the remaining liver and add to the mixture with the pistachios.

2 Press the mixture into an ovenproof terrine and cover tightly with foil. Place the terrine in a baking dish of hot water and cook in a preheated oven, Gas Mark 2-4/150°-180°C/300°-350°F, for about 1¾ hours.

3 Place a plate with a weight on top over the cooked terrine and leave to cool. Reserve any juices that are pressed out and skim these of fat.

4 Add a little water to the reserved terrine juices to make them up to 200 ml/7 fl oz and flavour with the meat extract, salt, pepper and Madeira. Stir this liquid into the previously soaked and dissolved gelatine.

As soon as the mixture starts to set, pour it over the terrine. Decorate with bay leaves and green peppercorns.

VEAL PIE

Makes approximately 8 portions

250g/8oz flour
1 tsp mixed dried herbs
Salt
200g/7oz quark
200g/7oz margarine
Margarine for greasing
Breadcrumbs

Filling

2 onions
1 red and 1 green pepper
100g/3½oz mushrooms
Margarine
Pepper, salt
2 hard-boiled eggs
500g/1lb lean veal, minced
1 egg
1 bread roll, soaked in water
Marjoram

1 Mix together the flour, herbs and salt on a pastry board. Place the quark and margarine on top and cut them in with a palette kinfe. Working quickly, mix everything together and knead to a smooth dough. Chill.

2 Grease a long loaf tin and sprinkle it with breadcrumbs.

3 Dice the onions and peppers finely, slice the mushrooms and sauté these vegetables in margarine for 5 minutes. Season and leave to cool.

4 Chop the hard-boiled eggs. Make a stuffing with the minced veal, raw egg, squeezed-out bread roll, salt, pepper and marjoram.

5 Roll out the dough and use to line the tin, leaving an overlap at the top edge. Spread half the chopped eggs on the dough,

then cover evenly with half the meat mixture.

6 Spread the vegetable mixture over, cover with the remaining meat, and finish with a layer of the remaining chopped egg. Fold the overlapping dough over the top of the pie. Brush the edges with a little water and press them together, to seal.

7 Bake the pie in a preheated oven, Gas Mark 6/200°C/400°F, for about 50 minutes. Serve hot or cold.

COLD TURKEY AND HAM PIE

Makes 15-20 portions

Pastry

500g/1lb flour
250g/8oz margarine
1 tsp salt
2-3 tbsps water
1 egg
Margarine for greasing

Filling

500g/1lb cooked turkey breast
250g/8oz cooked ham
2 tbsps chopped fresh parsley
½ tsp dried sage
6 hard-boiled eggs

To Finish

1 egg yolk
12 sheets gelatine
250 ml/8 fl oz chicken stock
5 tbsps brandy
Grated zest of ½ lemon
2 tbsps lemon juice
Salt, freshly ground black pepper

1 Make a smooth dough from the pastry ingredients. Chill.

2 Roughly dice the turkey and ham and mix with the herbs.

3 Roll out about two-thirds of the pastry to a thickness of 3 mm/⅛ inch and use to line a greased 30-cm/12-inch loaf

tin. Put half the meat filling into the pie. With the back of a spoon, make a hollow along the centre of the centre of the filling.

4 Peel the eggs, slice a little off each of the ends to flatten and arrange them in a line along the channel. Cover with the remaining meat filling.

5 Roll out the remaining dough and use to cover the pie. Press the edges together well to seal. Cut a small hole for steam to escape.

6 Mix the egg yolk with a little water and brush over the top of the pie. Cut decorative shapes from the pastry trimmings, fix on top of the pie and brush with egg yolk.

7 Bake in a preheated oven, Gas Mark 4/180°C/350°F, for about 75 minutes. Leave to cool in the tin.

8 Soak the gelatine. Drain it and dissolve it in the hot chicken stock. Add the brandy, lemon zest and juice. Season well with salt and pepper. Pour through the hole into the cold pie. Leave to set in the refrigerator.

ZINGY BREAD ROLLS

Makes 8 rolls

125g/4oz smoked bacon, diced
10g/½oz margarine
250g/8oz flour
3 tsps salt
Good pinch of mustard powder
60g/2½oz margarine
150g/5oz Gouda cheese, grated
1 egg
150 ml/5 fl oz milk
Margarine for greasing
Flour
Milk

1 Sauté the bacon in the margarine until coloured. Leave to cool.
2 Mix together the flour, baking powder, salt and mustard powder on a pastry board. Dot with margarine and cut this in with a palette knife. Add

125g/4oz of the grated cheese, the bacon and the egg, mixed with milk. Mix everything together well and knead to a smooth dough.
3 Shape the dough into eight balls and place these close together in a circle, in a cake tin with a removable base.
4 Brush a little milk over the sides and tops of the rolls, sprinkle them with the remaining cheese and bake in a preheated oven, Gas Mark 4-6/180°-200°C/350°-400°F for about 30 minutes.

SAVOURY LOAF WITH HERBS

Makes approximately 8 portions

1 red pepper
2 onions
1 large pickled gherkin
100g/3½oz margarine
4 eggs
1kg/2lb low fat quark
60g/2½oz semolina
200g/7oz ham, diced
1 bunch each fresh dill, parsley, chives
1 packet of cress
Salt, pepper, paprika
Garlic
Margarine for greasing

1 Dice the pepper, onions and gherkin and sauté in 1 tbsp of the margarine. Leave to cool.
2 Cream the remaining margarine until light, then gradually

beat in the eggs. Squeeze the quark in a cloth to drain, and add to the egg mixture together with the semolina, ham, herbs, cress and the onion mixture. Season with salt, pepper and paprika.
3 Turn into a well-greased loaf tin and smooth the top.
4 Bake in a preheated oven, Gas Mark 4/180°C/350°F for about 80 minutes.

Note: This loaf may be served hot or cold.

BACON AND TOMATO FLAN

Makes approximately 4 portions

250g/8oz flour
Salt
125g/4oz margarine
1 egg
Margarine for greasing

Topping

500g/1lb tomatoes
125g/4oz smoked ham, diced
1 onion, finely chopped
2 eggs
125 ml/4 fl oz milk

1 Put the flour and salt onto a pastry board, dot with the margarine and cut this in with a palette knife. Make a well in the centre of the mixture and drop in the egg. Mix in, and knead to a smooth dough.

2 Use to line a 22-cm/8½-inch flan tin, pinching up the edges well. Bake blind in a preheated oven, Gas Mark 6-7/200°-220°C/400°-425°F, for about 10 minutes.

3 Slice the tomatoes, arrange them in the flan case, and season with salt and pepper. Sprinkle over the ham and onion. Beat the eggs with the milk, season with salt and pepper and pour over.

4 Return the flan to the oven for a further 30-40 minutes.

AMERICAN CHEESE PIE

Makes approximately 4 portions

300g/10oz frozen puff pastry, thawed
250g/8oz Gouda or Camembert cheese, cubed
100g/3½oz walnuts, chopped
2 tbsps cranberries
50g/2oz raisins
½-1 tsp salt
2 egg whites
1 egg yolk, beaten

1 Roll out the pastry to a thickness of 3 mm/⅛ inch. Divide into two equal rectangles, prick with a fork and set aside.

2 Mix together with the walnuts, cranberries, raisins and salt. Whisk the egg whites until stiff and fold them in.

3 Rinse a baking tray in cold water, put one puff pastry rectangle on it and spread with the cheese mixture, leaving 1 cm/½ inch clear round the edges. Dampen the edges, place the second rectangle on top, and press the edges together well, to seal. Brush the pie with egg yolk. Decorate with the pastry trimmings, cut into shapes.

4 Bake in a preheated oven, Gas Mark 8-9/230°-240°C/450°-475°F, for about 20 minutes.

SALAMI CROISSANTS

Makes approximately 20 croissants

200g/7oz plain flour
200g/7oz low fat quark
175g/6oz margarine
Pinch of salt
Margarine for greasing

Filling

200g/7oz sliced salami, diced
1 small onion, finely chopped
200g/7oz cream cheese
2 tbsps single cream
Pepper, paprika
Egg yolk, beaten

1 Sieve the flour onto a pastry board. Squeeze the quark in a cloth to drain, and place it on the flour together with the margarine and salt. Cut in, using a palette knife. Mix well and knead quickly to a smooth dough. Chill.
2 Mix the salami and onion with the cheese and cream, and season with pepper and paprika.
3 Roll out the dough to a thickness of 5 mm/¼ inch. Using a pastry wheel, cut out 15-cm/6-inch squares and divide these into triangles. Put a little filling on each triangle, roll it up and twist into a croissant shape, then place on a greased baking tray.

4 Brush the croissants with egg yolk and bake in a preheated oven, Gas Mark 7/220°C/425°F, for 15-20 minutes.

Variation:
Roll out half the dough into a circle, cut out rounds to fit bun tins, spread with the filling and use the remaining dough to make lids. Bake for 35 minutes.

MINCED MEAT PIES

Makes approximately 15 pies

25g/1oz fresh yeast
200 ml/7 fl oz lukewarm milk
Pinch of sugar
500g/1lb flour
Salt
Grated zest of ½ lemon
2 eggs
25g/1oz margarine, melted and cooled
Margarine for greasing

Filling

500g/1lb mixed minced pork and beef
20 g/3/4oz margarine
1 tsp curry powder
1 small red pepper, diced
200g/7oz tomatoes, peeled and chopped
6 tbsps red wine
1 tbsp gravy powder
½ tsp paprika
Salt, pepper
2 egg yolks, beaten

1 Crumble the yeast into the lukewarm milk, and stir in a little sugar and flour. Cover and leave in a warm place for about 10 minutes, until frothy. Put the flour, salt and lemon zest into a bowl, add the frothy yeast, eggs, egg yolk and margarine. Knead to a smooth dough and leave, covered, in a warm place until doubled in volume.
2 Brown the meat in the margarine, then stir in the curry powder. Add the diced pepper and chopped tomatoes to the meat. Mix well and stir in the red wine and gravy powder. Simmer until nearly all the liquid has evaporated. Season well with salt, pepper and paprika.
3 Knead the dough again and roll out to a thickness of 5 mm/¼ inch. Cut out 12-cm/4½-inch rounds. Spread half with the filling mixture and cover with the remaining pastry rounds. Press the edges together well, to seal.
4 Put the pies on a greased baking tray, brush with beaten egg yolk and bake in a preheated oven, Gas Mark 7/220°C/425°F, for about 15 minutes.

SAVOURY HAM PUFFS

Makes about 20 portions

250g/8oz flour
1 tsp baking powder
Tomato ketchup
½-1 tsp salt
250g/8oz low fat quark
250g/8oz margarine

Filling

250g/8oz cooked ham, finely diced
2 small onions, grated
2 tbsps chopped fresh parsley
Good pinch of paprika

1 Squeeze the quark in a cloth to drain. Working quickly, make a dough from the flour, baking powder, 1 tsp of the ketchup, salt, quark and margarine, and chill for 1 hour. Roll out the pastry into a rectangle about 1 cm/½ inch thick, fold the two ends over each other and roll out again to the original size. Repeat the process, rolling in the opposite direction, then chill the pastry for 15 minutes.
2 Mix the ham, onions and parsley, and season generously with paprika.
3 Roll out the pastry to a thickness of 5 mm/¼ inch. Cut out 10-cm/4-inch squares or circles, and spread them thinly with tomato ketchup. Place a little of the filling on top.
4 Brush the pastry edges with a little water, fold the puffs into triangles or croissant shapes, seal the edges and decorate the tops with shapes cut out of the pastry trimmings.
5 Rinse a baking tray in cold water and line with greaseproof paper. Put the puffs onto it and bake in a preheated oven, Gas Mark 7/220°C/425°F, for about 10 minutes. Serve hot with tomato ketchup.

CHEESE BALLS

Makes approximately 20 pieces

250 ml/8 fl oz milk
60g/2½oz margarine
Salt
4 eggs
4 tbsps single cream
100g/3½oz grated cheese
Margarine for greasing
Flour

1 Bring the milk to the boil with the margarine and salt. Remove from the heat and pour in the sieved flour in a stream. Put back on a low heat and cook, beating continuously, until the mixture shrinks away from the sides of the pan in a ball.

2 Beat 1 of the eggs in immediately. Leave to cool slightly, then beat in the remaining eggs one by one, followed by the cream and cheese.

3 Use a wet teaspoon to drop little mounds of the mixture onto a greased and floured baking tray and bake in a preheated oven, Gas Mark 6-7/200°-220°C/400°-425°F, for 30-35 minutes, until golden.

Note: These are good served with fricassées or stews.

CHEESE HATS

Makes approximately 30 pieces

250g/8oz flour
1 egg
Salt
150g/5oz margarine
180g/6oz cheese spread with smoked ham
1 egg yolk, beaten

1 Working quickly, make a pastry dough from the flour, egg, salt and margarine; knead and chill in the refrigerator for 1 hour. Roll out thinly and cut out 5 cm/2-inch rounds.

2 Dice the cheese using a knife dipped in cold water. Divide the dice between the pastry rounds. Pull up the pastry round the cheese and press the edges together well to form three-cornered hats. Brush with a little beaten egg yolk.

3 Bake in a preheated oven, Gas Mark 6/200°C/400°F, for 15-20 minutes.

CHEESE PASTRY SNAILS

Makes approximately 60 snails

200g/7oz flour
Salt
100g/3½oz margarine
100g/3½oz cheese spread with herbs
1 egg yolk
1 tbsp water
Caraway seeds
Margarine for greasing

1 Using a palette knife, cut the margarine and cheese into the flour and salt. Working quickly, knead the mixture into a smooth dough.

2 Roll out the pastry to a thickness of about 5 mm/¼ inch and cut into 10-cm/4-inch-long strips with a pastry wheel.

3 Beat the egg yolk with the water, brush this over the dough and sprinkle it with caraway seeds. Roll up the strips into snail shapes and put on a greased baking tray.

4 Bake in a preheated oven, Gas Mark 6-7/200°-220°C/400°-425°F, for 12-15 minutes.

HAM ONION AND HERB BITES

Makes approximately 40 pieces

250g/8oz flour
1 tsp baking powder
250g/8oz low fat quark
200g/7oz margarine
75g/3oz smoked ham, diced

1 bunch each fresh parsley, dill and chives, chopped
1 small onion, very finely chopped
Good pinch of pepper
½ level tsps salt
Margarine for greasing

1 Knead all the ingredients together well. With floured hands, shape the dough into 5-cm/2-inch-thick rolls, cut these into 2-cm/¾-inch-thick slices and shape each slice into a ball.
2 Place the balls on a greased baking tray and make a small dent in the top of each one with your finger.
3 Bake in a preheated oven, Gas Mark 6/200°C/400°F, for about 20 minutes.

CHEESE AND PEPPER SLICES

Makes approximately 50 slices

250g/8oz flour
125g/4oz margarine
1 egg
Salt, pepper
250g/8oz cheese spread triangles

Margarine for greasing
1 skinned red pepper, thinly sliced
1 egg yolk, beaten

1 Make a shortcrust pastry dough from the flour, margarine, egg, salt and pepper. Working quickly, mix it well, knead and chill for 1 hour.
2 Using a hot knife, slice the cheese spread horizontally into thin triangles.
3 Roll out the pastry to a 25-cm/10-inch square. Place this on a greased baking tray. Arrange the cheese triangles on top, interspersed with slices of pepper. Brush with egg yolk.
4 Bake in a preheated oven, Gas Mark 8-9/230°-240°C/450°-475°F for about 20 minutes, until golden. Cut immediately into small rectangles and serve warm.

CARAWAY SEED STRAWS

Makes approximately 35 straws

300g/10oz frozen puff pastry, thawed
1 egg
Caraway seeds
Salt

1 Roll out the pastry, prick it several times with a cocktail stick and cut into strips about 1 cm/½ inch wide. Lightly beat the egg, brush it over the pastry strips and sprinkle them with caraway seeds and salt.

2 Twist the strips into spiral-shaped straws and leave for 15 minutes on a baking tray which

has been rinsed in cold water.

3 Bake the caraway seed straws in a preheated oven, Gas Mark 8-9/230°-240°C/450°-475°F, for about 10 minutes.

PARTY BOATS

Makes 12-14

200g/7oz flour
Salt
100g/3½oz margarine
1 egg
Margarine for greasing
375g/12oz cooked prawns
Parsley, sliced tomatoes, sliced gherkins, etc., to decorate

1 Sieve the flour and salt onto a pastry board, dot with the margarine and cut it in with a palette knife. Make a well in the centre of the mixture, drop in the egg and work everything quickly together to a smooth dough. Cover and chill.

2 Roll out the pastry and use to line greased boat moulds. Bake in a preheated oven, Gas Mark 6-7/200°-220°C/400°-425°F, for about 20 minutes. Turn out of the moulds and leave to cool.

3 Shortly before serving fill the boats with prawns and decorate attractively.

SAVOURY STICKS

Makes approximately 30 sticks

125g/4oz flour
100g/3½oz potato flour
2 level tsps baking powder
1 tsp salt
25g/1oz margarine
2 egg whites
5 tbsps milk
1 egg yolk for brushing
Poppy seeds, coarse salt or caraway seeds
Margarine for greasing.

1 Sieve the flour, potato flour, baking powder and salt onto a pastry board, dot with the margarine and cut it in with a palette knife. Lightly whisk the egg whites with the milk. Make a well in the centre of the mixture, put in the egg and milk and mix everything quickly to a dough.
2 Roll out the pastry immediately and cut into strips, 1½ cm x 15 cm/⅝ inch x 6 inches. Mix the egg yolk with a little water, brush it over the pastry strips and sprinkle them with the poppy seeds, coarse salt or caraway seeds.
3 Twist the strips into spirals and place them on a greased baking tray.
4 Bake in a preheated oven, Gas Mark 4-6/180°-200°C/350°-400°F, for 10-15 minutes.

CHEESE WAFFLES

Makes 10-15 waffles

250g/8oz margarine
4 eggs
Pinch of salt
7 tbsps lukewarm water
150g/5oz white flour
100g/3½oz buckwheat flour
1 tsp baking powder
100g/3½oz Gouda cheese, grated
Paprika powder
Pepper
Vegetable oil for greasing

1 Cream the margarine, eggs and salt until light and fluffy. Gradually add the water and flour, sieved together with the baking powder. Add the grated cheese and season.
2 Heat the waffle iron and brush it with vegetable oil. Put about 1 tbsp of the mixture onto the iron and cook for about 3 minutes until golden brown. Repeat until the mixture has been used up.

HAM CROISSANTS

*Makes approximately 12
croissants*

25g/1oz fresh yeast
150 ml/5 fl oz lukewarm milk
1 tsp sugar
350g/12oz flour
Salt
50g/2oz margarine, melted and cooled
1 egg, beaten
Margarine for greasing

Filling

2 egg whites
200g/5oz smoked ham, thinly sliced
150g/5oz pineapple chunks, finely chopped
2 egg yolks, beaten

1 Crumble the yeast into the milk and stir in a pinch each of sugar and flour. Cover and leave in a warm place for about 5-10 minutes, until frothy. Put the flour, sugar, salt, margarine and egg into a mixing bowl, add the frothy yeast, mix and knead to a smooth dough. Cover with foil and leave in a warm place until doubled in volume. Thoroughly knead dough a second time.
2 Roll out the dough to a thickness of 5 mm/¼ inch. Using a pastry wheel, cut out about twelve triangles measuring 14 cm/5½ inches from corner to corner. Brush with each with a little egg white, and top with a piece of ham and some of the pineapple. Roll up the triangles and twist them into croissant shapes.
3 Cover the croissants and leave in a warm place to prove. Brush the croissants with the egg yolk and bake them in a preheated oven, Gas Mark 6/ 200°C/400°F, for about 20 minutes.

SWISS CHOUX GOUGERES

250 ml/8 fl oz water
75g/3oz margarine
½ tsp salt
175g/6oz flour
4 eggs
1 tsp baking powder
2 triangles of Swiss cheese spread
75g/3oz Emmenthal, grated

Margarine for greasing
Flour
Egg yolk
Cress, to garnish

1 Bring the water, margarine and salt to the boil. Remove from the heat and beat in all the flour. Return to the heat and beat the mixture until it shrinks away from sides of the saucepan in a ball.

2 Beat one of the eggs into the hot mixture, add the cheese spread cut into pieces and 50g/2oz of the grated Emmenthal cheese. Beat in the remaining eggs one at a time. Leave to cool.
3 Spoon the mixture into a piping bag fitted with a plain round nozzle. Pipe mounds of the mixture onto a greased and floured baking tin. Mix the egg yolk with a little water and brush it over the pastries.

CHOUX PASTRY BUNS WITH CHEESE

Makes approximately 20 buns

250 ml/8 fl oz water
40g/1½oz margarine
Salt
Nutmeg
125g/4oz flour
2 eggs
2 cream cheese triangles
1 tsp baking powder
Margarine for greasing
Flour

Filling

3 triangles cheese spread with herbs
1 hard-boiled egg, chopped
Condensed milk
2 tsps chopped fresh herbs

1 Bring the water, margarine and a little salt and nutmeg to the boil. Off the heat, beat in all the flour at once. Return the mixture to the heat and beat continuously until the mixture shrinks away from the sides of the saucepan in a ball.

2 Beat one of the eggs and the cheese spread into the hot mixture. Leave to cool. Beat in the second egg and the baking powder.

3 Using two teaspoons, drop spoonfuls of the mixture onto a greased and floured baking tray. Bake in a preheated oven, Gas Mark 8-9/230°-240°C/450°-475°F, for about 25 minutes. Use scissors to cut off the tops of the buns as soon as they are removed from the oven.

4 Mix the herbed cheese spread with the chopped egg, condensed milk and fresh herbs and use to fill the buns.

Sprinkle them with grated cheese.

4 Bake in a preheated oven, Gas Mark 7/220°C/425°F, for 25-30 minutes. Garnish the finished gougères with the cress and serve hot.

INDEX